BEFORE
WE WERE
TRANS

BEFORE
WE WERE
TRANS

A NEW HISTORY OF GENDER

KIT HEYAM

SEAL PRESS
New York

Seal Press
Hachette Book Group
1290 Avenue of the Americas, New York, NY 10104
www.sealpress.com
@sealpress

Printed in the United States of America

Originally published in Great Britain in 2022 by John Murray (Publishers), Basic
Books UK, An Hachette UK company
First US Edition: September 2022

Published by Seal Press, an imprint of Perseus Books, LLC, a subsidiary of Hachette
Book Group, Inc. The Seal Press name and logo is a trademark of the Hachette Book
Group.

The Hachette Speakers Bureau provides a wide range of authors for speaking events.
To find out more, go to www.hachettespeakersbureau.com or call (866) 376-6591.

The publisher is not responsible for websites (or their content)
that are not owned by the publisher.

Typeset in Bembo MT by Hewer Text UK Ltd, Edinburgh

Library of Congress Control Number: 2022933909

ISBNs: 9781541603080 (print), 9781541603103 (ebook)

LSC-C

Printing 1, 2022

Love and solidarity to everyone who's ever felt alone
in their experience of their gender

Contents

Introduction
'I had a gown on in a lark': what is trans history?

On the night of Monday 8 June 1847, John Sullivan was drunk. Strolling unsteadily down the street in Aldgate, East London, the 22-year-old was wearing a bonnet, a gown, a silk apron, a pair of trousers and a pair of women's boots. Police Constable Henry Pye's attention was caught both by this attire and by the bundle John was carrying under one arm. Steering John to the local police station, he opened the bundle to find more items of women's clothing. Where, he asked John, had these come from?

John said, 'They're mine.'

Six days later, on 14 June, John Sullivan was tried for the theft of a cape, a handkerchief, an apron, two gowns, two petticoats and a pair of stays. The clothes belonged to local woman Frances Norton, and had a total value of thirteen shillings and sixpence. Under oath, John denied stealing the clothes, and dismissed the choice to wear them as a drunken joke, swearing, 'I had them given to me to carry to the market; the policeman caught me, and the person who gave me the things ran away; I had a gown on in a lark, but I had my trousers on; I was very much intoxicated.' The court, mindful that this was John's second offence (following a six-month prison sentence the previous year for a crime whose records don't appear to survive), was unsympathetic. John Sullivan was sentenced to be transported to Australia for ten years.[1]

Is this story part of trans history? It's unlikely that many people would treat it as such. John Sullivan lived before the word 'transgender', as we use it now, was widely available for individuals to describe their actions or identities. There's no evidence that John presented as female outside of the specific circumstances outlined in the trial records. Perhaps most conclusively, those trial records give us John's own testimony, framing the choice to wear women's clothes not as a matter of identity but as a drunken 'lark'. Surely there's no better metric by which to judge a historical person's gender than their own voice?

These are the criteria that usually determine whether trans people feel able to talk about someone as belonging to trans history. We look for evidence that their motivation for gender nonconformity was not external, but internal – ideally in the form of personal testimony. We look for continuous presentation as the gender 'opposite to' the one they were assigned at birth. And we look for histories that we can fit into contemporary Western ideas of what it means to be trans. Even if those criteria are met, we get anxious if the person we're dealing with lived before the advent of the terminology that we use to talk about trans identities today: often, this in itself is enough to dismiss their trans possibility altogether.

These criteria often make it difficult for us to talk about trans history at all. What makes this conversation even more difficult to have are the concepts that underpin it: gender and sex, internal and external motivations, personal testimony, stability of identity. If we poke at any one of these concepts, the whole edifice starts to crumble. When we talk about trans history, what are we even talking about?

This book is about the answer to that question.

Ask a trans person today what the adjective 'trans' refers to and, while the nuances will differ, the most common definition you'll get is 'anyone who doesn't identify with the gender they were assigned at birth'. It's important to us to put it in these terms. Talking about being trans as an identity, rather than an action, helps us to understand transness as relating to *who you are*, not *what you do* – a crucial step in undermining the argument that transitioning means adhering to gender stereotypes. It makes space for people who can't, or don't want to, transition socially or medically. And talking about moving *away from* the gender we were assigned at birth, rather than from male to female or vice versa, helps our definition to be clearly inclusive of non-binary people: people like me, who don't identify as male or female all of the time.

This modern understanding of 'trans' is usually dated back to early-twentieth-century sexology: an intellectual movement that attempted to examine sexuality and gender identity as scientific phenomena. The German sexologist Magnus Hirschfeld coined the term 'transvestite' in 1910, and although this word sounds to modern ears like a sensationalist term for 'cross-dressing' – something that relates to external gender expression rather than internal gender identity, and is probably sexualised in the vein of *The Rocky Horror Picture Show* – Hirschfeld intended it to cover a much broader range of trans identities, including people who transitioned medically, people who transitioned socially, and people who changed their gender expression some but not all of the time.[2]

The word 'transsexual' then came, by the mid-twentieth century, to primarily indicate trans people who accessed medical transition: who used hormones and/or surgery to change their body so that it aligned with the physical characteristics associated with the gender they identified as. By the late 1960s, American trans activist Virginia Prince was helping to popularise the word 'transgender' to refer to trans people who transitioned socially, but not medically: living as a gender other than the one they were assigned at birth, without changing their body.[3] While this distinction persisted in common parlance for some decades, by the twenty-first century – and in particular, following the influence of Leslie Feinberg's 1992 book *Transgender Liberation* – trans identities and practices of all kinds were becoming subsumed under the umbrella term 'transgender'.[4] The word 'transsexual', while still valued by some for its connection to the history of trans activism (and particularly to that of older trans women) – and while still persisting in some official quarters, like the UK Equality Act 2010, which uses it to refer to any trans person who transitions socially *or* medically – has become gradually replaced by 'trans', short for 'transgender', as the default word we use to describe ourselves.[5] 'Cisgender' or 'cis', an adjective that refers to the opposite of trans – anyone who does identify with the gender they were assigned at birth – dates back to at least the 1990s.[6] The word 'cis' is sometimes misunderstood as referring to stereotypes; much of the opposition to it rests on the idea that to call someone a 'cis woman' is to say she is comfortable with society's narrow idea of femininity. In reality, though, the way most trans people use it is to refer not to stereotypes, but to self-identification. A cis woman is someone who was assigned female at birth, and is happy to describe herself as a woman – regardless of how much she defies *society's* idea of what 'woman' should mean.[7]

Even in the past hundred years, then – a period in which the category of 'trans' has been relatively coherent – thinking about trans history is a difficult and messy business. Look back further in time, and the difficulty and messiness increases dramatically. It's not as simple as saying that while the terminology is new, the experiences are not; the advent of new terminology can genuinely shift how we *think about* gender, as well as what names we give to our experiences.[8] But it's also not straightforwardly true to say that the use of the word 'trans' to talk about gender has no history before sexology: literary scholar Joseph Gamble has recently discovered that the seventeenth-century writer Thomas Browne used the prefix 'trans-' and the word 'transition' to refer to the spontaneous sex changes of hares as early as 1646, and even coined the adjective 'transfeminated' to refer to a body that has transformed from what we think of as 'female' to what we think of as 'male'. * So the prefix 'trans-' was clearly relevant to thinking about 'gender malleability' long before Hirschfeld leveraged it to refer to the patients he saw at his Institute for Sexual Science.[9]

Yet this doesn't mean any of us can easily map our category of 'trans people', as I've defined it here, back onto the past. If we try to think about that contemporary definition – 'anyone who doesn't identify with the gender they were assigned at birth' – in historical terms, it immediately starts to break down. In England and Wales, civil birth registrations (as opposed to the noting of births and baptisms in parish records) didn't begin until 1837, and they didn't become compulsory until 1875 (twenty years later than in Scotland) – meaning that birth records are unlikely to include a gender marker before the nineteenth century. So what does it mean to be 'assigned' a particular gender at birth before that point? And what, for that matter, do we mean by 'gender' or 'sex' when we're thinking about the past?[10]

These terms aren't even stable in our own society. While popular discourse often defines gender as a social construct and sex as a biological reality – 'sex is between your legs, gender is between your ears' – this neat-sounding distinction belies the many socially determined aspects of how we think about bodies. The labels 'male' and 'female' are themselves socially determined: our society labels one configuration of body parts 'female' and one 'male', but what's stopping us from calling those biological trends A and B, or orange and purple? Similarly, why do we think of some sexual characteristics (like genitals and chromosomes) as 'fundamental' parts of sex, which make a difference to how we

---

* This looks odd to modern eyes, as we're used to using words like 'transfeminine' to describe people who have transitioned *to* living as female or feminine – but Browne used 'transfeminated' to mean the opposite.

categorise a person's body, and others (like facial hair and fat distribution) as comparatively insignificant? Why do we think of sex as binary, dividing humans into two clear biological types, when in reality it's a spectrum on which comparatively few people tick all of the boxes required to slot neatly into one of those two categories?[11] Why do so many societies still carry out violent, non-consensual and medically unnecessary surgery on intersex children (children whose bodies don't fit clearly into one of the categories we label 'male' and 'female')? The answer to all of those questions is that gender – that socially constructed idea which carries all of the social baggage we associate with 'male-ness' and 'femaleness' – informs, even *produces*, our ideas about sex.[12] In the words of trans writer and activist Shon Faye, 'Our sexed bodies never exist outside social meanings: consequently, how we understand gender shapes how we understand sex . . . The way we perceive and understand sex differences and empha-sise their significance is so deeply gendered that it can be impossible to completely divorce the two.'[13] To say sex and gender are both socially constructed isn't to say they're not *real* – like other social constructs, including race, money and crime, they have material and life-changing consequences for all of us – but it is to say there's no innate reason we *have* to think about them in the way we do.

Given that we don't think about 'gender' and 'sex' in a coherent way today, it's no surprise that these ideas were equally unstable in the past. The idea of 'gender' as socially constructed and distinct from sex didn't become common parlance in English until the mid-twentieth century.[14] That isn't to say that before this, it was only bodies that mattered. 'Gender' and 'sex' were used interchangeably – with 'sex' far more common – and both referred to a combination of the social and biological: to adapt the words of trans theorist and historian Susan Stryker, both 'gender' and 'sex' referred to 'the social organisation of different kinds of bodies into different categories of people'.[15] When the clergyman Thomas Stoughton complained in 1622 that 'men and women' had 'changed their sex (as much as they can) one with another' by 'Men wearing long hair like unto women, and women cutting off their hair like unto boys', he was referring *both* to their bodies *and* to their social experience. This was complicated even further by the fact that Stoughton and his contemporaries understood the biological makeup of the body, and its relationship to personality and society, very differently from the way we do today. As a result, we can't even straightforwardly apply our modern concepts of 'men' and 'women' to people in the past.[16] The term 'gender', until it started to refer more exclusively to 'men' and 'women' in the mid-twentieth century, just meant 'kind' or 'sort': when Shakespeare referred to 'one gender of herbs' in his play *Othello*, this is what he meant.[17] In this sense, 'gender' is related to the word 'genre', which we use to categorise different kinds of art (into many more groups than just two).

There's also the problem that, in any society, what constitutes 'male', 'female' or any gender is different for different people. How we understand gender is shaped by so many factors – personal, cultural, historical – that every individual's conceptualisation of gender is unique.[18] For some people, being a man necessitates not wearing dresses, even as a joke – meaning John Sullivan, our nineteenth-century gender-nonconforming thief, wouldn't qualify as male. In my own life, my wardrobe of floral shirts and dangly earrings means a visit to the shops can be a lottery in terms of whether I'll be called 'Sir', 'Madam', or (on one memorable occasion, equal parts validating and amusing) 'Young Person'. If I played professional sport, my testosterone levels would make me a 'man'; if I got pregnant, my doctor's computer system would force me to be labelled 'woman'. If you asked me, I'd tell you neither category is accurate – instead, I use the term 'non-binary' to describe myself – and yet the way I

7

understand that term is different from many of my non-binary friends. If what it means to *be* a man, a woman or a non-binary person is different for everyone and varies between contexts, how can we straightforwardly talk about 'people who don't identify as the gender they were assigned at birth', in either the past or the present?

Despite these difficulties and complexities, trans people love to tell stories from our history. Feeling a sense of community with the past is profoundly important for many of us, and particularly for those of us who are isolated in our day-to-day lives. As a teenager, struggling to articulate my feelings around gender and sexuality, I confided far more in the queer historical figures who populated my mental landscape than I did in the friends I saw every day at school. Talking about our history is politically important, too, helping to undermine arguments that (as I'll talk more about later) present trans people as newfangled inventions, simultaneously suggesting that we're a trend that shouldn't be taken seriously, and that we're a potent new threat.

The tales of trans history that we tell often, for personal and political reasons, have a familiar cast. They feature people like Billy Tipton, the American jazz musician who lived as male and whose family and friends were shocked when he was outed as trans after his death in 1989; and his nineteenth-century antecedent James Barry, the Irish surgeon who similarly lived as male for all of his adult life, and was outed against his will after his death in 1865. We talk, too, about pioneers of medical transition like Lili Elbe, the Danish trans woman made famous by the disappointing 2015 film *The Danish Girl*, who was one of the earliest recipients of a modern Western form of gender reassignment surgery; and Christine Jorgensen, who travelled from her native New York to Denmark to access medical transition and was made famous by the sensational 1952 *New York Daily News* headline 'EX-GI BECOMES BLONDE BEAUTY'.[19]

These stories, and their well-known characters, are profoundly valuable. There's a powerful, electrifying force to the resonance we feel when we realise someone else has felt our feelings before us; the queer theorist Carolyn Dinshaw uses the image of a 'touch across time', an image that always reminds me of the line about literature in Alan Bennett's *The History Boys* – 'as if a hand has come out, and taken yours'.[20] But when we look closely at these stories, we can see that they have a troubling amount in common. These well-known trans figures from the past aren't reaching out their hands to everyone.

This is the problem: the trans histories that we point to most often are the easy stories. They are stories of people who lived stably in a gender distinct from the one they were assigned at birth; people who, even if they didn't have access to the word 'transgender', lived recently enough to fit easily into modern Western understandings of sex and gender; people who pursued medical transition if they had access to it; people from whom we have first-hand testimony, saying that they wanted to be recognised as the gender they lived in. Even if we occasionally draw on long-ago stories – like that of the Roman Emperor Elagabalus, who, according to multiple contemporary accounts, presented as female and sought gender reassignment surgery – they tend to be those that are easily, uncomplicatedly recognisable according to these modern Western ideas of what it means to be trans.[21] And if we mention trans people of colour, like Marsha P. Johnson, they're often deployed tokenistically in an attempt to make sure our cast of trans historical figures isn't entirely white – without really taking the time to understand the specificities of their experience.

If we try to slot John Sullivan into this cast of trans historical characters, we fail on every count. But John's story is crucial. It's crucial because it represents the tip of an iceberg: just one of a huge number of difficult, complicated stories from the history of gender that we don't have a good way to talk about. And it's crucial because it forces us to confront the fact that there are two big problems with how we decide whether a story 'counts' as trans history.

The first problem – and one that the 1847 story of John's dress exemplifies – is that a lot of the evidence we have for gender-nonconforming lives comes from legal and medical contexts. These are the kinds of records in which gender-nonconforming people overwhelmingly become visible. But law and medicine aren't neutral contexts in which people give objective narratives of their experience: they're high-stakes environments in which we construct a narrative for an author-ity figure whose decisions have huge consequences for our lives. As a result, we might adopt a particular discourse or way of speaking suited to the environment; we might strategically edit the truth to give a more coherent or believable narrative; we might even simply lie, telling those authority figures what they want to hear. If, in a century's time, a historian looked at the records of gender identity clinics in the UK, their estimate of how many non-binary people accessed medical transition would be much smaller than the true number: knowing that clinicians can still be suspicious of non-binary identities, we've been taught to edit our stories, to present ourselves as trans men or women in the hope of accessing medical treatment more quickly. So we can't rely on the accuracy of legal or medical records to tell us about the truth of trans experience in the past.[22] What's more, even when trans people *do* tell the truth in these official contexts, we can't always rely on official documents to record their voices or wishes accurately – as demonstrated by the many obituaries of trans people that misgender their subjects.[23]

For John Sullivan, then, it was expedient to present the gender nonconformity of 8 June 1847 as a drunken 'lark': to choose the legal censure of theft over the moral censure of cross-dressing, which was associated with sexual deviance and thereby carried legal risks too.* Just because it was expedient doesn't mean that John's account wasn't true, of course – but it does call into question how much we can rely on it, and whether we can use it as a reason to definitively exclude John from our narratives of trans history.

The second problem with our existing criteria for inclusion in 'trans history' is that they privilege an incredibly narrow version of what it means to be trans. The trans histories we tend to tell are those that conform to the trans narrative that's centred and recapitulated in contemporary media. The non-binary writer and activist Jacob Tobia, in their memoir *Sissy: A Coming-Of-Gender Story*, has brilliantly likened this narrative to the game Mad Lib: a story with a pre-written skeleton format, where the teller fills in the specifics from a limited list of options.[24] The 'Mad Lib' trans narrative begins in childhood, with the trans person articulating their early, stable sense that they were 'in the wrong body', and conforming to stereotypes 'opposite' to those of the gender they were assigned at birth. After a long and traumatic struggle with themselves, they come out, medically transition to male or female, and live a conventional, gender-conforming and heterosexual life. While this is an accurate depiction of many trans people's lives – and nothing about its dominance makes these trans people's experiences any less valid or radical – it's inaccurate, indeed inadequate, for many more. And as Tobia suggests, the dominance of this narrative perpetuates and reinforces the idea that it's 'the only trans narrative that cisgender people want to hear; the only trans story that cisgender people can comprehend'.

As a result, this narrative shapes contemporary trans stories, and all trans lives appear fundamentally similar. In order to get

---

* I'll talk more about this in Chapter 3.

what we need – whether that be medical treatment, legal gender recognition, or social validation of our identities – we fit our stories around contemporary standards of coherence and validity. In doing so, we continue the cycle, perpetuating the idea that this is the only way to be trans.

For people today who are struggling with their gender, trying to work out whether social or medical transition is right for them, these narrow ideas of what it means to be trans can be genuinely harmful. They're certainly the reason it took me so long to figure out my own gender; the few piecemeal images of transness I had access to as a child were heavily medicalised, all suggesting that being trans was something you *did* to change your body, not something you *felt*. I didn't know it was possible for trans people to be anything other than straight, for them not to conform to gender stereotypes, or for them not to have 'always known' – in a kind of static, essentialised way – that they weren't the gender they were assigned at birth. When I tried to articulate my feelings about my gender to friends and therapists, none of them recognised them as transness either. It wasn't until I started volunteering for the charity York LGBT History Month in the autumn of 2014 – ostensibly as an enthusiastic LGBTQ+ ally looking for a way to engage the public with my PhD research on King Edward II's sexual reputation, but really (as I soon realised) as a way of forcing myself to finally confront the reasons why I cared so fiercely about queer history and rights – that I was able to truly get to grips with new ways of thinking about gender, and to real- ise where I fitted in. Nobody on the York LGBT History Month committee asked me to explain what I was doing there, but my involvement with them turned out to be the push I needed to explain it to myself.

But this difficult process – giving myself permission to finally take my feelings seriously, to present myself differently, and to ask for the name and pronouns that made me happy – turned out to be the tip of the iceberg. It was explaining it to everybody else that really revealed the perniciousness of the narrow trans narrative constructed by contemporary media. Friends and family alike contrasted being non-binary with being 'properly trans', some saying they were glad I wasn't the latter. A member of the HR department where I worked asked derisively whether 'genderqueer', the word I used to describe myself, was 'an official term' (a question that, grimly hilarious in retrospect, suggests a belief in a literal 'gender police' who legislate over what trans people are and aren't allowed to call ourselves). When I corrected one man I knew after he used my old name, he was surprised, asking, 'Do you always correct people?' – as if being non-binary meant my commitment to my gender was temporary or half-hearted. By the time I got to an NHS gender identity clinic, twelve months after my referral – a wait that was one of the worst times in my life, but which is far exceeded by most of today's inhumane waiting lists – I was prepared: I was going to tell them a version of the truth that stuck to the 'Mad Lib' trans narrative as closely as possible. As a white middle-class person, it was going to be far easier for me to have my gender taken seriously than it would be for many others – but I still wasn't going to risk them denying me the treatment I needed because my gender didn't fit the mould.[25]

The narrow trans narrative we see emphasised in contemporary media, then, makes life harder for people who experience their transness in a way that's not binary, stereotyped or stable. And this narrative also makes it difficult to tell histories that fully reflect the messy reality of trans life today.

Jacob Tobia describes the standard trans narrative as 'classical' – and the way it operates with regard to history is in fact comparable to the 'classics' of literature.[26] It determines which stories constitute the 'canon' of trans history: which stories get retold and reread while others languish in the dusty corners of second-hand bookshops or are confined to specialist university courses. The canon has – like the literary canon more generally – no space for people of colour, especially not for those whose experience of gender is culturally specific. It has no space for the history of gender fluidity: for people whose genders change throughout their lives, or are different in different contexts.[27] It has no space for the history of playful or creative approaches to gender: for people who experiment with different forms of gender expression or nonconformity. It has no space for the histories of people whose gender is ambiguous or messy. It has no space for people who feel like some or all of the factors that determine their gender come from outside themselves, rather than inside. It has no space for the histories of people who can't articulate their gender clearly, or resist the imperative to do so.

Often, what this means is that our narratives of trans history are *recent*, avoiding challenges of terminology or evidence; *binary*, including only those trans people whose identities are male or female; *stereotyped*, limited to those who live and present in a way that conforms to contemporary social expectations about that gender identity; and *medicalised*, restricted to those who have accessed medical transition wherever possible. And perhaps most damagingly, it also often means that our trans histories are white. In fact, our contemporary idea of what it means to be trans has itself been shaped by those well-known trans people, like Christine Jorgensen, who were able to conform to ideals of white femininity or masculinity.[28] More broadly, the impact of colonialist ideology on the way white historians write about history – and the impact of racism on whose history books get read – has led to a widespread failure to acknowledge the histories of people of colour whose experience of gender can't be contained within a modern Western binary.

Thinking about gender critically and expansively is a central and necessary part of any anti-racist project. This point isn't just relevant to history; challenging Western constructs of gender in the present day is essential to challenging racism. To deny the reality of any genders beyond male and female is also to deny the reality of many genders that white people in Western Europe and the USA aren't socialised to recognise, many of whose histories I tell in this book. Importantly, while white non-binary people might feel a sense of kinship or recognition with these genders, they're not *the same as* being non-binary or trans in a Western sense. White non-binary people often seize upon the existence of these genders to prove the validity of our own: tokenising, instru-mentalising and romanticising them, often without really taking the time to understand them on their own terms.[29] This is a prob-lem: when white people use the genders of people of colour in this way, it recapitulates a colonialist dynamic of exploitation. The desire to name and categorise people according to Western metrics reflects and re-enacts a similar colonialist impulse.[30] I've tried hard to avoid this dynamic when writing this book: it's why (as you'll see) I've continually emphasised the cultural specificity of gender, and the way we can't separate it out from factors like sexuality, spirituality and fashion, which work together to make gender what it is. It's also why I've continually emphasised the violent impact of Western colonialism on many of the people whose histories I'm telling here.

Black feminists like Kimberlé Crenshaw, Audre Lorde, bell hooks, B Camminga, Emi Koyama and many others have long emphasised that the way we experience and understand gender is inextricable from race.[31] In its simplest terms, this is one of the points that the anti-slavery activist Sojourner Truth made as long ago as 1851, emphasising that white women were treated as if they needed to 'be helped into carriages, and lifted over ditches, and to have the best place everywhere' – but 'Nobody ever helps me into carriages, or over mud-puddles, or gives me any best place! And ain't I a woman?'[32] Relatedly, many trans people of colour whose genders aren't binary have emphasised that their experience of gender is inextricable from their cultures: as Carrier First Nations two-spirited researcher[*] Michelle Cameron has described, the inter-tribal term Two-Spirit (used by Native American/First Nations people to describe a variety of culturally specific gendered experiences that are neither male nor female) 'is a reclaimed term designed by Aboriginals to define our unique cultural context, histories, and legacy'.[33] And as I mentioned earlier, the trans people whose genders are taken most seriously – and those whose construction of their trans identities came to define the terms in which others could articulate their own – have tended to be those who can perform the norms of white femininity or white masculinity most effectively.[34] This means that, even among trans people who *do* fit comfortably into the 'classical' narrative of male/female identity and medical transition, trans people of colour remain marginalised and must struggle harder to have their genders respected and validated. When combined with systemic racism and misogyny, this means that trans women of colour – especially Black trans women – are at devastatingly high risk of violence.

In 1977, the Combahee River Collective of Black lesbians issued a statement critiquing the way white feminism privileged gender – often understood as essentialised in a way that excluded trans women – as the most fundamental axis of oppression around which political organising should take place.[35] 'We know,' they asserted, 'that there is such a thing as racial-sexual oppression which is neither solely racial nor solely sexual.'[36] Similar ideas have been expressed by queer indigenous writers: as Cameron explains, the term Two-Spirit/Two-Spirited 'was chosen to emphasize our difference in our experiences of *multiple,*

* Cameron uses 'two-spirited' instead of 'Two-Spirit' to describe herself and others. In general, though, I've chosen to use the latter, which is more common and is the term officially adopted at the 1990 Native American/First Nations Gay and Lesbian Conference in Winnipeg (see Chapter 6).

interlocking oppressions as queer Aboriginal people'.[37] The Collective's work paved the way for Kimberlé Crenshaw's later articulation of the concept of intersectionality, and it has also been a key driving force behind the opposition of Black feminists to the trans-exclusionary factions of white feminism. As Emi Koyama has put it succinctly, to argue that trans women should be excluded from women's spaces 'because their experiences are different would have to assume that all other women's experiences are the same, and this is a racist assumption.'[38] To fail to consider race as one factor that co-constitutes gender, then, is to homogenise people of all genders, erasing both the experiences of people of colour and their intellectual and activist contributions, most importantly those of Black feminism.

This has important implications for how we think about trans history. Many cultures throughout history (including those I mentioned above) have had genders that aren't male or female because they're inherently spiritual, because they're linked to sexuality, or because they're partly about a person's social role. Contemporary Western ideas would tell us that these genders are less 'real' than others, or too complicated to fit under a trans umbrella. This book is full of genders like this: to ignore them is to prop up the racist idea that having genders that aren't male or female, or approaching gender disruptively and creatively, is something only modern people and/or white people do.

Stories of trans history can also support our anti-racist work in the present day because they reveal the racist origins of our contemporary ideas about sex and gender. In particular, the idea that sex is dimorphic – that there are two types of sexed body, and that they're clearly delineated – has a racist history.[39] As nineteenth-century scientists developed racist taxonomies of human beings, grouping people into the racial categories we've inherited today, they also developed theories about sexual dimorphism. For these scientists, sexual dimorphism was one of the things that divided people into different races: white people's bodies were the most 'perfectly' divided into male and female, while people of colour had fewer differences between the sexes.[40] We can see the legacy of these racist ideas everywhere today: they're behind the association of Black women with masculine-coded anger, and the feminisation of Asian men. Knowing the history of our contemporary ideas about sexual dimorphism can help us both to challenge these racist ideologies, and to dismantle transphobic arguments that there are 'only two genders' – or that our ideas about sex are based on neutral 'biology'.[41]

In the process of researching this book, I've wrestled a lot with the question of what exactly makes me – a white writer *using* the stories of people of colour – different from the colonisers whose actions I'm condemning here. One way I've tried to address this is by making visible the many forms of racism that led to these stories being insufficiently known in the first place.[42] Another is by emphasising that trans liberation and anti-racism are inextricable struggles, and commitment to the former *must* necessitate commitment to the latter; in the words of Leslie Feinberg, who showed that trans history can pave the way for the liberation of all marginalised people in a manifesto I can only hope to emulate here, 'we should aspire . . . to be the best fighters against each other's oppression, and in doing so, build links of solidarity and trust that will forge an invincible movement against all forms of injustice and inequality.'[43] Another is by doing my best to platform the voices of trans people of colour working within and outside the discipline of history; I hope people will read the notes and take my reading recommendations seriously. Not everyone will think this is enough; I'm not sure I think it is myself. But right now, one flawed step towards making these histories resonate more loudly – along with the anti-racist politics they demand – feels, cautiously, like a step worth taking. This, right now, feels like the best way of using the platform I've been given. To para-phrase the non-binary storyteller Ivan Coyote, it's still so rare for trans people to get the microphone that, when we do, it's often difficult to shake the feeling that we're being handed it on behalf of every trans person alive.[44] I hope fervently that I won't be the last trans person given the opportunity to talk about what our history can be, and I hope this book might play a part in creating the conditions where that's more likely and more possible.

How did we end up with historical narratives that represent such a narrow slice of trans life? How did we reach a point where so many of our trans histories erase people whose experience of gender hasn't been binary or stereotyped, who haven't transi-tioned medically, and/or whose gender can't be accurately described in modern Western terms?

One of the reasons is that historical methodology – the way we're accustomed to doing and thinking about history academi-cally – tends to demand a much higher standard of evidence to 'prove' that someone in the past can be called trans than it does to 'prove' that they can be called cis. Because trans people are a minority, we're seen as an aberration from the norm: our society treats cisgender-ness as the default, or 'unmarked', state of all human beings. (This is compounded for anyone whose body is seen as non-normative: in white Western culture, this includes not only trans people but also intersex people, disabled people and people of colour.) This pervasive *cisnormativity* means that the cis perspective is – just like the male perspective, as Simone de Beauvoir argued – positioned as objective truth.[45] This means historians tend to interpret people from the past as, effectively, cis until proven otherwise. Though we might not admit it (or even realise it consciously), this approach also enables historians to avoid the horror of (gasp) accidentally mislabelling a straight, cis person from the past as queer.[46] And if, as a result, we mislabel a queer or trans person as straight or cis . . . well, funnily enough, that doesn't cause as much anxiety. Our sense of what we need to be cautious about has been insidiously shaped by homophobia and transphobia.

Relatedly, trans people who write about our own history are – like many other marginalised groups – often accused of bias. To anyone who accuses me of rereading the past from a perspective that's biased towards finding trans history, I would say: you're absolutely right! But I would also say that I'm no less objective than any other historian. Because we live in a society that sees cis people as the default, the majority of histories are biased *against* finding trans history even when they try not to be. But funnily enough, it tends to only be marginalised groups who are accused of lacking objectivity.[47] While I'm keen not to constrain the possibilities of the past by fixing historical people in modern categories, I'm equally keen for us to remember that 'cis man' and 'cis woman' are modern categories as well. Making space for trans possibility, then, is no *less* objective than any other kinds of history: in fact, in many cases it might be *more* so.

Objectivity aside, though, I also want to make the case for the value of a trans gaze in historical research. The curator Margaret Middleton and the literary scholar Lindsey Row-Heyveld have both argued that we should acknowledge and value the expertise of marginalised people in recognising *people who are like us* in the past: as Middleton brilliantly puts it, this means valuing 'queer experience as expertise and gaydar as epistemology'.[48] Simply put, trans people can pick up on hints and signals in the historical record that others might overlook. This community recognition also provides an ethical alternative to subjecting historical figures to the same kind of diagnostic process that both disabled people and trans people have to go through in the present day to prove our 'realness'.[49]

This is a further problem in the way we currently do historical research: in the present day, our structures for validating trans experience are all built around *testimony*. Trans people access medical treatment through our testimony; and any attempt to convince the general public to support trans rights includes a personal narrative, a story of what it *feels* like to be trans that attempts to win sympathy by 'humanising' us. For the majority of trans writers, the most common genre in which we can get our voices heard is the memoir.[50] The problem with this emphasis on testimony is not just that it demands trans people cede our right to privacy, exposing our vulnerabilities in order to prove that we deserve basic human rights: it's that it creates an *expectation* of testimony. Without testimony, a trans narrative seems incomplete, inconclusive, invalid. And when we look at historical records and can't find that testimony – often because we're looking at periods when far fewer people had access to literacy and the means to publish, and many ordinary people's private records of their experience have been lost – we conclude that we can't find any trans people, because our standard of evidence hasn't been reached.

The other reason that our contemporary narratives of trans history are so limited is that political debates over trans rights, and pervasive media transphobia, are actually shaping trans people's very sense of our history.

On 27 November 2017, *The Times* published an article by Scottish writer and sociologist Stuart Waiton with the headline 'Transgender fetish is a truly shameful modern invention'. Responding to a moral panic about access to healthcare and gender recognition for young trans people, set against the backdrop of misinformation about the UK government's consultation on reforms to the Gender Recognition Act 2004, Waiton claimed that trans identities were 'the endpoint of our culture of narcissism': devoid of external sources of liberation and inspiration, twenty-first-century children and adults had turned to their own bodies as the last available site of experimentation.[*] This was a product of modern society, he argued: the idea that anyone had felt like this in the past was a 'total fantasy'. More than that, the idea of being trans was 'profoundly conservative': people were being encouraged to transition to fulfil gender stereotypes, to make sure that only girls liked 'all things pink and frilly', and only boys were into 'football and fighting'.[51]

Many contemporary arguments, of which Waiton's represents only the tip of the iceberg, focus on the supposed newness of trans identities. We're described by columnists as a 'fad'; commentators (and in some cases, psychiatrists) fret that young people[†] are coming out as trans 'because it's cool'.[52] Some anti-trans campaigners have taken these connotations of newness to their logical extreme, denying all possibility of trans history on the basis of our supposed absence from 'the historical record' and arguing that to even suggest our historical existence is 'anachronistic'.[53] Underlying these claims is a sense that historicity provides legitimacy: that the newfangledness of trans identities means policymakers and the general public do not need to, indeed should not, take them seriously. Presenting trans identities as a 'modern invention' also enables transphobic campaigners to frame us as a new and growing threat: something that has come out of nowhere to threaten an existing way of life, and against which women and children – groups positioned, often without their say, as vulnerable victims in this hastily constructed fight – must be protected at all costs. Like other campaigns over LGBTQ+ rights – in

* Waiton's views may seem extreme, or a product of a specific political climate a few years ago – but sadly, they're still not atypical in contemporary media. For more on how this situation developed, see Pearce et al., 'TERF Wars'; Faye, *The Transgender Issue*.
† Relatedly, the UK's most prominent campaign group positioned against the rights of trans children is called – tellingly – 'Transgender Trend'.

which the nebulous but powerful concept of 'tradition' is frequently weaponised – the battle for trans rights today is being fought on the battlegrounds of history.

It might be expected that this would lead to a resurgence of trans histories: that trans campaigners would fight these arguments by highlighting as many stories from our past as we could, and using those stories to emphasise how diverse (and very often non-stereo-typical) trans people have always been. But the problem – and the root cause, I think, of the narrow historical narratives I described earlier – is that anti-trans campaigners are not simply arguing, 'Trans people are new'. Instead, they're arguing, 'Trans people are new, *and that means they're not real*'. And by coupling our historicity with our *realness*, they've managed to tap into one of the most profound anxieties of trans communities today.

In January 2015, I screwed up enough courage to attend my local trans group for the first time. The people there were wonderful and welcoming, embracing my new name and pronouns with generosity and kindness – but I was convinced I didn't fit. Every one of them seemed so effortlessly at ease with their trans identities: so secure in their knowledge that this was how they were supposed to be. I knew that not living as female made me happy in a way I hadn't known was possible, but that didn't feel like enough. 'How do you know this is *real*?' asked a persistent voice in my head. 'What if you just *think* you're trans because it makes you feel special? What if you've just been talking to too many trans people on the internet? What if you've convinced yourself this is right, but you're wrong?'

Eventually, I managed to ask the question. 'Did anyone else here . . . when you first came out, did you have problems *believing* yourself?'

Every single person in the room raised their hand.

As trans people, the ways we navigate the world and claim our rights are all oriented around proving our realness: demonstrating that our genders are real and should be treated as such. We have to prove we're real enough to be referred to with the correct pronouns; to be given the medical care we want; to be given legal rights and access to gendered spaces. Our society asks us to re-assert our validity again and again. Anti-trans campaigners claim we're not real: that our genders are constructed and synthetic rather than 'natural', and that to acknowledge their validity – in particular, the femaleness of trans women – is to be asked to participate in a 'post-truth' world or engage in Orwellian double-think.[54] The experience of being misgendered chips away at our internal sense of security in the realness of our identities.[55] Even our defenders speak in these terms, implying that asserting our realness is the most effective way to remind people that we deserve human rights: 'Trans women are real women'; 'Non-binary people are valid'.

In this context, it's not surprising that we question ourselves. Nor is it surprising that we fight our opponents on the terms they've set. When we assert the realness of our identities, we're not just trying to convince anti-trans campaigners that we deserve rights: in many cases, I think, we're also trying to reassure *ourselves* that our genders are real, in the face of a world that continually tries to undermine them.

It's never clear what 'realness' really means, but there's a vague, unspoken community consensus over the things that might be considered to trouble it. They're all the messy things that our 'classical' trans narrative prefers to leave out: fluidity, non-binary identities, play, external motivations, ambiguity. When you're faced with a political landscape that says 'you're not real' – and when you're working in an exhausting, hostile political environment characterised by orchestrated online pile-ons and immediate Twitter amplification of out-of-context statements, which leaves no room for nuance – the overwhelming temptation is to avoid mentioning these messy aspects of trans experience altogether: to stay 'on-message', which, in Jacob Tobia's words, 'generally means catering to the least common denominator, watering down your community's story'.[56]

Make no mistake: clearly, this emphasis on our realness has considerable political value. It helps us to target many of the most pernicious transphobic arguments. It supports the growing consensus that we were 'born this way', which handily means we can't be morally blamed for being trans, or persuaded not to be.[57] And it has personal value too: it feels reassuring, solid, stable. But if we take these contemporary standards of realness anywhere outside our immediate cultural and historical context, they start to crumble. This means that when we come to research history, if we bring those standards of realness along with us, we can't get very far at all.

One key reason that these standards of realness aren't useful for looking outside our immediate cultural and historical context is because of the way they rely on asserting our deep, *internal* sense of gender. In order to prove our realness, we emphasise how strongly we feel ourselves to be male, female or non-binary on the inside. We draw a clear distinction between this *internal* gender identity and *external* factors like gender expression or gender roles. This internal/external distinction is essential to representing how we understand ourselves, and it's essential to combating arguments like those of Stuart Waiton, which see trans people as motivated by a desire to conform to gender stereotypes in our external appearance and behaviour. But the problem is that this internal/external distinction doesn't really stand up to scrutiny. For one thing, not everyone (in the past or in the present) understands themselves as *having* a core, stable internal self that remains the same at all times: there's a lot of evidence to suggest that this understanding of selfhood is culturally specific and, in Western Europe and the USA, dates back only to the late eighteenth century.[58] For another, people can have multiple motivations at once: a person in the past who was assigned female at birth and presented as male for a term in the army might well have been motivated *both* by a desire to overcome patriarchal assumptions about women's roles *and* by the affirmation they drew from being seen as male, and might well have struggled to separate the two (I'd challenge anyone today to separate out the internal and external motivations for the way they present themselves). For another, external gender expression can impact or reshape the way we feel inside, whether temporarily or permanently. And for another, even if someone's motivations for disrupting gender *are* completely external, their history still demonstrates the viability of moving – whether for an hour or a lifetime – away from the gender we were assigned at birth, providing a powerfully liberating precedent for all of us.

What can we, as trans people or as historians, do about this? Instead of continuing the exhausting fight to prove our realness in the past and the present, I think it's time we changed the terms of the conversation. If we start to treat our standards of 'realness' critically, we can open up space for so many more new ways to relate to gender, in both the past and the present. We can both widen the scope of trans history and enable people of every gender to live more freely and expansively. Being 'really' a man, a woman, a non-binary person or any other gender isn't incompatible with fluidity, situationality, ambiguity or creativity. And those of us who experience our genders in this way have a longer history than we might previously have thought possible.

Because of this, the way I use the word 'trans' in this book is deliberately expansive. Importantly, expanding trans history isn't the same as rewriting it. While in a sense everybody who writes a history book is rewriting history, in another sense it's not possible to rewrite the past: it happened, and nothing can change it. What is possible – and what I want to do here – is to re*read* the past.[59] Unlike historians a few decades ago – or even a few years ago – we now live in a society that equips us with the tools to realise that gender isn't simple, binary, stable, or inextricably linked to the body. These tools enable us to see things in the past that were always there, but which haven't been apparent to us until now.

What this doesn't mean is 'reclaiming' people from the past as part of trans history. That language of 'reclaiming' is used a lot, both by trans activists and by anti-trans activists – and every time I see it, I can't help but feel like this capitalist language of owner-ship is part of the problem, part of the system we're trying to dismantle.[60] As trans historian and literary critic Gabrielle M.W. Bychowski pointed out to me when I brought this up during an online discussion, thinking in this capitalist way also leads us to see historical representation as a scarce resource we need to fight over, rather than as something we can expand, reshape and share.[61] Instead, I want to propose that we use the language of *community*. In real life, we don't *own* or *claim* the members of our communi-ties; we certainly don't forbid them to be members of multiple communities at once. Instead, we make space for them: we support, validate and celebrate their presence in our community. We open our arms and shift things around to make them feel welcome. We're unlikely to share every aspect of our experience with every member of our community, but we have enough in common to create solidarity.[62] We might find that we benefit from the support of different communities, even communities that might seem at odds to some: one person might feel at home among both trans men and lesbians, for example, or among both non-binary people and women. And if we keep our communities expansive and welcoming, and continue to insist that they're not mutually exclusive, everybody's communities are richer. This is how, I hope, the histories in this book will enrich multiple present-day communities too. Expanding the scope of trans history doesn't mean erasing the history of others: with any story, but especially with stories this messy, emotional connection to the past isn't a zero-sum game.

Like Susan Stryker – who points out that we can use 'trans' as a verb as well as an adjective – I want to take the word 'trans' back to its roots, which reflect a sense of *movement* between places.[63] Many, if not most, of the individuals whose stories I tell in this book can't be uncomplicatedly described as 'trans people' – whether that's because they lived long before the term 'trans' was coined, or because their experience of their gender was specific to a culture that doesn't (or didn't) use it, in which case the imposition of a white, Western gendered paradigm would be an act of colonial violence.[64] But the history in this book is *trans history* nonetheless. It's history that shows us the *moveability* of gender. It's history that shows us that – notwithstanding the outraged claims of anti-trans commentators today – what constitutes a man, a woman, or gender itself has *continually* been defined, contested and redefined. It's the history of people who've troubled the relationship between our bodies and how we live; people who've taken creative, critical approaches to gender binaries; people who've approached gender disruptively or messily. Before our current moment, before we were trans, these people showed us that gender was ours to play with, ours to challenge, ours to change.

We don't know whether John Sullivan ever wore a gown again, in England or Australia. We don't know what John felt while walking down the street, drunk, on the night of Monday 8 June 1847; and we don't know whether 'These clothes are mine' was an excuse for theft, or something John genuinely felt. Perhaps John *was* female, or neither male nor female, for those minutes; perhaps John was male, but expressing femininity; perhaps John redefined masculinity to include the wearing of dresses. Each one of those possibilities tells us a new story about the history of gender, and provides us with a new promise about the way gender can be. Each one of the stories in the pages that follow does the same.

Author's note
Writing trans history differently

In writing this book, I was keen to do something different: to write a trans history that made space for complex and messy gendered experiences, and that had care and ethics at its heart, prioritising the dignity and humanity of people in the past and the present. As a result, I've made a few decisions that set the book apart from many other histories like it, which I want to explain here.

Pronouns

Most of the people in this book embody multiple gendered possibilities at once: we can interpret them, simultaneously, in several different ways. Because of this, I've chosen to use they/them pronouns to refer to the majority of the people in this book. In contemporary English, we use the pronoun 'they' in three distinct senses. Many non-binary people use it as a deliberately claimed singular pronoun, pointedly emphasising its neutrality; in many contexts, this is the pronoun I choose for myself. But we also use it as a default singular pronoun for someone whose gender we don't know; in this way, it can function as *passively* neutral as well as *actively* neutral. And of course, we use it as a plural pronoun to refer to more than one person. In this book, I'm partly using 'they' in the second way – avoiding presumption of gender, rather

than suggesting that the people I'm talking about would necessarily have actively chosen they/them pronouns – and partly in
the third way, emphasising the multiplicity and plurality of these
people's genders.[1] Choosing they/them as a neutral pronoun also
allows me to avoid imposing gendered pronouns on people who
wouldn't have used these in their native language. The exceptions, where I use he/him, she/her, or other pronouns, are people
for whom we have evidence not just that they used these pronouns
in life (which might, for many people, simply have indicated that
they didn't have another option) but that they clearly articulated
a male or female identity.

Sources

My research for this book has gone beyond archival records of
how people lived, and into the literary world. The real people in
this book rub shoulders with fictional characters – not because I
think it's irrelevant whether trans historical figures existed or not,
but because literature can often provide us with a fascinating
glimpse into how people in a particular society thought about
gender; and because queer fiction can sometimes provide new
ways of thinking about possible trans pasts and futures that historians might never have thought of.

One thing this book does is makes visible the trans dimensions
of other kinds of history: gay history, women's history, the histories of costume and theatre. In doing so, I engage with and cite
many people who've gone before me. Some of these are fantastic,
trans-affirming scholars and activists whose work I hope this
book lifts up; some others, though, are people who express
transphobic and/or racist views, and who I'm simply citing for
the facts they provide. Anyone who wants to pursue further reading should approach the sources in the notes with this in mind.

Treating the past with respect

I've avoided giving the invasive details about trans and intersex people's bodies that populate many other histories: nobody needs to know exactly what someone's genitals looked like to understand their story. I've also tried to minimise the number of times I refer to people as assigned male at birth (AMAB) or assigned female at birth (AFAB) – partly because (as I mentioned above) these don't fully make sense for contexts without official birth registration, and partly because I'm concerned that these terms often get used to suggest that the gender a trans person was assigned at birth is their 'real' gender, or to separate non-binary people into another artificial binary. I haven't always been able to avoid these terms completely, though; the problem is that in many historical contexts, the gendered experiences that are available to people have *depended on* what their body was like, and how they were categorised socially on the basis of that body. But I've still tried to be mindful of this kind of categorisation and the harmful impact it can have, and I'd encourage everyone who reads this book to be mindful of this too.

I

'The majesty of Him my daughter'
Colonising gender roles in West Africa

The Portuguese made their way into the Kingdom of Ndongo by river. Winding 600 miles through present-day Angola, the Cuanza River enters the Atlantic not far from Luanda, the city that was the first centre of Portuguese occupation following their invasion in 1575 (and which remains the capital today).[1] Ndongo centred around the banks of the Cuanza and its tributary the Lucala. Ruled by a monarch called the Ngola, who sat at the top of a complex network of hierarchies including local authority figures and hereditary rulers, it was a country with a well-developed military and strong international trade networks. The Portuguese initially wanted trade on an ostensibly equal, collaborative footing, but their efforts soon turned to Christian conversion and the establishment of political rule.[2]

From the beginning of their contact with the Portuguese, the rulers of Ndongo were assertive. Keen to establish a trading relationship, they had sent emissaries to Lisbon in 1520, four decades before the Portuguese first visited them in 1560–61.[3] They made it clear in negotiations that they would only accept a partnership on an equal footing.[4] But as the Portuguese established their fortress at Luanda, and began to abduct people in increasingly large numbers for enslaved labour in their Brazilian colonies, they became steadily more intolerant of Ndongo's independence. In particular, they were committed to diverting the flow of tribute away from the Ngola and into their own pockets. From the 1580s onwards, the Portuguese and Ndongo fought a series of battles as the Portuguese constructed forts on Ndongo land. During the earliest battles, Njinga Mbande was born.[5]

Njinga was a member of the Ndongo royal family: the child of the king, Mbande a Ngola, and his favourite concubine Kengela ka Nkombe.[6] They grew up alongside their three full siblings: their brother Ngola Mbande, and their two sisters Kambu and Funji. Distinguished from a young age by their intelligence and their interest in law and military strategy – all qualities perceived as masculine – Njinga actively sought out political education, and was known in their community for outperforming the men around them mentally and physically.[7]

In 1617, when Njinga was probably in their thirties, their father was murdered by his own soldiers. His death plunged the kingdom, and Njinga's secure family life, into turmoil. Succession in Ndongo was not strictly hereditary: instead, local rulers would elect a new monarch from various candidates with familial and/ or political claims to the throne. This time, there were multiple candidates to choose from: children of Mbande a Ngola's multiple concubines, other competing royal families, and rulers with important local power bases. In the end, the throne was secured not by diplomacy but by trickery. Njinga's brother, Ngola Mbande, gathered his supporters and seized the throne just minutes before the election could begin.

Aware of the fragility of his grip on power, Ngola Mbande consolidated it swiftly and brutally. While he didn't see Njinga, Kambu and Funji as serious rivals, since all of them had been assigned female at birth (AFAB), he was worried by their potential to produce male descendants who would have their own claims to the throne. As a result, he had all three of them forcibly sterilised. More traumatically still, he set about murdering his existing rivals – including Njinga's young son, their only child.[8]

In 1621, Ngola Mbande asked Njinga to undertake an embassy to Luanda, the centre of Portuguese rule. Their delegation was received by the Portuguese governor, João Correia de Sousa: the first delegation from an African country to be recognised in such a way. Njinga's embassy was a great success: they negotiated a peace treaty, recognising the then-established borders between Ndongo and Portuguese territory but asserting their country's sovereignty by refusing de Sousa's demands that Ndongo pay Portugal an annual 'tribute' of enslaved people.[9] Njinga also consented to Christian baptism and, with João as their godfather, took the name of Ana de Sousa.

With their embassy and strategic baptism, Njinga established themself as an important political figure, and a potent ally or threat, in Portuguese eyes – and they were soon to rise to greater prominence. In 1624, their brother Ngola Mbande died. His death may have been suicide, brought on by his inability to protect the integrity of Ndongo, or may have been poisoning. Several contemporary reports suggest that Njinga may have poisoned him: all these reports are written from hostile perspectives, but certainly Njinga, having endured forced sterilisation and the murder of their child at his hands, had reason enough.[10] Whether or not they were responsible for their brother's death, Njinga certainly seized the Ndongo throne with alacrity. And to the Portuguese, they presented themselves not as queen, but as king.

Throughout history and across the world, people like Njinga have occupied social roles coded as or associated with genders different from the ones they were assigned at birth, and have lived their gender differently as a result. In the vast majority of cases, it's impossible to tell with any certainty where the social role ends and the gender begins.

The intersection between gender and social role is one of the biggest factors that leads to the dismissal and erasure of trans possibility in history. People who lived as a different gender as part of their job or social position are overwhelmingly character-ised as 'disguised' or 'cross-dressing' men or women, the gender they lived as nothing more than a masquerade. This is particularly the case for AFAB people who lived as men while fulfilling a male-coded social role: these people, the mainstream narrative goes, were simply defiant women making their way in a man's world, concealing their 'real' gender in order to reap the benefits afforded to men in a patriarchal society. Anti-trans feminist activ-ists go further, claiming that if we read these histories in any other way, we're robbing young women of historical female role models, and writing the category of the masculine or nonconforming woman out of existence.[11]

Trans people find it difficult to talk about the ways in which gender intersects with social role, because we spend so much energy refuting arguments like this, which frame our desire to transition as solely motivated by restrictive and oppressive gender stereotypes. Certainly, the distinction between 'who I am' and 'what I do' is, for many trans people including myself, a crucially important one. Raised by a committed feminist, I've never under-stood particular roles or qualities to be exclusively associated with one gender or another; if moving away from living as a woman meant having to abandon crochet and compassion in favour of sports and stoicism, I'd never have done it. To adapt the words of a good friend, the non-binary activist and writer Ynda Jas, while I feel strongly that there's no singular way to be female – in fact, there are as many ways as there are women – I know equally strongly that that category doesn't *feel* like a good fit for my inner sense of self.[12]

But it would be equally untrue to say that my gender can be completely disentangled from the social roles I occupy. When I express care for a student I teach, for example, on one level I'm just following my pedagogical instincts and my sociopolitical values. But on other levels, I'm aware that I'm deliberately disrupting expectations of the 'male lecturer' role, which is *politically* important to me; fashioning my own 'not-straightforwardly-male' identity in the student's eyes, which is *personally* important to me; and carefully negotiating the power dynamics of the situation depending on the student's own gender, which affects both my gender expression and the way I experience my gender in the interaction. This sounds ridiculously complicated written out in such a way, and yet it's an accurate depiction of the complex way that social role works as a co-constituent of gender, in the same way as the other factors I've talked about. Who's to say that people in the past didn't experience their gender with the same complexity?

With this in mind, it doesn't make sense to automatically exclude people from trans history if their gender intersects with a social role they perform – for several reasons.

Firstly, in many cases, we simply can't know people's motivations with any certainty. We know, for example, that at least 400 AFAB people fought in the American Civil War – but most of their names are lost to us, let alone the complexities of how they understood their genders or the multiple factors that led them to enlist.[13] But if we assume that their gender must be 'disguise' until proven otherwise, we're privileging one possible interpretation over several others: bringing cisnormative assumptions to history, and letting them colour the way we read it.

Secondly, these stories provide a valuable history for the ways in which gender is often fluid and situational. Fluidity is often used as a reason to dismiss people's gendered experience as 'not real', which harms genderfluid people in particular, but also obscures the ways in which *everyone* can experience their gender differently in different situations.[14] Just because someone only lived as a gender different from the one they were assigned at birth for a short proportion of their life, then – such as living as male for a six-year term in the army – we shouldn't simply dismiss the validity of their short-lived trans experience.

And we should, I think, call it trans experience. This is the third reason I believe these stories must be treated as part of trans history: because regardless of what motivated them, the stories of people like the American Civil War soldiers show us that gender is malleable and has never been limited by birth assignment. To argue that gender fluidity and creativity are 'non-traditional' is to ignore this long history of gender disruption. It doesn't matter *why* they did it: the very fact they did it demonstrates that people living and being respected as a gender other than the one they were assigned at birth – temporarily or permanently – is far from a new phenomenon. This is an important point for both women's history *and* trans history, and both of these overlapping groups of people can find a sense of empowering historical community in these stories. In this respect, the message that young people of *all* genders can take away from these histories is not that there were no defiant women in history: it's that gender is flexible and disruptable, and this is liberating for all of us.[15]

People in Europe and the USA who have lived as a gender different from the one they were assigned at birth as part of occupying a particular social role are part of trans history. But I also have a broader point to make here. The fourth reason we must treat these stories as part of trans history, and perhaps the most important one, is that social roles work to co-constitute gender differently in different cultures. If it's hard to disentangle someone's inner sense of gender from their social role in white and/or Western cultures, it's completely impossible in many others.[*] If

---

* In her important 1997 book *The Invention of Women: Making an African Sense of Western Gender Discourses* (Minneapolis: University of Minnesota Press, 1997), Oyèrónké Oyěwùmí showed that Yorùbáland (situated in the west of what is now Nigeria) did not categorise people as 'men' or 'women' prior to Western contact and colonisation. While society recognised anatomical differences between AFAB and

38

we try to draw an artificial separation between what counts as someone's 'real gender' and what should be dismissed as 'just a disguise to enable them to fulfil a particular social role', we're imposing modern Western understandings of gender on cultures and time periods where they don't fit. And if we exclude people from trans history *unless* their gender can be clearly separated from their social role, we're contributing to the enduring whiteness of mainstream trans historical narratives. The neat separation of these ideas is a specifically Western construct, which was imposed on many societies through the process of colonisation. A truly inclusive trans history, then, must examine the devastating impact of Western colonialism, and the many gendered ruptures it caused, which continue to exert their impact today.

Because of the patriarchy and systemic misogyny that continues to pervade many cultures, AFAB people have often had more to gain from inhabiting male social roles than AMAB people have from inhabiting female ones. Many historians have told stories like these using the term 'female masculinity', which originates in the work of the trans theorist Jack Halberstam.[16] Halberstam's term has been transformative for gender scholars, enabling us to decouple 'masculinity' from 'men' and to realise it can be expressed and embodied by people of any gender. However, I've chosen not to use it myself. The problem with using 'female masculinity' uncritically, in my view, is that it can reify a distinction between an inner 'femaleness' and an outwardly expressed 'masculinity': it can leave unchallenged the assumption that the person you're describing is essentially, inherently 'female'. For some AFAB people in history, inhabiting male-coded social roles didn't just

---

AMAB people, people were not categorised along these lines; instead society, including the social roles people occupied and the ways they were addressed, was organised on the basis of relative seniority. This is another really good example of the way in which understandings of gender differ significantly in different cultures, and how this has been shifted by colonialism, as I'll talk about in the rest of this chapter.

make them 'masculine women', or make them express 'female masculinity'. Sometimes, it made them people who couldn't be categorised within a gender binary. At other times, it simply made them men.

The Pharaoh with the golden beard

In the fifteenth century BC, an ancient Egyptian treasurer named Tiy carved a piece of graffiti on the island of Sehel in the River Nile. 'I followed the good god, the king of Upper and Lower Egypt,' Tiy wrote, naming the Pharaoh who had led them into battle before exclaiming, 'may she live!' 'I saw,' Tiy continued, 'when he overthrew the Nubian Bowmen, and when their chiefs were brought to him as living captives. I saw when he razed Nubia, I being in his Majesty's following . . .'[17]

The Pharaoh whom Tiy had followed into battle, who had prompted this mixture of gendered pronouns, was Hatshepsut. Hatshepsut was the child of Pharaoh Thothmes I. When Thothmes I died, he was succeeded by his son, Thothmes II; Hatshepsut, Thothmes II's half-sibling, ruled as his queen. When Thothmes II died, his son with Hatshepsut, Thothmes III, was still a child and so for around seven years, Hatshepsut ruled as queen regent – but they wanted more. In a dramatic coup, Hatshepsut seized power, and had themself crowned Pharaoh.

The office of Pharaoh was a divine one – the Pharaoh was a god on earth – and so Hatshepsut's route to power took the form of a new religious mythology. The king of the gods, Amun, had declared Hatshepsut his male heir. 'He, greatest of all the gods, speaks to me,' Hatshepsut declared, 'as a father to his son!'[18] Having been declared not only male, but divine, Hatshepsut adopted the male dress of the Pharaoh, including the ceremonial gold beard. They also adopted a mixture of gendered ceremonial names, including male-coded names ('Son of the Sun'), female-coded names ('Lady of Both Lands', meaning Upper and Lower Egypt) and names that could be described as non-binary, in that they were grammatically female forms of male titles.[19] Statues and visual depictions, too, combined gendered representations. Statues produced early in Hatshepsut's reign as Pharaoh are particularly disruptive of the gender binary: one, for example, depicts them with breasts but wearing masculine dress, while another shows them with male-coded sex characteristics but describes them as 'daughter' of the god Re.[20] In these combinations of gendered characteristics, Hatshepsut arguably drew on the conventions surrounding particular Egyptian deities, who were also depicted in ways that disrupted binary understandings of gender.[21] As their reign progressed, though, they moved towards more strictly male depictions of themself. Their funeral temple, Djeser-Djeseru (also known as Zoser-Zosru), was lined with statues of Hatshepsut as a sphinx – an exclusively male creature in ancient Egyptian tradition – while at Karnak, an enormous 28-metre obelisk depicted Hatshepsut with their ceremonial beard and male-coded crown, with a caption describing them as king.[22] Their skin was depicted as red, the convention for depicting men in ancient Egyptian art, rather than the pale yellow conventional for women.[23]

Visual depictions of Hatshepsut as a child and teenager also show them wearing masculine clothing, and engaging in pastimes such as hunting that were associated with boys rather than girls.[24] Stone inscriptions produced during Hatshepsut's reign claimed that their father (the Pharaoh Thothmes I) had performed a religious ceremony to denote Hatshepsut his heir, crowning them not as Princess but as Prince.[25] Horus, the falcon-headed god of kingship, was depicted referring to Hatshepsut as a king, with he/him pronouns.[26] Yet the extent to which Hatshepsut was genuinely understood as male before they took the office of Pharaoh

is unknown. Most depictions of their youth were produced retro-
spectively, during their reign – at a point in their life when they
were deliberately fashioning their male identity. In order to
bolster their maleness as Pharaoh, then, Hatshepsut created a
male past for themself too. Signalling that they intended to
continue the tradition of AFAB maleness within their own family,
Hatshepsut had statues of their young child Nefrure carved with
a miniature beard.[27]

In an age where most Egyptians would never see the Pharaoh
in real life, these depictions of Hatshepsut as male, royal and
divine were intended to consolidate their power across their
kingdom.[28] Graffiti like Tiy's, and other written records, indicate
that their gender was understood partly as male, and partly as
both male and female. Depictions of Hatshepsut as a boy produced
during their reign would sometimes be accompanied by feminine
grammar.[29] Stone inscriptions referred to 'King Hatshepsut, she
whom the gods hath chosen'.[30] Their close servant Sennemut
called them both 'King' and 'Mistress'.[31] Their father, Thothmes
I, referred during his lifetime to 'the majesty of Him my
daughter'.[32]

Why did Hatshepsut go to such lengths to present themself as
a man, with a male origin story – and why did their subjects
understand their gender in this way too? The answer was not
simply that Hatshepsut was 'pretending' to be a man in order to
seize the throne: there is little doubt that their subjects knew they
were assigned female at birth. Nor was it that women were
considered unable to lead, as Hatshepsut's term as queen regent
– and the several other queen mothers or regents who had ruled
Egypt before them – makes clear.[33] It was that their gender was
inseparable from their social role: to be Pharaoh, in ancient
Egyptian culture, was to *be* male.

Ancient Egyptians understood gender in a largely binary way:
maleness and femaleness were complementary aspects of an

essential duality built into their religious stories of the world's creation.[34] While some deities were represented in ways that combined male- and female-coded characteristics, the royal roles of King (Pharaoh) and Queen were strictly defined as complementary male and female offices, and this gendering was reflected in their iconography: the Pharaoh was the living incarnation of the male god Horus.[35]

Hatshepsut was not the first AFAB pharaoh: 300 years earlier, the Pharaoh Sobekneferu had ruled as part of the Twelfth Dynasty.[36] But no records exist of Sobekneferu depicted with a beard, and very few of them wearing male dress.[37] The difference for Hatshepsut was that they were not the only person vying for the throne. Thothmes III, who Hatshepsut had supplanted as Pharaoh, was AMAB, and if Hatshepsut were to be depicted as feminine in any way, they would be understood as secondary ruler in comparison to him.[38] They would be seen as less close to the gods, and less able to embody the true office of Pharaoh as a result. This marginalisation of AFAB people was replicated throughout the ancient Egyptian religious hierarchy.[39]

Hatshepsut's visual depiction as male, therefore, was an intrinsic component of their role as Pharaoh – but it was *also* a response to patriarchal ideology, which would have understood a female-presenting ruler as secondary to a male-presenting one. It's impossible to separate these two factors: Hatshepsut's place in trans history is both a product of the way their social role was gendered, *and* of the way their society treated women. In what we might well understand as a product of the latter, Thothmes III ordered all images of Hatshepsut destroyed after their death. How they died, after seventeen years as Pharaoh – and what happened to their mummified body – remains an unsolved mystery.[40]

Colonising the rich men

Hatshepsut ruled over an independent kingdom, pursuing a policy of diplomacy rather than the conquests of their prede-cessors and sending diplomatic missions as far as present-day Somalia and India[41]. For much of more recent history, however, large parts of the African continent on which they lived have been invaded and occupied by European colonisers. The story of that process of colonisation has often also been the story of the imposition of European understandings and ideologies of gender.

For the people of precolonial Igboland, in the west of contem-porary Nigeria, gender was a fundamental aspect of social organi-sation. Land ownership was passed down through male relatives, but women worked the land and largely operated the subsistence economy, while men performed more ritual-oriented roles; industriousness was understood as an essentially female trait.[42] Igbo society before the nineteenth century, then, had 'male' and 'female' social roles, but these roles weren't tied to anatomy or to gender assigned at birth. Instead, the gender of individuals shifted *depending on* their social role.

'If Ekwe is coming to you,' an Igbo woman named Nwajiuba told researcher Ifi Amadiume in the 1980s, 'it shows you the sign and throws in money for you.' The title of Ekwe was understood to attach itself to AFAB people through possession by the goddess Idemili, which first manifested itself as extraordinary good fortune: successful harvests, economic prosperity, and charisma that encouraged others to want to work for the person concerned. Once a person took the title of Ekwe, they were gendered male. This gender didn't manifest itself linguistically – Igbo pronouns are gender-neutral – but socially. Ekwe people could own land; they married women, including paying the 'child-price' for them, which enabled any children these wives bore to carry on the

Ekwe family name;[*] and they occupied important political positions within their local community.[43]

People who did not bear the Ekwe title could also become male through marriage and land ownership. If a household was left without men – for example, if a husband died, leaving his wife and daughters as sole occupiers of the family's house and land – the family's continuing right to work the land depended on one of the children becoming a son. Like Ekwe people, these sons could marry one or more wives, and any children those wives had would bear their husband's family name. There was no assumption or expectation that the husband and wives would have a sexual or romantic relationship – and the husband's maleness was defined by social role, not by sexuality – though it must, of course, have provided an opportunity for women or AFAB people who did want to have sex or live as a romantic couple to do so.[44]

To perform these social roles was, in precolonial Igbo culture, to *be* male. These men weren't obliged to modify their presentation in order to be treated as male: the position they occupied in society was enough. The social role and the gender were intrinsically entangled.[45]

British invasion of Igboland, along with the rest of contemporary Nigeria, changed all this. Christian mission activities began in earnest in the early 1840s and as the new religion became established – through a mixture of force and coercion – so practices associated with indigenous deities were suppressed. Since the Ekwe title was intrinsically associated with possession by and worship of the goddess Idemili, it was banned, eliminating a key aspect of Igbo gender fluidity, and depriving AFAB people of a

---

* As Nwando Achebe points out, it's more accurate to describe the money paid to secure a marriage as the 'child-price' rather than the 'bride-price', as its main purpose is to integrate any children the wife has into the husband's line of succession.

route to political influence.[46] The newly imposed patriarchal Christian ideology, and education informed by it, led to a reorganisation of Igbo society in which men were the primary holders of political and economic power, and AFAB people could no longer become men in the same way. Christian-influenced moral censure also meant that Ekwe people no longer married women, instead arranging marriages for their sons.[47]

As the Christian missions spread through Nigeria, Britain also began its campaign of colonial rule. In 1851, the Royal Navy bombarded the city of Lagos, enabling Britain to install a new leader who served British interests more effectively. (With apparently unacknowledged irony, these interventions were justified in part as efforts to abolish the trade in enslaved people – from which Britain had, of course, benefited significantly.[48]) From 1891, the British colonisers delegated leadership of areas of Igboland to local leaders by issuing them with 'warrants' to rule; ostensibly this was a way of allowing Nigerian people to govern themselves, but in practice it was a way of entrenching surveillance across a large and decentralised nation, and a way of rewarding people who served British interests.[49] These 'warrant chiefs' were, with one notable exception (who I'll talk more about later), all AMAB people. As a result, this entrenched a foreign system of male leadership in colonial and postcolonial Igbo culture; and once again, AFAB people were denied the opportunity to move into leadership positions by becoming men. Though the warrant chief system was abolished in 1929, the newer Igbo royal title of Igwe remains restricted to AMAB people.[50]

This context was devastating for AFAB people – but some fought back. Historian Ndubueze L. Mbah tells the story of how AFAB people in the region of Ohafia, in the south-east of contemporary Nigeria, responded to being shut out of colonial power structures by manipulating precolonial social roles in new ways, and were able to reshape gender accordingly. In Ohafia, the category of *ogaranya* referred to people who accrued what Mbah calls 'wealth–power masculinity': a form of maleness that necessitated both 'wealth in commodities' and 'wealth in people'.[51] Before British colonisation, ogaranya were overwhelmingly AMAB. But as the AMAB people in Ohafia began to take on commercial, political and religious roles within the new colonial structure, in the early twentieth century, AFAB people moved into their previous spheres of influence. They practised ritual specialisms such as medicine, cultivating yams, and developing trade partnerships with other regions in Nigeria and beyond.[52] In fulfilling these roles, they were already understood as masculine. But as they accrued wealth through these practices, they were able to fashion themselves as ogaranya. Through this, they cemented their social maleness, including becoming able to marry one or more wives.[53] As eyewitness Tessy Uzoma recalled of one well-known early-twentieth-century ogaranya, Unyang Uka, 'Because of her ogaranya performance, she was no longer considered a woman': Unyang had instead 'transformed herself into a man'.[54]

In early-twentieth-century Ohafia, then, reduced opportunities for women's power and influence led to more AFAB people fashioning themselves as male ogaranya. But even as they strove against the tide, the imposition of colonial British values entrenched restrictive gender roles and reduced options for fluidity both within Igboland and across the rest of Nigeria. (The fact that contemporary Nigerian anti-trans laws focus on AMAB people is, in part, a reflection of how invisible these options for AFAB maleness have become.)

It's important, though, that white historians don't treat women or other AFAB people as passive victims in this process. On the contrary, many of them have cleverly and strategically negotiated the new gender norms that colonisation has brought. The stories of Ohafia's ogaranya are examples of this at the level of the local community – but the stories of Njinga Mbande and Ahebi Ugbabe show us that the history of gender disruption in West Africa goes right to the very top.

The kings and the invaders

It was when Njinga Mbande seized the throne of Ndongo that their gender became an issue. While the title of Ngola wasn't inherently gendered (meaning it can't be accurately translated as either 'king' or 'queen'), Ndongo's previous rulers had all been male.[55] The Portuguese, concerned about Njinga's propensity to assert Ndongo's sovereignty rather than submitting to colonial rule, exploited this fact to argue that Njinga was an unsuitable monarch: as the new governor Fernão de Sousa wrote in a letter to the Portuguese king, 'a woman had never governed this kingdom'.[56] They worked to undermine Njinga's rule by convincing local authorities within Ndongo that their gender disqualified them from sovereignty, and set up an alternative puppet monarch, Ngola Hari, who had a far weaker claim to the throne than Njinga but was much more pliable.[57]

The Portuguese authorities' understandings of how gender operated in Ndongo politics were simplistic and inevitably informed by their own patriarchal society and Christian worldview. The contemporary sources that record resistance to Njinga's rise to power are all informed by these ideologies too. In reality, women in Ndongo had substantially more political agency than Portuguese norms led the authorities to expect.[58] Moreover, AFAB people could be understood as masculine in Ndongo society, as Njinga's childhood makes clear.[59] While the role of Ngola was heavily associated with masculine symbolism – and while Ngola Mbande, Njinga's brother, clearly only saw AMAB people as potential rivals – the throne of Ndongo was not automatically barred to AFAB people. In seizing the throne and the title of Ngola, Njinga could also build upon their already established masculinity and seize a form of symbolic maleness.[60]

The precise ways in which Njinga's maleness manifested itself are difficult to determine. Most of the contemporary evidence comes from Portuguese chronicles, which were informed by a racist, anti-African worldview that associated people of colour (and particularly Black people) with sexual transgression and gender inversion. Did Njinga really, for example, keep a retinue of male concubines who were forbidden, on pain of death, to sleep with anyone but the monarch?[61] Were these concubines really forced to dress in women's clothes?[62] What does seem likely is that Njinga asked to be addressed as King in gendered languages like Portuguese (Kimbundu, their native language, does not have gendered pronouns); that they commanded their troops in battle; and that they wore what was perceived by the Portuguese as masculine dress.[63] As the Scottish mapmaker and travel writer John Ogilby wrote, they used 'a man's [name]', 'especially in the Army, and will acknowledge no otherwise'.[64]

If this maleness was an intrinsic part of occupying the role of Ngola, it was also clearly a strategic advantage in negotiating with the Portuguese. As their claims that women couldn't rule Ndongo suggest, the Portuguese were liable to not recognise the authority of a female monarch. In fact, they had form in this respect: when negotiating with the Makua people in northern Mozambique, they recognised only the male leaders (mwene) and not the female leaders (ipwiyamwene), despite their equal status as co-rulers.[65] While the colonial context of seventeenth-century Angola wasn't the *only* driving force behind Njinga's gender fluidity, then, the two things also can't be disentangled. Being male was, in part, a strategic decision that enabled Njinga to command respect – or at least to be taken seriously.

And Njinga did need to be taken seriously by the Portuguese. Despite the alliance the two parties had developed after Njinga's embassy and conversion to Catholicism, harmonious relations did not last long. The Portuguese reneged on their agreement to remove a fortress they had built without permission on Ndongo lands, and objected to Njinga's decision to shelter people fleeing enslavement on Portuguese coastal plantations, who fled inland and sought asylum in Ndongo.[66] They were then scandalised when Njinga developed alliances with the Imbangala, militarised groups who also lived around the Cuanza River, and abandoned their Catholic faith in the process.[67] Njinga spent some time hiding from Portuguese pursuit on the islands in the river, before conquering and becoming monarch of the nearby Kingdom of Matamba (a nation that did have a tradition of female rulers).[68]

During this time, letters sent by the Portuguese colonisers back to Portugal demonstrate how serious a threat they considered Njinga to be. Governor Fernão de Sousa wrote regularly to the Portuguese king, and his letters reveal that relations with Njinga consistently preoccupied him. In one 1625 letter, he outlines the tactics the Portuguese used to avoid giving Njinga 'the occasion to make war', and emphasises the need to 'understand [Njinga's] determination' in order to succeed in their colonial project.[69] In 1626, he wrote with frustration that Njinga 'continues to endanger the conquest of the region'.[70] Most concerningly for the Portuguese, when Dutch armies seized control of Luanda in 1641, Njinga reached out to them in search of an alliance, and in 1647, the combined force of Njinga's army and the Dutch defeated the Portuguese at the Battle of Kombi.

In 1648, however, the Portuguese recaptured Luanda. It was at this point that Njinga began to alter their military strategy. Apparently realising that it would be impossible to drive out the Portuguese completely, their priority shifted to securing the liberty of their sister Kambu. Both of Njinga's sisters, Kambu and

Funji, had been captured and imprisoned by the Portuguese and used as hostages to manipulate Njinga. Funji had been murdered by her captors in 1646 after Njinga and the Dutch planned to rescue her, making Kambu's rescue ever more urgent.[71] As a result, Njinga pursued reconciliation with the Portuguese, and re-converted to Catholicism, writing a series of deferential letters to the Pope to secure his recognition of their sovereignty.[72] The Portuguese finally released Kambu (who had also converted to Catholicism, taking the name Dona Barbara) in 1656, in return for 'tribute' from Njinga, which took the form of hundreds of enslaved people. For the next seven years, Njinga co-operated harmoniously with the Portuguese: adopting Catholic religious practices across their kingdoms, entering into a Catholic marriage to a young courtier named Sebastião at the age of seventy-five and largely accepting the transportation of enslaved people from their kingdoms: in fact, these transports increased substantially under their watch.[73] They died in 1663 from a lung infection, at the age of eighty, and were succeeded by their sister Kambu, whose life they had fought so hard to preserve.

Since Angola regained its independence from Portugal in 1975, Njinga has increasingly been treated as a national hero. A statue of them stands in Luanda; films, songs and poems tell their story; their name has been used to lend prestige to streets, schools, coffee and beer.[74] Angolan narratives present them as a leading figure of anti-colonial resistance who opposed Portuguese conquest and obstructed the slave trade – and as a heroic female leader.

The truth, of course, is more complex. Njinga certainly opposed the Portuguese invasion of Ndongo fiercely, and they offered asylum to people fleeing enslavement during the years when they were fighting the Portuguese. But at other times, they engaged in the slave trade themself, competing with other local rulers in this economy of human beings.[75] In the last years of their life, they were increasingly motivated by regaining the freedom of their sister Kambu, even if their efforts cost hundreds of lives. Their letters to the Portuguese governor from the 1650s betray their desperation: if only the Portuguese would return Kambu, Njinga promises, there would be peace.[76] In a 1655 letter, Njinga complains that they have 'given infinite slaves', and yet Kambu has still not been freed.[77] Clearly, the Portuguese were using Kambu as a bargaining chip, exploiting Njinga's love for her to extort money and ensure a steady supply of enslaved people to labour in their Brazilian colonies. But the negotiations surrounding Kambu's release cannot entirely account for Njinga's toleration of the slave trade in the later years of their life, during which the number of people captured and transported increased dramatically.[78]

Modern narratives of Njinga's life don't just simplify their relation to the history of colonisation and the slave trade; they also simplify the story of their gender. Njinga's role as male Ngola is downplayed, or presented as strategic cross-dressing to enable them to navigate a patriarchal world.[79] This interpretation of Njinga obscures the ways in which their social role intersected with and shaped their gender. It also squeezes them into a Western gender framework, by which gender is fixed and binary – ironic, given that this same understanding of gender is what motivated the Portuguese attempts to strip Njinga of sovereignty altogether.[80]

Despite the complexity of their political legacy, Njinga certainly made the Portuguese realise that they needed to take seriously the rulers of the countries they sought to colonise – and that they couldn't take the success of the slave trade for granted. And despite limited historical recognition of the ways in which they disrupted gender, they also shifted the landscape for monarchs of Ndongo and Matamba. While Njinga had been treated as male on the throne, after their death a succession of women ruled the two combined kingdoms, and were treated as queens rather than kings. Not only did Njinga disrupt gender in their own lifetime, then, they also effectively shifted the gender of the title of Ngola, transforming it from a male role to a gender-neutral one. For 80 of the 104 years following Njinga's death, the monarch of Ndongo and Matamba was a woman.[81]

250 years later and over 2,000 miles north, Igalaland, a nation in modern-day Nigeria, also crowned an AFAB king. Like Njinga Mbande, Ahebi Ugbabe did not straightforwardly resist the colonisation of their country; indeed, far more than Njinga, they collaborated with them. Unlike Njinga, however, Ahebi was not born of royal blood. Instead, they worked their way up. From a teenage runaway who had to engage in sex work to make ends meet, they became the only AFAB warrant chief in colonial Nigeria, and were later crowned king of their neighbouring nation – before falling spectacularly from power when they pushed their disruption of gender too far.

We owe our knowledge about Ahebi's life to the historian Nwando Achebe, who pieced together a detailed biography through painstaking oral history research for her 2011 book *The Female King of Colonial Nigeria*. Ahebi was born in Igboland, in the village of Umuida within the Enugu-Ezike region, during the second half of the nineteenth century.[82] At the age of fourteen or fifteen, in around 1894, they ran away to neighbouring Igalaland: a self-imposed exile from their community, following a traumatic period in which they were raped and narrowly evaded forcible dedication to the goddess Ohe as punishment for a crime their father had committed.[83] There they survived through sex work and, later, by developing a professional network as a trader.[84] Through both of these jobs, they developed three commodities that would prove very valuable to them: understanding of pidgin English, knowledge of the local road networks, and contacts among the British colonisers.[85]

When they returned to Enugu-Ezike around 1915, Ahebi put all of these to good use. As the sole line of communication between their village and the British colonial officials, they soon ousted the existing headman (village leader) and were appointed in his place.[86] The British – who appointed them to this colonial office – clearly admired them, describing them as 'loyal', 'of a quiet disposition', and with 'far more intelligence than the men'.[87] Shortly after Ahebi's promotion to headman, they were promoted to the position of warrant chief: leaders given 'warrants' by the British to rule in their stead over particular local areas, and to sit on the local Native Court.[88]

Both of these positions – headman and warrant chief – were intrinsically male ones, and Ahebi's appointment to them as an AFAB person was unique and unprecedented. There were plenty of established routes to maleness within precolonial Igbo culture: indeed, as warrant chief, Ahebi also became a male household head and married wives for their brothers in the same way as the Ekwe people I described earlier, paying the child-price on behalf of their brothers and ensuring that these wives' children would become Ahebi's heirs.[89] This meant that they were treated as a man by their local Igbo community. Their main role was as judge in the local court, and they were carried to court sittings on a hammock, accompanied by musicians singing songs that reiterated and upheld their maleness.[90] But within the British culture of colonial Nigeria, Ahebi was still regarded as female: British reports refer to them as 'a lady'.[91] Only a few astute observers among the British recognised what was going on: as V.K. Johnson, the Assistant District Officer for Enugu-Ezike, wrote in his 1934 'Intelligence Report', Ahebi had 'had to . . . become a man' and had been 'regarded [as such] ever since'.[92]

Ahebi's acquisition of male titles did not stop there. At some point in the second half of the 1920s, they were crowned *eze* – a quasi-portable title best translated as king – by the king of

Igalaland, the Attah-Igala.[93] Their intention was to use their *eze* status to exert power in their native Igboland. While Igalaland had a tradition of kings (and one AFAB person, Ebulejonu, had previously ruled there), Igboland was not monarchical at all; as Achebe describes in her book, by being crowned king, Ahebi was importing an alien, Igala system of hierarchical, singular leadership into Igboland.[94] And yet they managed it. Having been crowned in the city of Idah, the Igala capital, Ahebi returned to Igboland in great pomp, accompanied by music and gunfire, and bearing the staff of male kingship.

For the next decade or so, Ahebi ruled as king from an increasingly elaborate palace compound, which included farmland, stables and housing alongside its own market, school, prison and brothel.[95] The school was unusual in providing education to girls, and the palace provided asylum for women fleeing abuse.[96] Ahebi married multiple wives, including some of the formerly abused women. These wives could sleep with male friends, bearing children who would carry on Ahebi's family line, and some were also encouraged to engage in sex work with important Nigerian and British men who visited the palace.[97] Through these political and sexual networks, Ahebi exerted influence both over their local area and within colonial power structures, consolidating the social role that saw them treated as male by their community.

It was in 1939 that Ahebi discovered the limits of their maleness. Although AFAB people could become male in Igbo economic and political contexts, the one area exempt from this gender fluidity was the spiritual realm. Ahebi had already begun to antagonise local male elders through their corruption, autocracy, and abuses of power such as abducting wives – but their foray into a male spiritual role was what led to their downfall.

Perhaps the most strictly male-coded role in Igbo culture in this period was that of invoking *mma*, or masked spirits. The masked spirits – physically represented by tall figures in elaborate costumes – represented the return of souls from beyond the grave, visiting Earth to reassure their families that all was well following their death. Men who wished to learn to invoke mma must endure a gruelling initiation ceremony, including being covered entirely in mud and subjected to several rounds of flogging. The association of masked spirits with men was so strong that women were expected to run away at the sight of one; and if a woman – or an uninitiated man – were to invoke one, the spirit would be desecrated.[98]

Ahebi was understood as a man by their local community, but the events that followed their decision to bring out a masked spirit showed that they were not understood as *enough of* a man – certainly not an initiated man – to perform this role. Their action was seen by the local elders as an 'abomination'.[99] Apeh Azegba, the oldest man in the community, regarded Ahebi's spirit with disgust before exclaiming, 'Do you not know our culture?'

Incensed at the rejection of their mma, Ahebi took Apeh and his fellow elders to court. Ahebi hoped that the British colonial officials, who they had served so loyally for so long, would back them up in court by ruling in their favour – but they were wrong. For the British, Ahebi had long become surplus to requirements. The office of warrant chief had been abolished ten years earlier, and now the very fact Ahebi had quarrelled with their local community over the masked spirit showed the British that they were no longer a useful ally.[100] The Resident, who oversaw the regional colonial court, heard the case and ruled that Ahebi, as a woman, did not have the right to invoke a masked spirit. Once it became clear that the British would no longer support Ahebi in every dispute, Ahebi's authority in their local community was severely damaged.

Thereafter, Ahebi was a king in name only. They never served as a judge or court official again: local people simply stopped attending their palace court. But they retained their palace servants, and with them their comfortable lifestyle. It also appears that they retained their maleness in the eyes of the community, but with the understanding that they were not male in a spiritual context. At some point in the early 1940s, they held a lavish, ritu-alised 'burial' ceremony while they were still alive, in which they were given male burial rites. When they died for real, in May 1948, their burial was accompanied by far less pomp. No one in the local area could recall to Nwando Achebe how they were treated in their genuine funeral: as a man, as a woman, or – just as they lived – as a non-binary, complex mixture of the two.[101]

Like Njinga, Ahebi's legacy is complicated. They gave the British indispensable local knowledge that actively advanced their invasion of and consolidation of power over Igboland, though it would be reasonable to argue that the colonisation process would ultimately have proceeded with or without their help, and that Ahebi simply took what little chance they had to better their own position.[102] They stuck closely to British colonial laws rather than indigenous justice as a judge, and abused their power over the local community as headman, warrant chief and king – but their community had often not been kind to them either, particularly during their teenage years.[103] It's unclear how much choice the women of their palace compound had about engaging in sex work, though it's important to say that the Igboland sex industry was in any case far more female-led, and granted sex workers much more autonomy, than its European counterparts.[104] In any case, the compound also provided a refuge for survivors of abuse, as well as a rare co-educational school. Like everyone living through the brutality of European colonisation, Njinga and Ahebi were human beings, negotiating their own emotional and politi-cal interests alongside those of their communities and countries – and though some of their actions had harmful consequences, we should never lose sight of the fact that those actions were themselves responses to that colonising process.

Similarly, we must understand the fluidity and complexity of their genders within that colonial context. The story of the relationship between colonialism and gender isn't as simple as the imposition of European gender hierarchies and binaries on cultures to which those ideas were unfamiliar. Instead, European colonisation enabled and necessitated some forms of gender disruption – like Ahebi's promotion to headman and warrant chief, and Njinga's use of male kingship to gain respect from the Portuguese – while suppressing others, like the banned Ekwe title in Igboland.

It's notable, of course, that Njinga and Ahebi were both assigned female at birth, but were understood as male within their political roles. AFAB maleness, and particularly AFAB royal maleness, was a phenomenon that the patriarchal European colonisers could come to understand: they already associated maleness with rule and prestige, so the idea that AFAB monarchs could be kings did not feel completely alien. AMAB femaleness, on the other hand, was treated by European colonisers with far more suspicion and disgust, and far less tolerance.

Fighting the patriarchy

For similar ideological reasons, the decisions of some European AFAB people to live as male while inhabiting a male-coded social role were celebrated, rather than censured. During the eighteenth century in particular, stories of people known as 'female soldiers' or 'female sailors' circulated with increasing regularity.[105] The crucial difference between these military personnel and people like Njinga and Ahebi, though, was that their recognition and treatment as men was often dependent on *passing*. Njinga and Ahebi's contemporaries – just like the inhabitants of precolonial Igboland, and the subjects of Hatshepsut – knew they'd been assigned female at birth, but understood them as men regardless, because of their social roles. Most of the people who lived and worked with the soldiers and sailors of eighteenth- and nine-teenth-century Europe, though, treated them as men because they genuinely thought they had been assigned male at birth. When they discovered they hadn't been, they largely reverted to using she/her pronouns and understanding them as women. The fact that these people's recognition as male was often contingent on their passing successfully doesn't make their maleness inher-ently inauthentic, and it doesn't exclude them from trans history. But it does mean that the experiences of AFAB men in eight-eenth- and nineteenth-century Europe were very different from those in nineteenth- and twentieth-century Igboland, or in seventeenth-century Ndongo.

The narratives of AFAB soldiers published in eighteenth-century England quiver with the constant threat of discovery. The soldiers experience thrilling close shaves, narrated with a level of bodily detail that is clearly, in some cases, designed to titillate the reader. Christian Davies, who enlisted in the British army in 1693, for example, writes of putting on one of their husband's suits, 'having had the precaution to quilt the waistcoat to preserve my breasts from hurt which were not large enough to betray my sex'.[106] Hannah Snell, who lived as James Gray in the British Royal Marines from 1747 to 1750, and who collaborated with publisher Robert Walker on their memoir *The Female Soldier* (which was an immediate sellout success), records how they were forced to remove their shirt for a flogging on the ship's deck. Later a musket wound in the groin threatened almost certain discovery (though given that they were not outed during their time in the Royal Marines, it seems more likely that they were actually hospitalised with scurvy or a tropical disease, and that the 'groin wound' story was concocted to add an element of jeopardy to their published memoir).[107]

Though there were many moments in military life that could pose the threat of being outed – sleeping, changing, going to the toilet – the cramped, communal existence of soldiers and sailors led everyone to keep their heads down, giving their comrades as much space as possible rather than scrutinising their every move.[108] This means that beyond the numbers we know – 83 in the Netherlands in the seventeenth and eighteenth centuries, 400 in the American Civil War – probably lie far more soldiers who were never outed, and who thus remain invisible to history too.[109]

Why did they do it? As with any large group of gender-nonconforming people, there's no way we can attribute all of their actions to a single cause. Military life was certainly a route to excitement, professional fulfilment and money that was inaccessible to women. Many of the published narratives cite romantic motivations, or their protagonists are depicted as following their natures, having preferred 'masculine' activities as children.[110] At least some people were also motivated to enlist as men by their sense of their own maleness.[111] But we don't need to get bogged down in teasing out individual motivations in order to realise that all of these people disrupted gender by inhabiting a male-coded social role, and taking on male names and pronouns as part of that process: that they lived, however temporarily, as genders distinct from the ones they were assigned at birth. Their stories demonstrate the malleability of gender according to clothes and context; they deserve, therefore, to be included in narratives of our rich and diverse trans history.

Throughout this chapter, the story of the intersections between gender and social role has been bound up with the story of patriarchy and systemic misogyny. It's important to say again that, if we understand these stories as part of trans history, this doesn't mean that they aren't also part of women's history. Both women and trans people (and of course, people who belong to both groups) can find inspiration and historical community in these stories, and all of us can benefit from recognising that there's nothing 'traditional' about seeing gender as fixed or essentialised.[112]

Like all the people in this book, the people we've encountered in this chapter are from both periods and cultures that did not have the concept 'trans' as many people understand it today. And like many contemporary societies, the cultures Njinga, Ahebi and Hatshepsut came from continue to understand gender differently from many Western cultures. But their stories still show that there is a long, cross-cultural history of understanding gender as not binary, not fixed, and not tied to the body. Indeed, understanding social role as a co-constituent of gender is not something that's confined to history. It continues today, both at an individual level (my experience of teaching, for example) and at a societal level too. In rural Albania, burrneshë or 'sworn virgins' take on the male role of household head and are consequently treated as men by their community, including using male names and pronouns.[113] In several Native American nations, people known today by the inter-tribal term 'Two-Spirit' – who I'll talk more about in Chapter 6 – are distinguished in part by taking on work associated with a gender different from the one they were assigned at birth, or with more than one gender.[114] In Samoa, an intrinsic part of being a fa'afafine – a person who lives as a girl or woman from a young age – is taking on a female-coded social role, performing domestic and caring duties.[115] All of these people, for whom their social role is not the totality of their gender but is inextricably bound up with it, deserve to have their histories told, without erasure or oversimplification. To do otherwise is to perpetuate the misogyny that has deprived, and continues to deprive, so many AFAB people of agency in so many areas of their lives, and the colonialist ideologies that suppressed and/or shaped the disruptive genders of Africa and beyond.

2

'She liked me in my greatcoat and hat'

Fashion and trans panic in early modern Europe

By the time he reached his sixties, the Reverend Thomas Stoughton was ready to leave the world behind. Stripped of his clerical duties – and of the stipend that came with them – as a result of his nonconformist Christian beliefs (a form of non-mainstream Protestantism that was subject to legal discrimination in seventeenth-century England), Stoughton was, in his own words, 'old and poor'.[1] In his postscript to his fourth and final book, which he described as his 'last Will and Testament', he instructed his seven surviving children not to grieve that he could leave them no inheritance.

This book, *The Christian's Sacrifice*, printed in 1622, is a hefty folio volume that chastises a world fraught with everyday sin. In it, Stoughton manages to extract 258 pages' worth of sermonising from just two Bible verses – Romans 12, verses 1–2:

> I beseech you therefore, brethren, by the mercies of God, that ye present your bodies a living sacrifice, holy, acceptable unto God, which is your reasonable service.
>
> And be not conformed to this world: but be ye transformed by the renewing of your mind, that ye may prove what is that good, and acceptable, and perfect, will of God.

Despite Stoughton's emphasis on his own frail and destitute state, his commentary on these verses is far from charitable. The text is often antisemitic, emphasising the virtue of Christians above that of Jewish people. And when it comes to advising his readers on how they might 'be not conformed to this world', Stoughton seizes upon gender as an example of everything that is wrong with his contemporary society. One of the 'deep abominations of these times, drawn from the deep pit of hell itself' – one of the 'monstrous' phenomena of seventeenth-century England – is that 'men and women' have 'changed their sex, (as much as they can) one with another'.[2]

Stoughton's horror at the practice of 'changing sex' – rhetoric that wouldn't look out of place in a transphobic blog post today – sounds to twenty-first-century ears like revulsion at bodily transformation. Though the people of early modern Europe did believe that bodies could spontaneously alter their sexual characteristics, here Stoughton's outrage was directed at a somewhat more ephemeral – though no less radical – kind of alteration. He was talking about fashion.

> Men wearing long hair like unto women, and women cutting off their hair like unto boys, or beardless young men, wearing nothing thereon but hats, putting them also off to such as they meet. Oh monstrous, oh monstrous.[3]

For Stoughton, to adopt hairstyles, headwear and gestures associated with a different gender was to 'change [your] sex'. His younger contemporary, the Puritan lawyer and polemicist William Prynne, agreed. As a result of the 'unnatural Tonsure' hairstyles adopted by the 'Female sex', Prynne argued, they were 'Hermaphrodited, and transformed into men'; while 'diverse of our Masculine, and more noble race, are wholly degenerated and metamorphosed into women' through the 'Womanish, Sinful, and Unmanly, Crisping, Curling, Frouncing, Powdering, and nourishing of their Locks'.[4]

While Prynne and Stoughton's claims about 'changing sex' work partly on a metaphorical level, dress was also one of the factors that *made* sex (a term used to refer both to bodily configuration and social identification) in early modern culture. Early modern European people saw clothing as 'a largely accurate indicator' of a variety of factors that affected one's place in the social hierarchy: not just sex, but also social status, race, age and profession.[5] For the early modern antitheatrical writer Philip Stubbes, this was one of the *purposes* of clothing: 'Our apparel was given us as a sign distinctive to discern betwixt sex and sex, and therefore for one to wear the apparel of another sex, is to participate with the same, and to adulterate the verity of his own kind'.[6] Clothing was not simply a covering, but a 'second skin', and so gender nonconformity *adulterated the verity of one's own kind*: changed the truth of one's very nature. To change one's appearance and hairstyle, then, *was* to change one's sex, in a real as well as a metaphorical sense.[7]

As a result, gender-nonconforming dress provides us with a potentially rich seam of trans history. But stories of people who dressed in gender-nonconforming ways aren't often included in narratives of the trans past. This, I think, is because they epitomise a problem that plagues the history of gender: the problem of motivations.

Simply put, it's rare that the motivations for dressing in this way can be attributed to gender alone. Sometimes we can identify people whose attachment to gender nonconformity clearly suggests a form of trans identity – such as the thief Glaudyne Malengin, who was arrested in Belgium in 1510 for wearing men's clothes, but still stated in court that they would continue doing it in the future – but more often, there are several possible reasons that any given individual might have dressed in a gender-nonconforming way.[8] People assigned female at birth (AFAB), for example, might present as male for economic reasons, or – as I'll talk more about later – for sexual ones. Widespread fashionable gender nonconformity of the kind Stoughton was complaining about inevitably concealed multiple individual motivations and experiences.

Lack of clarity about motivations – owing to lack of testimony – means that the trans possibility of these histories is very often erased. If historians start investigations of gender-nonconforming people by referring to them as 'women dressed as men', this immediately closes off any possibility of trans history.[9] Words and phrases like 'transvestism' or 'cross-dressing', which suggest disguise – a disruptive form of gender expression that definitively *doesn't* reflect the reality of a person's experience underneath their clothes – have the same effect. Even leaving aside all mention of gender can't, by itself, encourage readers of history to notice trans possibilities, because we live in a society that encourages us to assume everyone is cis and straight unless they explicitly state that they're not (after all, it's only people whose gender or sexuality is marginalised who are expected to 'come out').[10] Consequently, if we're not reminded that transness is a possible interpretation of a particular historical narrative, it's unlikely that it will simply occur to us.

Trans history can be explained away, and thus erased, in a way that much of the history of queer sexuality resists. Even if a historian avoids calling a historical man 'gay', they can't avoid confronting the fact he had relationships with other men. They might misrepresent him in other ways – in particular, bi history is often erased, as if it would be too complicated to confront the fact that a historical person had relationships with people of more than one gender – but the fact of the relationship still allows the history to transcend wrangling over terminology. But to prove that people who disrupted norms of gendered dress 'count' as trans history, we're expected to prove that they were *motivated by* gender identity alone – even in periods when 'gender identity' meant a very different thing from what it means today.

In fact, though, people who dressed in gender-nonconforming ways have always had *multiple* possible motivations. And this was truer than ever in societies like Stoughton's, where people were 'changing their sex' everywhere you looked.

Pearl earrings and perfumed hair

In many Western cultures today, the expression of femininity by people assigned male at birth (AMAB) is often stigmatised. While masculinity among AFAB people is considered acceptable (or even gender-neutral), AMAB femininity is the subject of comedy – think groups of young men in sports teams or stag parties wearing dresses 'for a laugh' on drunken nights out – or worse, of hostility.[11] The unspoken suggestion, reflecting underlying misogynistic ideologies, is that these 'men' have debased themselves by 'dressing like women', and thus deserve any ridicule and/or violence that comes their way. This means that people who are perceived as AMAB and who *want* to express femininity – whether they be trans women, non-binary people, gay men, or anyone else; and whether their motivations relate to identity, aesthetics, play, or some combination of factors – have to negotiate these risks, and make difficult decisions about whether feminine expression is worth potentially compromising their psychological or physical safety.

But in early modern society, the people who 'metamorphosed into women' by way of their dress were not stigmatised social outcasts: they were the court elite.

The reign of Elizabeth I in England saw the rebirth of a threatening category of people: AMAB court favourites who posed a sexual danger, in that they might gain favour and power through being sexually attractive to the unmarried queen.[12] Under most previous kings, male favourites had access to political influence, but couldn't intensify their power through sexual influence; female favourites could get close to the king sexually, and use their position for political persuasion as best they could, but couldn't be given official political positions.[*] Under Elizabeth, though, a courtier could aim for political *and* sexual dominance.

This new situation coincided with changing trends in men's fashion from mainland Europe, particularly France and Italy. In these countries, AMAB people[†] were wearing colourful, richly embroidered doublets with decorative puffed sleeves, along with accessories that had previously been restricted to women's fashion: lacy collars, earrings and other jewellery.[13] As these trends made their way to England, the Elizabethan court became a more colourful – and sweeter-smelling – place. Courtiers followed their mainland counterparts in donning embroidered doublets and accessorising with previously female-coded lace and jewellery. They set off these outfits by paying newly fastidious attention to their hairstyles, visiting barbers to have their hair and beards cut, curled and misted with perfumed water.

As a result, sixteenth- and seventeenth-century European writers characterised the court as a place of gender nonconformity. In England, the poet Richard Niccols described courtiers with a 'soft maiden voice and flickering eye', whose 'perfumed' clothes, 'curled locks, and thin beards' betrayed their 'woman's manhood'.[14] A set of three popular pamphlets published in 1620 pitted the figure of 'Hic Mulier' (Latin for 'that woman', but using the grammatically masculine version of 'that') against 'Haec

---

[*] This, of course, applied only if the king wasn't attracted to men: in the early fourteenth century, Edward II's subjects were worried that his sexual and romantic attraction to his male favourites was affecting his political decisions.

[†] I'm using the term AMAB here for clarity: these people were presumed male on the basis of their bodies, but weren't strictly 'assigned' male in an institutional way, since the state kept no systematic record of individuals' genders in this period.

Vir' ('that man', with a feminine 'that'): the 'feminine masculine' Haec Vir took more time to 'curl, frizzle, and powder your hairs . . . than ever Caesar did in marshalling his Army', and only their slight moustache and beard distinguished them from their 'fair mistress'.[15] In France, the diarist Pierre de L'Estoile compared the favourites of King Henri III to the (female) 'whores in the brothels' on the basis of their 'long hair, curled and re-curled by artifice, teased up over their little velvet caps', and described the king's dress as like that of 'court ladies'; his contemporary Agrippa d'Aubigné wrote that onlookers were 'hard put to say' whether they 'beheld a female King or a male Queen'.[16] In Venice, the nobleman Girolamo Priuli wrote in his diary that 'Young Venetian nobles and citizens tricked themselves out with so many ornaments, and with garments that opened to show the chest, and with so many perfumes', that 'Truly they may be called not youths, but women'.[17]

All of these accounts have a derogatory tone. Their writers pointed out courtiers' gender nonconformity in order to suggest, by drawing on wider sexist ideologies of gender, that these courtiers were not fit for political office. Henri III's favourites drew particular ire because of their association with an often unpopular king (Henri's attempts to negotiate a ceasefire to the bloody French Wars of Religion through concessions to Protestants made him unpopular, particularly with the polemical Catholic League); and because they made a serious faux pas when they accompanied him on a progress through Paris meant to raise funds for the war effort, wearing expensive, fashionable dress and jewellery while asking ordinary people to donate money to the Crown. Even in countries without such specific reasons for anti-courtier sentiment, concern for fashion was seen as opposed to concern for serious matters of religion, war or politics – reflecting gendered ideologies that saw women as trivial and inconstant, men as serious, thoughtful and steadfast. So pointing out courtiers' gender nonconformity was one way of suggesting that these young, fashionable people were not really fit to be political advisors.

These courtiers were also often accused of being 'effeminate'.[18] Importantly, though, this word had different associations in the early modern period from those it carries today. 'Effeminate' wasn't associated with gay men: instead, it was associated with excessive desire for *women*. People who wanted to attract women, the thinking went, would focus too much on their appearance – which was itself seen as a feminine trait. When the Italian poet Ludovico Ariosto depicted the North African Muslim warrior Ruggiero helplessly in love with the sorceress Alcina – in a passage also informed by the racist early modern European association of people of colour with sexual transgression – he described Ruggiero's newly 'womanish' concern with appearance: they wear 'golden bracelets' instead of 'warlike weapons' and two dangling pearl earrings (men typically wore just one), and 'bedew' their curly hair with 'waters of sweet savour'.[19] In letting their sexual desire determine their actions, people like Ruggiero were also betraying what was seen as a 'womanlike' lack of sexual control. If 'effeminate' people *were* accused of having sex with men – as in the diaries of both L'Estoile in France and Priuli in Venice – this was less because 'effeminate' meant 'gay' than it was because their 'womanlike' lust meant they would give in to any and all sexual impulses.[20]

But even though these accusations of gender nonconformity were made for polemical reasons – and even though they rarely name specific individuals, probably to avoid falling foul of defamation laws – their frequency and consistency indicates that such gender nonconformity was widespread. The extent to which these courtiers understood their *own* gender expression as feminine is likely to have varied. Some will have experienced their adoption of jewellery, lace and embroidered garments, combined with new attention to their appearances, as taking on feminine traits; others will have experienced these practices as reshaping what constituted masculinity, just as lesbian writer Jenn Shapland argues, 'I occupy the category woman, and that category must expand to contain *me*. In all my outfits.'[21] Motivations to present in this way will have differed between individuals, too: for some the femininity of contemporary fashion might be attractive because of its aesthetics, the way it made them feel modern, or the way it helped them fit in with the in-crowd; for others, it might be an opportunity to present in a way that felt more comfortable for them; for still others, the enjoyment they took in feminine expression might have been unexpected. The extent to which this expression *counted as* gender nonconformity will have varied in different contexts, too: in a court, surrounded by people who presented in this way and affirmed each other's male identities, lace and jewellery may not have constituted gender nonconformity in the same way as they did outside of that bubble.

The gender nonconformity of early modern courtiers resists easy categorisation – and that's precisely why it's a story we ought to tell. In part, it's important because it helps us understand that gender nonconformity and fluidity in fashion, and the transfer of trends from womenswear to menswear and vice versa, isn't a new or unprecedented trend in our contemporary society. But it also helps us to understand how gender expression means different things in different contexts, and how what counts as gender-nonconforming, as feminine, or as masculine is contextually contingent too. And it reminds us that, within a large group of people engaging in gender nonconformity, gendered experience is unlikely to be homogenous. All of these facts mean that, just because gender nonconformity has been fashionable at different points in history, this doesn't mean we should expel all cases of gender-nonconforming dress from how we think about trans history.

Ruffianly hats and wanton feathers

As the tirades against gender nonconformity penned by Stoughton and others made clear, gender nonconformity in early modern Europe wasn't a practice restricted to people assigned male at birth. The flow of influence between men's and women's fashion went in both directions. As AMAB people embellished their doublets with decorative embroidery, AFAB people themselves embraced doublets for the first time – constructing the doublet as a 'gender-neutral' item of clothing (and a far more interesting one than the neutral-coloured, loose-fitting garments that have often characterised gender-neutral fashion lines in recent years). They also adopted short hair and masculine-coded accessories such as daggers, spurs and hats. In doing so they would become, in the eyes of society, what the satirist Henry Fitzgeffrey called 'a woman of the masculine gender': a figure neither clearly male nor female.[22]

By 1619, when this gender nonconformity was the height of fashion, King James I of England had had enough. The gentleman John Chamberlain (an independently wealthy man-about-town who spent his days gathering news in the crowded nave of St Paul's Cathedral, which was used as a marketplace and hub of gossip) wrote to his friend Sir Dudley Carlton on 25 January 1620:

> Yesterday the bishop of London called together all his clergy about this town, and told them he had express commandment from the King to will them to inveigh vehemently against the insolency of our women, and their wearing of broad brimmed hats, pointed doublets, their hair cut short or shorn, and some of them stilettos or poniards [daggers], and such other trinkets of like moment; adding withal that if pulpit admonitions will not reform them he would proceed by another course; the

truth is the world is very much out of order, but whether this will mend it God knows.[23]

James was no stranger to personal interventions in religious practice (as his introduction of the 1611 Authorised Version of the English Bible shows), and he had already made it clear that he subscribed to the misogynistic ideologies of his period: his 1597 book *Daemonologie*, which asserted the dangers and realities of witchcraft, argued that women were more likely than men to become witches because 'that sex is frailer than man is', making them 'easier to be entrapped' by the Devil.[24] But his intervention here – asking every preacher under the jurisdiction of the Bishop of London not just to preach, but to preach *vehemently* against gender nonconformity – is nonetheless striking. John Chamberlain clearly agreed with James that this was an issue worth intervening over: for him, gender nonconformity indicated that 'the world is very much out of order'.[25] Both James's and John's reactions indicate that, like the gender nonconformity among courtiers – or perhaps more so – this disruptive gendered dress and behaviour was widespread.

Hot on the heels of James's intervention, later in 1620, came the *Hic Mulier* pamphlets I mentioned earlier: three texts that themselves 'inveighed vehemently' against gender nonconformity in fashion. The first, *Hic mulier: or, The man-woman*, depicted on its title page a barber cutting short the hair of a person in a doublet and skirt. Beside them, a companion in a similar outfit, with the addition of a broad-brimmed hat with a feather, looks at their reflection in a mirror.[26] The image is a caricature of sorts, but it's nonetheless a powerful reminder of the individual experiences behind invectives like those of James and Thomas Stoughton. What does the person gazing in the mirror *think* of their gender-nonconforming expression? How are they evaluating what they see? Thinking about the gender-nonconforming people of early modern England as *reflecting* on their appearance – rather than just as going about their days in hats and spurs – reminds us that they had internal lives, and that they made the decision to present themselves in this way with agency and purpose.

The anonymous writer of *Hic Mulier* delineates every gendered transgression that 'the masculine-feminines of our times' have made. They have exchanged feminine-coded headwear ('the comely Hood, Caul, Coif, handsome Dress or Kerchief') for 'the cloudy Ruffianly broad-brimmed Hat, and wanton Feather'. They have swapped 'the modest upper parts of a concealing straight gown' for 'the loose, lascivious civil embracement of a French doublet'. They have gone from 'the glory of a fair large hair' to 'most ruffianly short locks'; from 'needles' to 'swords'; from 'Prayer books' to 'bawdy jigs'; and from 'women's modesty' to 'apish incivility'.[27] In doing so, they have overturned a tradition of clear gendered differentiation in dress dating back to the Creation: 'Remember how your Maker made for our first Parents coats, not one coat, but a coat for the man, and a coat for the woman . . . the man's coat fit for his labour, the woman's fit for her modesty'.[28] As such, they have transformed their gender: they are now 'so much man in all things, that they are neither men, nor women, but just good for nothing'.[29]

Dress, here, is clearly not just about appearances. Men and women's different 'coats' reflect what are presented as their divinely ordained social roles ('labour' versus 'modesty'), and many aspects of 'masculine-feminine' gender expression are sexualised: the doublet is presented as 'all unbuttoned to entice . . . and extreme[ly] short-waisted to give a most easy way to every luxurious [sexual] action', while the repeated word 'ruffianly' has connotations of sex work.[30] While AMAB gender nonconformity was stigmatised because it was seen to indicate an inappropriate interest in the trivial rather than the serious, then, AFAB gender nonconformity was associated with sexual transgression and disruption of the patriarchal order.

The latter problem was, in part, behind John Chamberlain's comment that 'the world is very much out of order'. Indeed, the claims of Stoughton and others that people had 'changed their sex' through dress also had sociopolitical meaning: early modern writers sometimes used the phrase 'changed their sex' to indicate that someone had taken on a different social role, such as an AFAB person commanding an army.[31] Clearly one motivation for gender nonconformity among AFAB people must have been the economic and political benefits that came with masculine presentation. Masculine-presenting people could move more safely through the streets of an early modern city, giving them access to more economic opportunities as well as greater personal liberty.[32] Among these 'opportunities' were jobs that were often restricted to men, such as military roles. Perhaps counter-intuitively, though, one of the other jobs that masculine presentation facilitated was sex work.

The association of AFAB gender nonconformity with sexual attractiveness and licentiousness – and, especially, with sex work – was pervasive. As well as suggesting that the 'masculine-feminines of our times' wore doublets 'unbuttoned to entice', the writer of *Hic Mulier* suggested that they had paid for their haircuts and fashionable masculine clothes with sexual favours: 'She that hath given kisses to have her hair shorn, will give her honesty to have her upper parts put into a French doublet'.[33] When people were prosecuted for masculine presentation, the most common charge was that they were 'concubines or whores'; and in trials for defamation or slander, the accusation that someone 'wore the breeches' was treated as tantamount to calling them a sex worker.[34]

The exciting and yet dangerous sexualisation of this kind of gender nonconformity had its roots in the conventions of men's and women's clothing. Before about the middle of the fourteenth century, male- and female-coded clothing in Europe was differentiated, but similar: tunics created a similar silhouette regardless of gender. During the fourteenth century, however, the rise of features such as buttons led to men's clothing becoming more sexualised, revealing much more of the legs and – by the sixteenth century, as a tight doublet and hose became the most fashionable attire – emphasising the crotch. In women's clothing, by contrast, the legs remained hidden under full skirts.[35] If people adopted masculine presentation, then, observers would be granted a tantalising glimpse of their legs.

As a result, such masculine presentation was seen as automatically sexually exciting. In a dialogue by the Italian erotic writer Pietro Aretino, the fictional sex worker Nanna advised her daughter Pippa on how to excite potential clients, suggesting that Pippa 'Put on his cap and doublet. No sooner does the gentleman see you transformed from a woman into a man than he will leap on you as hunger does on a hot loaf.'[36] Thomas Stoughton clearly felt the same way: his explanation for AFAB gender nonconformity was that people wanted to 'be taken for young men', so that 'they may also be bed-fellows to such young men, and so play the harlots with them'.[37] For those who wanted to attract a sexualised gaze, this presented a potent opportunity.

Breeches and skirts

On Christmas Day 1611, the liberating and sexual potential of gender nonconformity was displayed in an unexpected venue. Evening had fallen over London, and the nave of St Paul's Cathedral was crowded. The old Gothic-style building (this was fifty-five years before it was to burn down and be replaced by the neoclassical building we know today) was always busy – the nave was used as a meeting place and marketplace, as well as a place of worship – but on Christmas evening it was busier than ever. Huddled together in retreat from the cold, dark streets outside, the St Paul's congregation was a captive audience for the person who stood concealed in one of the cathedral's high galleries, wearing a skirt and a man's cloak. Before the eyes of all who gathered there, the figure raised their skirts to reveal their legs – not bare, but, as the arrest records later recorded, with their 'petticoat tucked up . . . in the fashion of a man'.[38]

The St Paul's 'flasher', who was quickly arrested, was something of a celebrity in early-seventeenth-century London – and the scandalous display of leg, far from causing their downfall, helped to cement their personal brand. The exploits of Moll Cutpurse, or Mary Frith, gripped the gossips of London. Frith used gender nonconformity to facilitate petty crime, and embraced the freedom it brought to walk alone through the streets of London, to drink and to smoke; but they also knowingly manipulated the sex appeal it carried. Their self-exposure at St Paul's was calculated to excite onlookers – the tucked-up petticoat resembled breeches and revealed Moll's shapely legs – without actually baring any flesh; in fact, this technique may well have reminded Londoners of the association between breeches and sex work. Frith also performed at London's second-biggest playhouse, the Fortune, probably in a variety show following a play; the performance records suggest that it was a kind of smutty musical stand-up in masculine dress, 'with a sword by [their] side and a lute in [their] lap'. The lute, an instrument held between the musician's legs, was sexually suggestive enough, but Frith played on this further, telling the audience that while they might think they were watching a man on stage, if they came to Frith's lodgings 'they should find that she is a woman'.[39]

Frith's celebrity influenced at least three plays: John Day's *Mad Pranks of Merry Mall of the Bankside* (1610), which has since been lost; Nathan Field's *Amends for Ladies* (acted 1610–11); and Thomas

Dekker and Thomas Middleton's *The Roaring Girl* (first printed in 1611, but probably written earlier). Dekker and Middleton's play casts a fascinating light on how the people of early modern England perceived gender nonconformity. The character of Frith, known alternately as Moll and as Captain Jack, is talked about at length before we meet them, and it's immediately clear that they defy gendered categorisation. They're described as 'A creature . . . nature hath brought forth / To mock the sex of woman'; 'a thing / One knows not how to name'; someone whose 'birth began / Ere she was all made'; 'woman more than man, / Man more than woman'; someone who, in the sun, has 'two shadows to one shape'; and several more.[40] When the actor playing Frith finally enters the stage in the second act, wearing a gender-nonconform-ing outfit of a masculine 'frieze jerkin' and a feminine 'black safe-guard' (practical over-skirt), their celebrity status is immediately apparent: characters stop talking and turn to them in the street, calling 'Moll, Moll, pist Moll', and they bat off the admirers, saying coolly, 'I cannot stay'.[41] Their gender nonconformity facili-tates social freedom and attracts a gang of followers – including a character with possibly the best name in all of early modern litera-ture, Sir Beauteous Ganymede, whose name roughly translates in modern queer language as 'pretty bottom' – but it also leads the play's villain, Laxton, to assume that they're an easy sexual conquest.

The play allows Moll/Jack to assert their honour and virtue: they agree to Laxton's suggestion that they 'be merry and lie together', then surprise him by challenging him to a duel, which they win.[42] But it never lets the audience forget that their charac-ter is sexualised, as a conversation with a tailor about the way Moll/Jack's breeches stand 'stiff between the legs' makes clear.[43] Importantly, though, even throughout this sexualisation, Moll/Jack is never straightforwardly understood as female. The tailor is, ostensibly, explaining to Moll/Jack that if they want 'Dutch slops' – fashionable, baggy breeches – they will need more fabric:

Tailor Your breeches then will take up a yard more.

Moll Well pray look it be put in then.

Tailor It shall stand round and full I warrant you.

Moll Pray make 'em easy enough.

Tailor I know my fault now, t' other was somewhat stiff between the legs, I'll make these open enough I warrant you.

Alexander Here's good gear towards, I have brought up my son to marry a Dutch slop, and a French doublet, a codpiece daughter.[44]

On one level, the conversation here is about fabric. The tailor will need a yard more fabric to make baggy breeches; the extra fabric will stick out quite a lot, but the tailor will take care to make the breeches loose and open rather than stiff; and Sir Alexander, a concealed observer who is worried that his son wants to marry Moll/Jack, is outraged to hear details of their gender nonconformity. But on another level, the conversation is about penises. 'Yard' is an early modern term for penis, and the subsequent commands to 'put it in', and references to something that 'stands round and full' and is 'stiff between the legs' continue this innuendo. Yet even the penis jokes work on two levels. When Moll/Jack says 'put it in', the audience understands them both as a sexualised woman who could be penetrated *by* a penis, and as someone who is aspiring to *have* a penis, crafted for them along with their breeches. A 'codpiece daughter', meanwhile, might simply be a gender-nonconforming woman – a daughter who wears a codpiece – but might also, given the preceding innuendos, be a daughter who *needs* to wear a codpiece because of the penis that comes along with their gender-nonconforming dress. Underlying all of these jokes is the additional gendered confusion caused by the fact that no women could act on the English stage in the early seventeenth century – so Moll/Jack is a gender-nonconforming AFAB character being played by an AMAB actor.

The narrative of *The Roaring Girl* may be fictional, but its depiction of Moll/Jack provides a powerful insight into how early modern people understood gender-nonconforming dress as reshaping gender – as well as hinting at what the real Frith's gendered experience was like. It's important, though, that we think about this area of trans history beyond celebrities like Frith, and consider the lives of more marginalised gender-nonconforming people.

You can learn a lot about the early modern Republic of Venice from the shoes. Surviving examples of women's 'chopines' look startlingly like the fashionable platform shoes of today, but their purpose went beyond trendsetting. They allowed the wearer to tower over their companions: one of many fashion technologies that helped to entrench a strict hierarchy in Venetian society. And just as importantly, they protected trailing skirts from the marshy mud, rubbish and even sewage that could line Venice's narrow streets.

In the early modern period, Italy was a collection of states that shared various political alliances (and, increasingly, a common language), but was not a unified country. The independent Republic of Venice was a centre of intercultural dialogue and trade, a history still visible today in its architecture, which combines European and Arabic influences. As the chopine-wearers teetered through the piazzas and over low canal bridges, they would hear traders and market stallholders calling to each other in a multitude of languages – but they would also, inevitably, smell their refuse, along with the stench of stagnant, marshy water carried by the southerly winds.[45]

Despite the muck, Venice was also a centre of early modern tourism, enticing visitors from all over Europe. Travel books provided rich, enticing descriptions of cities like Venice, encouraging tourists to visit for its architecture, carnivals, culture – and courtesans. Demographic pressures and food shortages in sixteenth-century Venice pushed many people of all genders into the sex industry.[46] Of these, 10,000–12,000 were elite, high-status sex workers known as courtesans.[47] Courtesans sought not just one-off clients, but the regular patronage of young Venetian gentlemen, cleverly playing their suitors off against each other to increase their earnings. They stood in the doorways of their houses, calling out to passers-by and singing improvised love songs. Their services were not just sexual: they engaged customers in witty and learned conversation, ranging from gossip to poetry.

Among them was Julia Lombardo.[48] Julia owned a three-bedroom apartment in Venice that they filled with art, ceramics and books. As with many courtesans, their home was constructed as a jewellery box to display Julia – its most important contents – as learned, cultured and beautiful. As well as earning money from sex work, they received produce from vineyards and land that they owned. They used their income not only to support themself, but to support their disabled sister, Angelica, who inherited all Julia's possessions after their death in 1542.

The inventory of Julia's possessions taken after their death includes a substantial wardrobe. Among the dresses, blouses, stockings and shoes are seventeen pairs of 'women's breeches' and eight 'masculine women's shirts'. Like other courtesans, Julia habitually wore a mixture of male-coded and female-coded clothing. The masculine shirt and breeches were often hidden beneath a dress, enabling courtesans to provide brief, teasing hints of their body and suggestions of what they could offer to clients.[49] This process of revelation – exposing the transgressive sexual excitement that lurked beneath the courtesan's conventional exterior – was far more titillating than openness would have been.

Lift-the-flap prints of courtesans enabled tourists to enact the reveal again and again, lifting up a courtesan's engraved skirt to see their breeches underneath, while the painter Titian depicted an attractive sitter perpetually frozen in the process of removing men's clothing to reveal their breasts.[50]

Julia's gender nonconformity, then, was partly a business technique. It advertised their body and the potential sexual pleasure they could offer to clients. It also suggested that they might be able to provide sex of a kind that was considered gender-nonconforming, such as anal sex, or sex with a woman on top. This caused some anxiety to Venetian authorities, who were worried that heterosexual anal sex would prove a gateway drug to anal sex between men. In 1480, a law was passed banning women in the sex industry from cutting their hair short, since this was considered an attempt to 'please men by pretending to be men' (it's telling, of course, that they assumed the way to please a man was to look as male as possible) and in 1500, a woman named Rada de Jadra was sentenced to death for arranging for men to be able to have anal sex with female sex workers.[51] These attempts to suppress anal sex, along with others, provide evidence of its continuing popularity.

In both cases, we might see the courtesans' gender nonconformity as economically motivated. Julia was not the only courtesan to provide for a family member; many others were sole earners for their families, and sex work – including its conventions of gender nonconformity – provided a route to this economic independence.[52] But it's also important to think about both the possibility of gender-related motivations for this kind of expression, and about how different individual courtesans *experienced* their gender nonconformity, regardless of what their original motivations for it might have been.

It's clear that the people of early modern Italy understood courtesans' genders as complex, and as reshaped by their gender nonconformity. The Venetian authorities' persistent concern that courtesans were stimulating men's appetites for sex with men – as shown in their anxiety about their haircuts and their provision of anal sex – suggests that they were worried clients would think of AFAB courtesans as male, or as having male attributes.[53] Pietro Aretino, the erotic writer who penned the dialogue advising aspiring sex workers to wear men's clothes, also wrote to a courtesan called La Zufolina, who came from the Tuscan city of Pistoia, describing them as 'a man when you are chanced on from behind and a woman when seen from in front'. 'Certain it is,' he continued, 'that nature has so compounded you of both sexes that in one moment you show yourself a male and in the next a female'.[54]

If the courtesans' dress could affect how others saw their gender, how did it affect Julia and La Zufolina themselves? Just as with their courtier counterparts, it's essential that we acknowledge the diversity that must have existed between the courtesans. It's likely that some courtesans saw masculine expression as simply a work uniform or a means to an end, which didn't reflect or affect their underlying sense of self. But for others – especially given the early modern understanding of clothing as a 'second skin', one of the factors that helped to *make* gender – it's likely to have changed the way they saw their own gender. It's inevitable that some courtesans felt more comfortable with this change than others. It's possible, too, that the knowledge of the courtesans' gender-nonconforming 'uniform' was one among many motivating factors for some of those who chose to join the sex industry. If we neglect this diversity, we not only do ourselves a disservice by homogenising the historical evidence; we also, much more problematically, erase the individuality of a marginalised group who are so often spoken of in relation to the gaze and experience of their clients.

'Womanizing me too much'

Doing justice to these historical people means resisting the temptation to explain gender-nonconforming dress as motivated by factors unrelated to gender. It's so easy, and so common, to rationalise gender-nonconforming dress as 'just' something else: just fashion, just sex appeal, just something people did to gain economic opportunities. Thinking about the role of dress in trans history doesn't mean doing away with those motivations – but it does mean embracing the multiple simultaneous motivations, meanings and possibilities that gender-nonconforming dress carried.

I learned the hard way about the importance of acknowledging this multiplicity. In 2015, I was living in York and volunteering with the charity York LGBT History Month, coordinating a programme of events for the charity in and around the city. Working with a local academic, Helen Graham – a clear-sighted, warm and interesting woman who I admired for the skilful balance she struck between guiding and empowering local activists – we'd co-organised an event that invited people to mark the spaces in York that they felt were significant to LGBTQ+ history, defining significance as widely as possible, from the personal to the local to the global. We created cardboard rainbow plaques – a visibly queer version of the iconic blue plaque – and for twenty-four hours, York's LGBTQ+ history became visible all around the city. Some plaques marked personal milestones: I marked the shop where I'd tried on men's clothes in the changing room for the first time, while another person marked the place she'd come out to her mum. Some marked York's social and activist history: discos raising money for the local Lesbian Line and the Campaign for Homosexual Equality, and a flat passed between gay couples for generations that became known for its wild parties. And two of them marked York's association with an icon of lesbian history: Anne Lister.

Born in Halifax, West Yorkshire, on 3 April 1791, Anne is best known today for their diaries, which recorded their daily life and business transactions in plain English and encrypted some of their personal recollections in a code combining mathematical symbols, punctuation and Greek letters. The coded sections turned out to contain Anne's records of their romantic and sexual affairs with women. After their descendant John Lister deciphered the code with the help of his friend Arthur Burrell, he considered burning the diaries, but instead kept them concealed behind a panel at Anne's home, Shibden Hall. The coded sections were not published until the historian Helena Whitbread edited the diaries in the late 1980s and early 1990s, revealing a wealth of lesbian history. Beginning with an affair with their schoolmate Eliza Raine, Anne had several meaningful relationships with women throughout their life. They had an intense long-term relationship with fellow schoolmate Marianne Belcombe, which persisted even after Marianne's marriage to Charles Lawton; and they finally committed to Ann Walker in 1834, in a union the two appear to have considered a marriage.

Anne's connection to York was twofold. They attended the Manor House girls' school (now King's Manor, part of the University of York), which is where they met Eliza and Marianne. And on Easter Sunday 1834, Anne Lister and Ann Walker solemnised their commitment to each other at Holy Trinity Church, Goodramgate. The pair exchanged gold rings privately at home, before attending morning prayers and staying behind to take Holy Communion together. It's clear that Anne saw this as a form of marital commitment. They had planned to do it with Marianne, before their relationship ended: in 1821, they wrote in their diary, 'We have agreed to solemnise our promise of mutual faith [to each other] by taking the sacrament together'.[55] Following their communion with Ann Walker, Anne wrote, 'The first time I ever joined Miss W— in my prayers – I had prayed that our union might be happy' – though as they noted, that early sense of commitment had not quite been mutual: 'she had not thought of doing as much for me'.

Anne didn't use the word 'lesbian' to describe themself in their diaries, but they expressed their attraction to women in plain terms: 'I love and only love the fairer sex and thus, beloved by them in turn, my heart revolts from any other love than theirs.'[56] Some local men appear to have perceived them as a sexual threat: as they wrote in their diary, a 'Mr Lally' had visited Marianne at home and told them 'he would as soon turn a man loose in his house' as invite Anne over.[57] But the majority of censure Anne received from their local community focused not overtly on their sexuality, but on their dress. Nicknamed 'Gentleman Jack', they were mocked for their masculine cloth-ing: they sometimes wore a 'greatcoat and hat' (recording in their diary that one woman, Mrs Milne, found this attractive), and at other times they wore black bodices 'which resembled men's coats'.[58] In this choice of dress, Anne undoubtedly had multiple motivations: it was practical, facilitating their love of outdoor exercise; it put off male attention (the connotations of masculine clothing had shifted since the early modern period, making Anne's dress a turn-off rather than a turn-on for their potential male suitors); and it was, in many but not all cases, attractive to women.[59] Anne also understood their sexuality as masculine, referring to their desire for women as 'manly feelings' and recording their discomfort when one partner, Mrs Barlow, touched their 'queer' (genitals) in gendered terms: 'This is womanizing me too much . . . she lets me see too much that she considers me too much as a woman'.[60] They scoured classical literature for stories of androgyny and gender fluidity, turning them over and over in their notes, diaries and conversations.[61] Indeed, Marianne, though she wasn't always attracted to Anne's masculine appearance or behaviour, nicknamed them 'Fred'.

This was in line with the developing connection between sexuality and gender in Anne's period of history, whereby same-sex attraction was considered to reflect and/or affect your gender identity; and it's also in line with a convention in lesbian culture by which some lesbians have long used male names and/or he/him pronouns. Anne's description of discomfort during sex reads like a description of what some people today would call stone butch experience – drawing on the origin of the term 'stone butch' as a partner who is 'untouchable' during sex, focusing instead on touching their female partner – but it also, simultaneously, reads like an instantly recognisable narrative of gender dysphoria.[62] Anne's relationship to their gender, then, was by no means simple or easy to categorise – something that paying attention to their gender-nonconforming dress helps us to appreciate.

From the very beginning of our cardboard Rainbow Plaques initiative, people were telling us that Anne Lister deserved a 'real' plaque at Holy Trinity Church. The church could, after all, be seen as the site of one of the first lesbian marriages in the UK. In 2018, when York Civic Trust and York LGBT Forum were both named the Lord Mayor's Charities of the Year, conversations between the two made that 'real', permanent plaque possible for the first time. With the Churches Conservation Trust (who care for the church today) on board, the conversation turned for the first time to what the plaque should say.

It was at this point that the commemoration of Anne Lister collided with all the challenges I've been discussing in this chapter. Anne's gender-nonconforming dress, their love of women, and their complicated relationship with gender meant that, after a series of consultations, the plaque wording was set as 'Anne Lister, 1791–1840. Gender-nonconforming entrepreneur. Celebrated marital commitment, without legal recognition, to Ann Walker in this church, Easter, 1834.' But within hours of the plaque unveiling, I was receiving angry and often abusive messages on social media. Within a day, this had escalated: a petition was launched against the plaque and several people had got hold of my work phone number. It quickly became clear just how many people Anne Lister was important to, and how few of those people our consultation had managed to reach. The problem was, firstly, that the plaque didn't name Anne explicitly as a lesbian. No one had highlighted this word as important in our consultation, and (with what seems in retrospect like enormous naivety) I'd assumed this was because everybody *knew* Anne Lister was a lesbian: the plaque was going to say they married a woman, so what did it matter whether we used the word or not? But many of the women who identified with Anne saw this as erasing the connection they felt to them. The second problem was that we'd used the phrase 'gender-nonconforming'. To everyone on the decision-making committee, this was a description of Anne's *behaviour*, reflecting the dress and activities that saw them nicknamed 'Fred' and 'Gentleman Jack'. But to many people, it read as a label for Anne's *identity*: a statement that they weren't a woman, and were therefore not a lesbian either.

Some of the angry messages (and all of the abuse) came from anti-trans activists who saw Anne's plaque as a symptom of how, in their eyes, advances in trans rights were eroding the rights of lesbians. Their arguments were easy to dismiss on a logical level, though the abuse took longer to deal with, and is the reason I haven't written about the whole episode in detail until now (I still haven't been able to bring myself to watch the BBC drama about Anne and Ann, *Gentleman Jack*). But the majority of anger and hurt came from lesbians and bi women who were explicitly supportive of trans rights, but still felt Anne was an important part of their historical community. Respect for their concerns led the plaque to be recast, naming Anne as a lesbian.

The new plaque makes no mention of Anne's gender nonconformity, and this still saddens me. This isn't because I think Anne wasn't a lesbian, but because the description of their dress and behaviour as gender-nonconforming was never untrue, and because we've lost an opportunity to commemorate how Anne represents an overlap between lesbian history and trans history. They're a part of trans history because of their complex relationship to their gender, and because of the way they disrupted gender through their dress. They didn't want to be straightforwardly seen as female by their partners, and they used their dress to express this – *as well as* to attract women, to facilitate their active lifestyle, to be taken seriously in business contexts, and doubtless because they simply preferred the way it looked and felt. As a result of their dress, their gender was seen differently by the men and women around them.

Anne Lister encapsulates the way that gender-nonconforming dress is rarely motivated by one single factor. As I've shown in this chapter, when we're researching trans history, this is often compounded by the fact that we find huge numbers of anonymous individuals (like the courtesans and the courtiers) who all dressed in gender-nonconforming ways – whose experiences of and relationships to that gender nonconformity are unknown, but were undoubtedly diverse. Our inability to know their individual experiences doesn't exclude these people from trans history. In a period where clothing helped to make gender – when to change your dress *was* to change your gender – contemporary responses show that the genders of gender-nonconforming people were understood in non-binary ways. This chapter of the past, then, underlines how the way we think about gender has shifted over time, and how we need to be expansive in our thinking about what counts as part of trans history.

We often think of dress as a costume: something that we put on *over* our internal self, which might reflect or obscure our true identity, but never reshape it. But while the distinction between 'gender identity' and 'gender expression' is a useful teaching tool, helping to underscore the point that we can't tell anyone's gender just from looking at them – I use it myself every time I deliver trans awareness training – the reality of our experience is often more complex. My own dress both reflects *and* reshapes my gender: sometimes it's the case that I put on jewellery and a bright, fitted cardigan because I'm feeling less male and more non-binary on that particular morning, but sometimes the reverse is true. Both kinds of gendered experience are equally true for me: my gender isn't less authentic because a pair of dangly earrings can change how it feels.

When we put on something that changes the way we feel about our gender, then, we share that experience with thousands of people from the past. And when we look at the history of gender-nonconforming dress, we should focus less on the impossible task of identifying which historical figures are 'really' trans and which aren't, and more on acknowledging the diversity of creative, nonconforming and fluid approaches to gendered dress in the past, and appreciating both the individuality and the shared experiences they represent.

3

'I took especial pleasure in masquerade costumes'
Living and performing as women in
First World War internment camps

The doctors called it 'barbedwirelitis'. The writer and artist Paul Cohen-Portheim, who experienced it, called it 'monstrous, enforced, incessant community'. Confined in wooden huts with 200 other people – just a six-foot-by-four-foot quadrant to call their own – the prisoners were '*never alone*. Not by day, not by night, not for a second, day after day, year after year.'[1] Cohen-Portheim's vivid description of the unremitting sensory assault – the noise of conversations, snores and musical instruments, the vibrations as other people moved around the hut, the constant sense of being watched and overheard – would set even the most determined extrovert's teeth on edge. It's not surprising, then, that the prisoners' mental health suffered. Industrial Superintendent James T. Baily, who was tasked with improving their well-being, described observing 'moroseness', 'avoidance of others', and 'aimless promenading up and down the barbed-wire boundary of the compound, like a wild animal in a cage'.[2]

Cohen-Portheim and his fellow prisoners had not committed any crime. Though their imprisonment took place during the First World War, they were not prisoners of war: they had never fought against Britain. In fact, a significant number of them considered themselves British; some even had children in the British army. They were civilian internees: waiters, bankers, musicians, businessmen and other ordinary people, who had been present in Britain when the war broke out and who suddenly, overnight, found themselves nationals of 'enemy' countries. It didn't matter whether they were on holiday, or whether their families had emigrated from mainland Europe three centuries ago: if they were assigned male at birth and of military age, and they had (whether deliberately or not) never acquired British citizenship, they were considered a potential threat.[3] From the very start of the war, the British authorities began to lock them up.

Initially – after issuing, and then quickly rescinding, an unrealistic order to intern *all* German AMAB people aged between seventeen and forty-two – the authorities focused only on people deemed to be acting suspiciously. The febrile wartime atmosphere clearly shifted the parameters for suspicion: almost a thousand people were arrested within the first week of the war, rising to 14,500 in the first three months.[4] Though the pace of internment slowed at this point – the government had simply run out of places to lock people up, even after imprisoning people on ships moored off the coast as an emergency measure – the reprieve was short-lived.[5] On 7 May 1915, a German U-boat torpedoed the British ship RMS *Lusitania*, killing over a thousand civilians. In the aftermath of the sinking, mobs of angry British people attacked German civilians in Manchester, Liverpool and London, throwing them through windows along with their furniture and tearing the clothes from their backs.[6] The riots catalysed a change in government policy. For their own protection, and to appease the mobs, every AMAB national of an enemy country aged between seventeen and fifty-five would be interned for the duration of the war.[7]

The hastily rounded-up internees, shocked and newly separated from their families, were transferred to camps. Around two thirds of them – over 20,000 – were sent to a purpose-built internment camp on the Isle of Man. Situated at Knockaloe Moar, on the island's west coast, Knockaloe Internment Camp had been built as a solution to overcrowding at Cunningham's Holiday Camp in the island's capital, Douglas.[8] When the first internees arrived, the camp was still unfinished: the wooden huts let in the rain, the sanitation system hadn't been properly built, and the fields quickly became such a mudbath that internees were forced to construct makeshift stilts from wooden blocks.[9] As the site developed, it grew to comprise four sub-camps, each with several compounds within it. With a three-mile circumference by the time it was completed, Knockaloe was the largest internment camp in the British Isles.[10]

Though the internees ostensibly shared the same fate, the camp quickly stratified along class lines. As Cohen-Portheim recorded in his memoir, which details his internment at Knockaloe and then at Lofthouse Park in Wakefield, internees could withdraw £1 per week from the camp bank if they had any disposable income, a system that created 'two sharply divided classes'. 90 per cent of the internees, he recalls, served the other 10 per cent in order to acquire spending money: they charged the wealthier internees to cut their hair, shine their shoes, act as a valet, even peel their potatoes.[11] While all of the four sub-camps at Knockaloe were initially alike, Camp IV evolved into a 'privilege camp': for a monthly rent of eleven shillings, wealthier internees got superior accommodation, tennis courts, and wine with their meals.[12]

But no amount of money could exempt internees from the confinement, regimented structure, and 'enforced, incessant community' of camp life. Their days were structured by roll-calls and communal mealtimes; their nights interrupted by the sound of guards calling to each other and of other internees snoring.[13] Cohen-Portheim wrote passionately, 'It is inhuman cruel and dreadful to force people to live in closest community for years'.[14] Compounding this was the fact that the internees had, at least initially, nothing to take their mind off the horrors of their situation.

Prisoners of war – former soldiers who had been captured by the enemy – could be forced to work while imprisoned. But under international law, civilian internees like those at Knockaloe were exempt from forced labour.[15] At the same time, however, as internees they were forbidden from working at the jobs that had previously filled their days, and separated from their friends and family. There was only so much potato-peeling one could do. 'Barbedwirelitis' was not just depression and sensory overload: it was a crushing, deadening, absolute lack of purpose.

To remedy the situation, the camp administrators called in a Quaker craftwork teacher.[16] Industrial Superintendent James T. Baily's pacifist beliefs meant he had chosen to undertake non-combatant war service, and he was determined to use this opportunity to improve the mental health of the internees at Knockaloe. Drawing on funds raised by a Quaker humanitarian organisation, the Friends Emergency Committee, he set up workshops in every compound of the camp. Internees could now devote their time to woodcarving, sculpting, weaving, wickerwork, sewing, constructing toothbrushes and walking aids for military hospitals, and making shoes and hosiery for women and children in need.[17] Not only did the workshops provide the internees with a sense of purpose, they also increased their disposable income, as the goods they produced were sold by international Quaker networks.[18] Alongside this, the internees developed sports leagues including gymnastics, boxing and golf; ran and attended classes in languages, maths, literature and veterinary medicine; produced camp newspapers; grew flowers and fruit and vegetables to supplement their daily rations; and set up camp orchestras.[19] But the activity that commanded their attention above all others was one that enabled them to step, however fleetingly, outside of their grim situation: camp theatres.[20]

Knockaloe had no fewer than twenty separate theatres, seven of which were located in the 'privilege camp', Camp IV.[21] Each camp saw an average of one show per week, with over 1,500 performed during the period of the camp's operation.[22] Unsurprisingly, given the role of the theatre as a distraction from day-to-day suffering, the majority of shows performed were comedies.[23] The selection reflected the multinational nature of the camp: internees saw well-known plays from Germany, Spain, France, Denmark and the UK.[24] The numbers of people involved give an idea of its popularity: in Camp IV alone, 170 internees were actors,[*] and a further 74 worked in supporting roles including lighting, costume-making and scenery-painting.[25]

On the stage, roles of all genders were played by the internees. Since only AMAB people were interned at Knockaloe, this meant the camp theatres were hubs of gender nonconformity. This was no comic drag that invited the audience to laugh at 'a man in a dress': as Cohen-Portheim recalls, while early efforts struck the audience as 'men rather clumsily disguised as women', 'this changed very quickly and they developed into very plausible actresses'.[26] Camp workshops constructed elaborate outfits, wigs, makeup, and prostheses to bulk out the chest and buttocks.[27] The objective was for the audience to read the people acting female roles *as* female – and it seems to have worked. In contemporary trans language, the actors 'passed' as women consistently, with many developing reputations as leading ladies and starring in multiple productions. They were accompanied by other female-presenting internees, who acted as waitresses and theatre attendants.[28] Rehearsals took up a substantial portion of each day, meaning that for some actors, presenting as women must have been the norm.[29]

None of this was strictly unprecedented. Onstage gender nonconformity of this kind was common in early-twentieth-century Europe, especially (though not exclusively) when no

---

[*] I'm using the term 'actor' here in its gender-neutral sense, not its male sense.

AFAB actors were available: the internees' theatrical activities would have caused no great stir outside the camp. What is more striking, though, is that for some internees, presenting as women was not confined to the stage. When they stepped out of the spotlight, they retained their dresses, their wigs, and even their women's names. They were no longer just playing female roles: they were living, full-time, as women.

Toxic confusion?

In January 2020, *RuPaul's Drag Race* alumni Carmen Carrera and Detox made headlines when they criticised the show for its exclusionary selection criteria. The lineup for *Drag Race* Season 12 had just been announced, and at the time the show was aired, it looked like a lineup of thirteen cis men.[30] Detox's response on Twitter was scathing: 'To @RuPaulsDragRace: Enough with the feigned inclusivity. Time to start putting your money where your mouth is. #AllDragIsValid'.[31] RuPaul's prioritisation of cis male drag queens was, for Detox, 'the conscious exclusion of an integral part of the drag community': trans women.

As media commentators noted, this was far from the first time that the drag superstar RuPaul had been accused of trans-exclusionary tactics. *Drag Race* had come under fire in 2014 for its use of transphobic slurs like 'tranny' and 'she-male', and in 2018, RuPaul drew further outrage after an interview with UK newspaper the *Guardian*, in which the interviewer, Decca Aitkenhead, asked him whether trans women could be drag queens. 'Drag loses its sense of danger and its sense of irony once it's not men doing it,' he told Aitkenhead, 'because at its core it's a social statement and a big f-you to male-dominated culture.' *Drag Race* Season 9 contestant Peppermint, a trans woman, was only acceptable because she 'didn't get breast implants until after she left our show; she was identifying as a woman, but she hadn't really transitioned'.[32]

In the outcry that followed the interview's publication, RuPaul at first doubled down, comparing medical transition to 'performance-enhancing drugs' — a comparison that highlighted his show's narrow standards for what constitutes successful drag, which (despite his self-proclaimed playfulness) often reward thin, glamorous hyper-femininity over more creative looks that disrupt gender norms and binaries.[33] Within days, though, he had changed his tune, issuing a conciliatory apology via a tweet that described 'the trans community' as 'heroes of our shared LGBTQ movement'.[34] Yet as Detox and Carrera's 2020 criticisms show, it took some time for these sentiments to be matched by meaningful action. And it remains hard to shake the feeling that the show's new-found trans inclusivity is primarily a PR decision, much like the abandonment of the term 'she-male' after the 2014 complaints: RuPaul explicitly clarified that this was the TV network's doing, and that had it been up to him, he 'would not have changed it'.[35]

At the heart of these arguments is the idea that drag and transness are mutually exclusive. In many ways, this understanding can be a helpful one for trans people. If a drag queen, according to popular understanding, is a man dressed up as a woman, then it's important for trans women to underline that their experience is different: that their femaleness is a matter of identity *as well as* expression. (The same, of course, applies to trans men and drag kings, but since drag culture has been dominated by queens for so long, it's trans women who are disproportionately affected here.) In 2014, trans writer, YouTuber and activist Zinnia Jones published an essay titled 'How modern-day drag hurts trans women and achieves little or nothing of value'.[36] Condemning the way 'cis people mistakenly conflate' drag queens and trans women, she asked:

If a cis person is told that drag queens are 'transgender', what are they going to think of me when I tell them I'm transgender? This is a situation where collapsing these very different phenomena into one word directly affects me in a way that's more than just theoretical or philosophical. Will they take this as meaning that the entirety of my appearance is just an elaborate artifice – a fragile shell that falls away the moment my clothes come off? That, underneath, I'm still just another cis guy . . . ?[37]

This suggestion that trans women are just men in drag has, she argued, 'been exploited by conservatives and other transphobes in their campaigns against basic non-discrimination protections for trans women'. Consequently, describing drag queens as members of a wider 'trans family' (as trans writer and producer Andrea James did in an article defending RuPaul's use of transphobic slurs) can result in a 'toxic confusion' that blurs the clear dividing line between the two groups, legitimising transphobic arguments and harming trans people in the process.[38]

But while the reification of the border between transness and drag – drag performers are just dressing up, trans people are expressing their inner self – can be a helpful strategy for encouraging people to take trans identities seriously, the truth is often messier and more complicated. In particular, once we start to consider the history of gender nonconformity in performance and theatre, the dividing line starts to look very shaky. The vast majority of research into the history of drag and other theatrical gender nonconformity focuses on the way audiences have responded to it: did they find it funny, threatening, sexy? But like the history of gender-nonconforming fashion, this history also encompasses diverse gendered experiences on the part of the performers, many of which underscore its place in trans history.

Trans and drag communities have long overlapped, and the

status of trans women as 'an integral part of the drag community' (in Detox's words) has an extensive history.[39] For some, drag has been one of their only employment options. For others, it's provided a gateway to coming out as trans: a low-stakes way to test out presenting as a gender different from the one they were assigned at birth, or an experience through which they unexpectedly realise that being treated as a different gender feels right. For still others, drag facilitates a kind of temporary trans experience: an hour, or a day, during which people experience their gender differently. And many trans people, just like cis people, have seized the opportunity that drag offers to play with gender: to mix it up; to disrupt it with makeup, sequins and prosthetics; to perform it outrageously.[40]

These experiences, like those of the internees at Knockaloe, blur the line between performance and trans experience. Importantly, this isn't the same as the idea that 'gender is performative'. Judith Butler's influential – and incredibly useful – theorisation of gender relies on a crucial distinction between *performance* and *performativity*. 'Gender is a performance' suggests that we have an essential, un-gendered self who can simply choose which gender (or which aspects of gender) to act out on any given day. 'Gender is performative' is a more complex idea, indicating that our gender is itself *made by* the things we cannot choose but do every day – the way we talk, dress, interact – and thus there's no un-gendered self underneath.[41] When anti-trans commentators use the idea that 'gender is performative' to mean 'trans identities aren't valid', they're often conflating performance and performativity, suggesting that our gender is just a costume we put on over our 'real', essentially sexed body. But when I talk about performance in this chapter, I mean not the theory of performativity, but performance in a theatrical sense: the portrayal of a character (who may or may not share qualities with the actor) for the purpose of entertainment. For centuries, the theatre has been a

BEFORE WE WERE TRANS

space where the malleability of gender becomes – however tran-
siently – impossible to ignore.

Feminine spirits

When historians have written about Knockaloe and other internment camps, they've often analysed them as 'all-male environments'. But that isn't a fully accurate description of how internees
experienced their lives. As onstage gender nonconformity gave
way to offstage, the gender makeup of internment camps ceased
to be fully homogenous. In these supposedly 'all-male environments', there were people who didn't live as male at all.

Cohen-Portheim's recollections of internment at Wakefield
suggest that for some internees, female presentation onstage was
a gateway to female presentation offstage. 'Our greatest actress,'
he writes, 'really remarkable in tragic parts, was originally very
much of an athlete':

> He* came from one of the Hanseatic towns, looked bursting
> with health, and was very good at and enthusiastic about all
> games. I don't know how he ever came to be cast for a female
> part, but he was a success from the start and later on really
> powerful. He was tremendously hardworking, and his evolu-
> tion was really curious and one of the most convincing proofs
> I have seen of the predominance of the intellectual or spiritual
> over the physical. '*Es ist der Geist, der sich den Korper baut*' (It is
> the spirit which builds itself its body) is a famous saying of

* In this quote, I've deliberately retained Cohen-Portheim's use of he/him
pronouns and the male-coded term 'youth' alongside the female-coded term
'actress', since they show clearly how he understood the gender of internees who
performed female roles onstage and lived as women offstage in a way that wasn't
binary.

Schiller's, the truth of which impressed me then; for as that youth became more and more of what I do not hesitate to call a great actress on the stage, he also became more and more feminine off the stage, and after some years of this he no longer played hockey or football or whatever it used to be but walked about mincingly with a little dog, called Toutou, with a pink bow. I used to think that he and some of the others would end by developing truly feminine physical characteristics if the war lasted long enough.[42]

Onstage female presentation was the catalyst that transformed this Hanseatic internee from masculine to feminine. Clearly, their femininity was partly about stereotypes – walking 'mincingly', giving up sports, even adopting a feminine-coded dog – but Cohen-Portheim suggests it was also more than that: for him, the actor's physical femininity was the *result* of their feminine 'spirit'. The reference to this actor as 'a great actress' who was 'really remarkable in tragic parts' suggests that their femininity was not – or at least not always – affected or played for laughs. In language that echoes the sexological discourse of the period,[*] Cohen-Portheim even suggests that the actor's femininity might eventually come to manifest itself in physical changes to their body, underlining how complete he felt the transformation to have been.

All around Cohen-Portheim, and at other internment and prisoner-of-war (PoW) camps – as well as, sometimes, in theatres at the front lines – internees and PoWs were treating some of their fellow captives as gendered differently in every sense. They lived and presented as women full-time; were referred to by female names; attracted performance reviews and fan-mail addressing them in feminine terms ('fair', 'sweet', the feminised

* I'll talk more about this in the next chapter.

diminutive German suffix '-chen'); and earned devoted followers who acted as attendants, washing and ironing their female clothing. German internee Frederick Dunbar-Kalckreuth travelled to the Isle of Man in the company of Frida, an internee who flirted with their fellow travellers and commanded chivalrous protection and jealousy from the men around them.[43] Dunbar-Kalckreuth also visited another internee who performed female roles onstage, and described their tent as 'a genuine boudoir, scented white roses in a slender vase, everything covered with floral cretonne'.[44] Sometimes these internees were referred to in terms that disrupted the gender binary – mixtures of pronouns, scare quotes in some contexts but not others – and sometimes in universally female terms.[45]

Similar stories abound from elsewhere: even prisoner-of-war camps, where theatrical performances typically had to make do with a far more straitened budget, had their residents who performed female roles onstage and lived as women offstage. These actors were the main attraction of camp theatre, and the main factor in its status as the most popular activity for internees and PoWs.[46] Diaries from PoW camps uncovered by historian Clare Makepeace record the theatre's leading ladies hosting sewing parties, tea parties and dances; speaking at debates from the 'women's point of view'; and gracing the dining tables of senior officers.[47] Sergeant Andrew Hawarden, who was imprisoned at Stalag 383 in Bavaria, demonstrated just how accepted their femaleness could be, when he recorded a performance of *HMS Pinafore* in his diary: he used scare quotes to refer not to the female actors, but to 'the "Male Part" of the chorus'. It was their maleness, not their femaleness, that seemed inauthentic.[48]

Impersonation?

What made the gender nonconformity of the camps possible was the long tradition of onstage gender nonconformity in Britain and elsewhere. The theatres of Ancient Greece, of sixteenth- and early-seventeenth-century England, and of early-twentieth-century British and American universities all had AMAB actors playing female parts; in the latter two contexts, this led to anxiety that male audience members would experience inadvertent but inescapable queer attraction.[49] Not all cultures saw a linear progression from theatrical segregation to theatrical diversity: in Beijing, for example, women had been performing on stage for over 500 years when they were banned from doing so in the eighteenth century.[50] But in Europe and the USA, the trend did move gradually towards mixed-gender casting, often (and with particular intensity in the twentieth century) because of growing anxieties about the connection between onstage gender nonconformity and offstage queer sexuality.[51]

There is plenty of evidence to suggest that this widespread onstage gender nonconformity acted to create or facilitate trans experience. In early modern mainland Europe, particularly Italy, the popularity of operatic *castrati* meant that theatrical performance facilitated both a form of medical transition (castration) and social transition (in Rome, *castrati* often presented as women offstage, using this in part to signal their availability for queer sex).[52] Literary scholar Simone Chess has researched the careers of the young people who played female roles on the early modern English stage, and found that many of them did not transfer smoothly to normative male roles when they reached adulthood.[53] Instead, they continued to play roles that emphasised their androgyny or femininity, disrupted heteronormative plots, and sometimes even relied on the audience's knowledge that they had previously performed as women – suggesting that their early reputations for female presentation meant they were never straightforwardly read as male again. One, Edward Kynaston – who gained a reputation as 'the last male leading lady of the Renaissance stage' – was described by Samuel Pepys as both 'the prettiest woman in the whole house' and 'the handsomest man in the house' during the same performance.[54] After their death, the theatre historian John Downes doubted 'whether any Woman that succeeded [Edward] so Sensibly touch'd the Audience' as they did.[55]

Onstage gender nonconformity did not, of course, disappear from the European or American stage once AFAB actors were permitted (which happened in England as early as the 1660s). 'Female impersonators' (AMAB actors playing women) and 'male impersonators' (AFAB actors playing men) had different origins, but both reached high levels of popularity in theatrical comedies and music-hall acts.*

AMAB vaudeville, music-hall and blackface minstrel performers began to add characters of older, working-class Black and white women to their acts during the first half of the nineteenth century; soon afterwards they found their way into pantomimes, and their popularity was bolstered significantly by the caricatures of men in deliberately unconvincing female 'disguises' who filled the stage of plays like *Charley's Aunt* (1892).[56] In early British cinema, too, female disguises were used by comic criminals, lovers and practical jokers, and reviewers praised the technological ingenuity of their quick transformations.[57] By contrast, 'male

* Terminology poses a problem here: these performers were *called* 'female impersonators' and 'male impersonators' at the time they performed, but if we use the word 'impersonator' uncritically, it suggests that their femaleness/maleness was never anything more than a disguise. As I'll go on to show, for some of these performers, it's not accurate to say they were simply 'impersonating' men or women. Consequently, I've chosen to keep these phrases in quotation marks in order to strike a balance between calling these performers by the names they used, and acknowledging their complex gendered experiences.

impersonation' was a separate tradition from the AFAB 'principal boy' of the pantomime. 'Male impersonation' was born in the music-hall in the second half of the nineteenth century, and was far removed from the working-class characters of the 'female impersonator', instead skewering the pretensions of dandies, cads and fashionable lovers. While white music-hall 'male impersonators' declined in the early twentieth century, particularly after the First World War, Black performers, particularly in New York City, continued to thrive.[58] The 'principal boy', meanwhile, had their origins in the vulnerable young waifs of the eighteenth- and nineteenth-century stage (female actors, the thinking went, could induce so much more pathos than awkward adolescent boys), but received a boost from the Victorian near-hysteria about the display of women's legs: the pantomime stage was a rare opportunity for an audience to see them on show.[59]

If they have been read as queer at all, the 'impersonators' have often been scrutinised for their sexuality. It's certainly true that many of them had partners of the same gender as the performers were assigned at birth, and had queer fans and admirers too. But in addition to this, we only have to scratch the surface of their histories to find trans experience. The huge popularity of plays like *Charley's Aunt* (in which two Oxford students, finding themselves without a chaperone during their girlfriends' visits, persuade their friend to dress up as an old woman) provided opportunities for trans actors to express themselves. Joyce, an American trans woman, wrote of her 'secret pleasure' at being cast in *Charley's Aunt* and being able to 'wear a skirt like the rest of the girls', and advised others who enjoyed presenting as women to do the same.[60] Several 'female impersonators' are known to have presented as women offstage too: when the German 'Dr W.S.' spoke to fourteen 'female impersonators' in 1901, he found that over half wore women's clothes at home.[61] Fanny Park and Stella Boulton, who were arrested in women's clothes at London's

Strand Theatre in 1870, both lived as women much of the time (Stella's mother told the court they had both worn dresses as children; Fanny signed her letters as a 'sister'; Stella was treated sometimes as a woman, sometimes as neither a man nor a woman, by her partner Lord Arthur Clinton and their friends) *and* performed as women on stage; the latter fact was enough to get them acquitted of the charge of 'solicitation to encourage others to commit sodomy'.[62] Similarly, Annie/Charles Hindle, an early American 'male impersonator', shaved their face regularly as part of their 'costume'; married their dresser, Anna Ryan, under the name of Charles, and lived with her as a woman thereafter; and was happy to be addressed as 'Sir' or 'Madam' in letters.[63] Their former dresser and later fellow 'male impersonator', Ella Wesner – who also had relationships with women – requested that they be buried in men's clothes.[64] Annie/Charles and Ella might simply have adopted male presentation for the purpose of marrying women, but the other details of their lives might also indicate that they experienced their gender in fluid or non-binary ways.

Other gender-nonconforming actors described their performance as a form of temporary trans experience. Principal boy Fay Lenore argued that 'You've got to think of yourself as a boy and act like one', while Shakespearean actor Sarah Bernhardt said of playing Hamlet that 'It is not sufficient to look like a man, to move like a man, and to speak like a man. The actress must think and feel like a man'.[65] Audiences also saw the genders of these performers differently: Charlotte Cushman, who played Romeo on the mid-nineteenth-century American stage, was described by a spectator as 'a very dangerous young man', while theatre producer Leonard Sillman described 'female impersonator' T.C. Jones as not an 'impersonator' at all, but 'simply an extraordinarily talented woman'.[66]

In accordance with their own natures

But why did this happen at Knockaloe? What was it that led to internees and prisoners of war not just presenting as female on stage – a time-honoured way to fill female theatrical roles in the absence of cis women – but living as women offstage too?

For some historians and theorists, female presentation was a 'safety valve': a mechanism by which the pent-up homoeroticism and anxieties about emasculation that haunted the camps could be released in a controlled environment, thus allowing the masculine, heterosexual order to continue to function outside of the theatre.[67] This argument, though, relies on the idea that normative gender and sexuality were reasserted outside of the theatre – something that the internees and PoWs who lived as women *off*stage explicitly undermined.[68] Consequently, some commentators have turned it on its head, suggesting instead that female presentation actually legitimised, or provided an excuse for, sexual and romantic attraction between captives.

Certainly, contemporary diaries and camp newspapers make it clear that internees and PoWs profoundly missed the presence of cis women, and the opportunity for sex with them: one of Knockaloe's camp newspapers, the *Knockaloe Lager-Zeitung*, referred to the internees as '22,000 Germans and Austrians in enforced monkhood, with a powerful thirst for earthly love and heavenly beer'.[69] As a result, there is ample evidence for this queerer interpretation of female presentation, from photographs of internees posed as heterosexual couples, to the devoted, romantic fan-mail some captives who performed and lived as women received. British PoW officer Dr Arthur Munk wrote in his diary that some 'dancers and other dramatic personnel' were effectively employed as sex workers by 'their admirers'.[70] The British internee (and later actor) George Merritt recalled that 'The boys that were girls . . . were wanted a bit you know. They played their courtesan role in the camp to a certain extent. They could get . . . free wine and things like that, but I don't think there was anything excessive.'[71] German internee Willi Hennings wrote of a dream in which he was 'completely immersed' in the vision of actor Bodo Wildt wearing 'short dresses' that showed off 'slim legs', and asks, 'Were we not sometimes a little bit in love with you?'[72] At Knockaloe, a camp newspaper review of one production reported that 'the pretty Parisian chambermaids of Henderson and Krause were delightful, and will have caused many a sleepless night'.[73] At the USA PoW Camp Alva, as former prisoners recalled in a jointly authored 1992 memoir, 'several ladies of the harem . . . (from the enlisted men's camp, as young as possible*) brought quite a number of visitors into gay-trouble [*Schwulitäten*]', while sexual attraction sometimes found its outlet in sexual harassment: 'A Lieutenant dressed in a mini-skirt appeared as number-girl "Lissy"', who developed bruises from numerous pinches on the bottom.[74]

Internees and PoWs who presented as female onstage recognised that others were attracted to them (Emmerich Laschitz, interned in the Siberian camp Achinsk, recalls experiencing 'an often peculiar gallantry . . . which did not entirely lack the scent of abnormality'), as did outside observers.[75] The German sexual reformer Magnus Hirschfeld, who was keen to demonstrate that relationships between men could lead to greater feats of military bravery (and who, as I mentioned in my introduction, had recently coined the term 'transvestite'), was confident that sexual and romantic relationships took place within internment and PoW camps, and supported his arguments with evidence from Munk's diary.

---

* Younger PoWs were preferred as it was easier for them to 'pass' as women; this may well, of course, have led to problematic power dynamics in sexual relationships.

Not all contemporary observers agreed that internees or PoWs were actually having sex with each other. Cohen-Portheim is adamant that it would have been impossible because 'the camp offered no possibility of isolation'. He complains that the 'author-ities responsible for prisoners' camps apparently gave [sex] no consideration whatsoever', noting that married internees occa-sionally saw their wives, but only at very infrequent, supervised visits, where they sat on either side of a table.[76] However, the phrasing in his memoir is revealing: he writes that, '*With the insig-nificant exception of the few single huts* (hardly a dozen), there was no possible privacy for anybody', thus specifying possible opportuni-ties for sex even as he dismisses them. He also notes reports that 'in the last year or so homosexuality became almost general at Knockaloe': while he cites no evidence to support this, he does acknowledge that it is 'quite possible'.[77]

Whether substantiated or not, these rumours suggest that internees were discussing and acknowledging the possibility and likelihood of sex within the camps with relative freedom. Moreover, other contemporaries disagreed with Cohen-Portheim that there was no opportunity for sex. Despite claiming that 'Homosexual practices are probably not as frequent as may be imagined', Swiss physician Dr Adolf Lukas Vischer (in his psychological study of PoWs, including civilian internees) reports that 'it is not uncommon for two friends to associate like lovers', and that 'homosexual epidemics' took place in several camps.[78] Similarly, when two internees at the Douglas camp, not far from Knockaloe, were prosecuted for 'what would appear to be a homosexual act', the judge's response suggested that he believed such acts were rendered more likely by the circumstances of internment: he 'took into account the trying circumstances under which the prisoners lived' when granting them the comparatively lenient sentence of 'one month's imprisonment with hard labour'.[79]

It's important to say that, while some of the captives who were attracted to other captives probably understood themselves as innately attracted to men, in a way roughly corresponding to today's gay or bi identities, it's likely that not all of them did. This is partly because, given the extent to which some internees and PoWs lived as women, some of their admirers and partners probably understood themselves as attracted to women rather than men. Others may well – as historians including Makepeace, Helen Smith and Emma Vickers have shown – have seen themselves as simply taking the sexual opportunities that were available, and seen sex or relationships with men as an activity they enjoyed in a particular context rather than something that raised larger questions about their identity or their longer-term preferences.[80] Cohen-Portheim corroborates this, noting that while 'there certainly were a very great number of friendly couples considered to belong together . . . I could not say how far any of them were self-conscious'.[81] His internment taught him to understand friendship, romance and sexuality as areas on a continuum rather than as clearly defined kinds of relationship: 'there is no hard and sharp division between what [people] admit to be sexual acts or sensations and a great many other things which they like to consider perfectly "harmless" or maybe of a spiritual nature'. Consequently, while he writes that 'To my own knowledge there was nothing of what is called homosexuality', this is mainly because 'what I learnt was that homosexuality is not what it is called'.[82] Cohen-Portheim makes it clear here that relationships between internees may have existed, but they weren't thought of as 'homosexual' or 'gay' in the way we understand those terms today.

One reason that internees and PoWs embraced female presentation so wholeheartedly, then, was probably because it legitimised these different kinds of queer attraction. Another reason, many historians have suggested, relates more closely to its theatrical origin. If an internee or PoW acted a female role onstage, and then continued to present as a woman offstage, this enabled them to *sustain the illusion*: to make their *on*stage female presentation ever more convincing. It's certainly true that internees and PoWs were hyper-concerned about this. They wanted to believe that they were watching cis women perform on stage. The Knockaloe camp newspaper *Quousque Tandem* advised internees playing female roles on stage to 'plump out and ennoble your silhouettes with cushions', lest their feminine 'full face' appearance be undermined by a 'flat profile'; and in diaries and memoirs, one of the most frequent and highest compliments given to these actors was that they were indistinguishable from cis women.[83]

Convincing the audience that they were watching cis female actors was, in part, an act of escapism, helping them – if only for a moment – to forget that they were interned at all. Living among women took that escapism one step further. Several historians have argued that internees and PoWs who lived as women provided the camp with 'substitute women', creating a sense of normality and 'home'.[84] The presence of women tapped into the longing of German captives for *Heimat*, a German word that means more than simply 'home', carrying connotations of roots and homeland alongside the home as a domestic and female-coded space.[85] Women, it was felt, would provide the love and care that they so desperately missed. In a poem published in the German field newspaper *Der Flieger*, one officer wrote of wishing they were a girl, in part so that they could cook for and comfort the men around them.[86]

All of these explanations implicitly suggest that internees and PoWs performed and lived as women for pragmatic reasons. The theatre needed some people to play female roles, and those female roles needed to be perfectly convincing; the camp needed some women in order to safeguard everyone's mental health; people needed a strategy to legitimise their queer sexual desires. In light of this, it's important to recognise that no one was being *forced* to live as women in the camps: acting female roles onstage didn't commit you to living as a woman offstage. At Knockaloe, one actor responded to being described in feminine terms with a three-page article in *Quousque Tandem*, articulating his male identity clearly: 'I am not a Fraulein, and I'm certainly not beautiful!'[87] In other words, the captives had *agency* over whether or not they accepted being seen as women: the fact that some could refuse it strongly suggests that others, for whom we have no record of resistance, embraced it.

What's missing from the explanations I've described so far – just as it was missing from the stories of widespread gender nonconformity I told in the previous chapter – is any suggestion that some internees and PoWs were living as women, part-time or full-time, *because they wanted to*. For some, it's likely that these pragmatic factors (the need for actors, the need for women) provided access to an experience that felt unexpectedly comfortable – or presented a valuable opportunity to live and present in ways they already knew felt comfortable for them.[88]

We can gain fleeting glimpses into the experiences of those who lived as women from the letters they wrote, evidence collected by historian Lisa Z. Sigel. In letters written for publication in magazines that often covered gender nonconformity, serving soldiers extolled their love of performing as women onstage: 'Tight lacing and high heels for ever!' Some had known they enjoyed this already, but had concealed it until the war presented 'opportunities of publicly displaying my hitherto secret garments': 'I gladly embraced the opportunity of taking a girl's part in our concert party'. Others began the war as 'one of many who looked down on female impersonation as something to be despised', but eventually found they 'used to look forward to the evening when I had to dress up', and that presenting as female changed their sense of gender: one former soldier wrote that 'play-acting a girl's part has changed my whole existence', while another reported, 'once I am attired in feminine frills and garments I am another being, and feel myself to be a real woman'.[89] Still others leave us guessing at their motivations, but in no doubt of the satisfaction that presenting as female brought them: for Laschitz, who became Achinsk's preeminent female actor, the war was 'the happiest time of my life'.[90] The soldiers' letters Sigel has uncovered often use the word 'kinky' to describe their experience, but it's important to note that this word didn't take on the primarily sexual connotations it has today until the middle of the twentieth century: the soldiers were describing themselves as weird or eccentric, not identifying their enjoyment of female presentation as solely sexual.[91] We should also remember that this was a period when sexual and gendered experiences were understood in overlapping ways. As I'll explain more in Chapter 4, same-sex attraction was understood as a kind of gendered inversion − AMAB people who were attracted to men, for example, were understood as inherently more female − and so enjoying female presentation in a sexual way may well also have affected the soldiers' sense of gender.

At the same time, case studies published by sexologists show us that late-nineteenth- and early-twentieth-century trans people were explicitly using theatrical gender nonconformity as an opportunity to present their gender in the way they wanted to. One trans woman told the influential sexologist Richard von Krafft-Ebing that, since the age of twelve or thirteen, she had 'had a definite feeling of preferring to be a young lady', that she had 'first expressed to a friend the wish to be a girl' when she was fifteen, and that she wanted to have gender reassignment surgery; she also said that from a young age 'I took especial pleasure in masquerade costumes, − i.e., only in female attire'.[92] Another, who had a 'secret and fixed desire to be a girl' from an even younger age, describes feeling 'delight' when, as a teenager, 'I had an opportunity to play a female role in a love-scene'.[93] Of another, Krafft-Ebing wrote, 'As [she] grew up, [she] managed it so that, when [she] was a participant in theatricals, [she] always had a female part'.[94] Krafft-Ebing's younger colleague Havelock Ellis, who coined the term 'Eonism' (after the gender-nonconforming eighteenth-century spy and diplomat the Chevalier d'Éon) to refer to what we would now call transness, quotes a trans woman who, when watching theatrical gender nonconformity, would 'sit and admire' the actors and 'long enviously to be doing the same': 'the performance would leave me sad with a hungry desire and envy'.[95] Although not everyone felt the same way – Roberta Cowell, a trans racing driver, who we'll meet again in Chapter 5, refused to play female roles on stage because she saw them as 'a public declaration of homosexuality' – these accounts show us that many trans women found happiness in onstage female presentation *because* it allowed them to express their female identities.[96] Among the internees, PoWs and soldiers who acted female roles and/or lived as women offstage, it's likely that there were some who felt the same.

Some contemporary observers recognised that this was going on. For Magnus Hirschfeld, the 'joy' some soldiers found in onstage female presentation is evidence of 'unmistakable transvestitism' (a term he uses in its early sense to encompass gender identity as well as expression).[97] He also quotes a revealing 'communication from a lieutenant':

Recently I had a proof of the incredible naiveté and ignorance of the majority in these matters. Our battalion arranged a party at which the most popular feature was a lady in very elaborate costume and blonde wig. This soldier sang soprano and in all his movements and bearing was thoroughly feminine. Our whole staff was represented at this party and at the table we all discussed the matter. The other men all expressed their admiration for the performer and opined that he must have studied very long in order to imitate a woman so successfully. I expressed the opinion, however, that the man was acting in accordance with his own nature, that his performance was virtually an expression of his real self and probably brought him intense satisfaction. Neither the general, nor the priest, nor the older gentlemen understood me. I cautiously tried to be a little more explicit but found complete lack of understanding in every gentleman, but most of all in the case of the priest. If this was true of him, how much truer is it of the common soldier.[98]

The lieutenant's account testifies to the fact that, far from being mutually exclusive, theatrical gender nonconformity and trans experience could be seen by some early-twentieth-century people as symbiotically linked. Equally notable, however, is the fact that the lieutenant's companions had no idea what he was talking about. Understanding of trans experience was patchy and variable in this period, something that doubtless intensified the diversity of experiences within the camps.

We shouldn't forget, though, that evidence of trans experience doesn't depend on us proving that some of the captives who lived as women felt female on a long-term, static basis. Fluid, fleeting and non-binary experiences still count. Hermann Pörzgen, who published a book based on his first-hand observations of theatrical performances in internment and PoW camps, argued that those who lived as women underwent 'soul changes': they hadn't previously understood themselves as female, but their experience in the camps changed their experience of their gender.[99] As the letters I quoted earlier show, some people also experienced female presentation as a form of gender fluidity: they felt more female when they were presenting as female, and less when they weren't.

For civilian internees in particular, these fluid, temporary trans experiences were perhaps enabled by the way they understood their camps as spaces separate from the rest of the world.[100] As Cohen-Portheim put it, 'The world ceased at the barbed wire, and what lay outside it might as well have belonged to a different planet.'[101] Unlike PoWs, who were often forced to work outside their camps, civilian internees had little interaction with the outside world.[102] As a result, the camp became a contained space where norms and expectations could be reshaped – including norms of gender and sexuality.[103]

Beyond the dame

The drag queens who compete in *RuPaul's Drag Race* today are descendants of both the 'female impersonators' and the gender-nonconforming PoWs. After the Second World War, drag shows starring members of the forces toured the UK to huge acclaim: an opportunity that, according to contemporaries, provided a haven for gay men (as well as, presumably, for trans people).[104] The success of performer Danny La Rue in the 1960s and 1970s then paved the way for drag acts to become a staple of the 1970s pub entertainment night.[105] In the USA, more direct antecedents of RuPaul's approach to drag were to be found in the ballroom communities of Black and Latinx people in New York City, and in the communities of performers and sex workers in San Francisco.[106] These communities formed a home for people of diverse gendered experiences: trans women, trans men, gay men, lesbians, people who lived as men or women some or all of the time but didn't label themselves as such. Some called themselves transvestites, some queens, some gay.[107] Among the communities that fought for queer liberation at San Francisco's Compton's Cafeteria, and later at New York's Stonewall Inn, were drag queens and kings, trans women and men, and people who saw themselves as belonging to overlapping categories.[108] For trans women in particular, performing onstage became a way to legitimise living as women, and/or to save money for medical transition.[109] For many, femaleness was both part of their professional performance, part of their nightlife glamour, *and* part of their everyday.[110]

This is the history of the shared community that Carmen Carrera, Detox and many other contemporary drag artists have celebrated. It's a community in which, today, some drag artists still find that drag is a gateway to discovering their trans identity.[111] Some, particularly in conservative environments, find that drag communities provide a valuable outlet for self-expression and access to information about transition.[112] Some experience drag as a form of gender fluidity, temporarily shifting their sense of their gender.[113] As one trans woman, Jennifer, wrote in *Transvestia* magazine in 1966, drag artists may be distinct from trans people in some ways, but they have one crucial thing in common: the artists 'seem to share with us the supreme joy of becoming, for a while, a woman'.[114]

Theatrical performance and trans experience have always been intertwined. If we try to cleanly separate the two – especially when we're talking about history – we misrepresent the experience of individuals for whom the two things overlap, and erase some of the multiple motivations that coexist within groups of gender-nonconforming performers. Onstage gender nonconformity is multivalent, but few of its manifold meanings leave gender unchallenged, whether in the mind of the performer or of the audience.

At the same time, onstage gender nonconformity – and particularly AMAB drag – is politically multivalent too. The normative feminine drag promoted by people like RuPaul has been criticised for promoting gender stereotypes; the caricature of the pantomime dame, which encourages audiences to mock older, working-class, assertive women for failing to live up to established standards of femininity, has similarly been seen as classist and misogynistic.[115] Some gay and lesbian rights groups have seen drag artists as propping up the stereotype of gender-nonconforming gay people, harming their efforts to emphasise that gay people are just like everybody else (as I'll show in Chapter 4, this is closely related to the history of how some gay rights groups threw trans people under the bus by disavowing gender nonconformity in the name of assimilation and respectability, and was often about class just as much as gender).[116] In recent decades, the categories have splintered further as many drag artists (like RuPaul) have sought to distance themselves from trans people as a route to mainstream popularity; in doing so, as I talked about earlier, they have popularised transphobic discourse and slurs that have prompted anger and hurt from trans communities.[117] Drag, especially in contexts like pantomime where it's played for laughs or framed as a man's 'unconvincing' disguise – combined with systemic misogyny, which encourages us to see femininity as debasing and unserious – has also played a large part in creating a climate where the idea of a 'man in a dress' is seen as inherently funny, with harmful consequences for trans people.[118] It's no coincidence that the writer Germaine Greer titled a transphobic chapter in her 1999 book *The Whole Woman* 'Pantomime Dames'.[119] As the trans cartoonist Sophie Labelle puts it, 'every time you laugh at the idea of a man dressed as a woman, a trans girl gets more scared to come out'.[120]

But it would be a shame to let this fraught relationship overshadow the past – and the present – that trans and drag communities share. Instead, knowledge of the trans history of drag might draw our attention to its potential to dismantle gender structures in ways more radical and less binary than it has hitherto been allowed to. Many contemporary drag artists use drag not just to present as a different gender, but to blur the boundaries between human and non-human, between body and artwork, and this is starting to make its way into mainstream drag.[121] When asked about the future of drag she would like to see, trans drag artist Daphne Always told interviewer Tim Mulkerin that she 'would like to see a drag where the importance is not about breaking down [the] gender binary, because that has already happened'.[122] Until that day, perhaps the knowledge that drag history *is* trans history might help everyone to realise its radical potential: its still-too-often untapped capacity to do what gay drag artist and activist Joan Jett Blakk declared themself to be doing in 1991, 'stomping on that line between male and female and erasing it'.[123]

Internees and camp authorities recognised that the norms of Knockaloe could not hold outside of the barbed wire: Baily, for example, noted that photographs of internees who lived as women 'should not be shown outside the camp'.[124] This, of course, had profound implications for the internees after the war ended. It took until October 1919 for Knockaloe to be emptied: at the end of the war, many of the internees – who Cohen-Portheim described as 'hordes of completely brutalised or broken men' – suddenly found themselves having to fight the attempts of the British government to deport them to Germany, and remained interned as their appeals were processed.[125] While the fates of most of the internees who had lived as women remain unknown, Cohen-Portheim's memoir tells us what happened to one:

A Viennese youth in our camp was the leading lady of society comedies or dramas; he is one of the few I have met again in later life, when I found him holding a high position in a bank in Vienna and married to an extremely pretty woman who looked not at all unlike him in some of his great stage-parts, which he then did not seem to care to be reminded of.[126]

This chance meeting, and the scant detail Cohen-Portheim provides, is tantalisingly ambiguous. Why did the Viennese banker not 'care to be reminded of' their days in the camp? Did they simply not want to remember the gruelling experience of internment? Were they embarrassed by the memory – either because they had consistently thought of it as sinful, or because they were ashamed of having enjoyed it? Were they made uncomfortable by their struggle to reconcile their past experience in the camp with their present-day experience of normative heterosexual masculinity? Did the presence of their wife make it more difficult to articulate their feelings, either to Cohen-Portheim or to themself? Did they miss living as a woman, and find it painful to remember? We can't know, but among all the internees released back into society, many of these emotions must have circulated.

Whether or not any of these people lived as women again after the war was over, their trans experiences left a legacy in the way their fellow captives thought about gender. Cohen-Portheim and Dunbar-Kalckreuth both used accounts of their internment to reflect on the fluid and non-binary nature of gender, and its independence from the body. Cohen-Portheim writes of his discovery that 'a predominantly masculine nature may belong to a person of the female sex and a predominantly feminine one to a person of the male sex'.[127] Similarly, Dunbar-Kalckreuth writes that 'Male and female characteristics ... occur in different percentages in both sexes': 'Whatever innate femininity there is in this one-gender world of men [i.e. in the camps] gradually takes form, on the stage and elsewhere'.[128] Both writers are articulating contemporary sexological theories – but they present their attitudes as shaped not by reading, but by camp life. As Dunbar-Kalckreuth recalls, when watching onstage female presentation, 'We felt, not for the first time, how much better the world would be if certain men were ladies and certain ladies men'. This opinion is not, he specifies, based on internees *appearing* stereotypically feminine: 'Alas! This is not a matter of aesthetics!'[129]

The story of gender nonconformity in wartime camps is a story of hundreds of thousands of people, and almost as many different kinds of history. It's the history of theatre, and how performances have adapted to new and challenging contexts. It's the history of human resilience, and how people work to create a sense of normality in situations that are so far from normal. It's the history of queer sexuality, and how gender nonconformity has often enabled, sanctioned and signalled it. And it's trans history, in several ways. Living as women provided some captives with an outlet for existing trans experiences. For others, it changed the way they experienced their gender, whether fleetingly or forever. And beyond their individual experience, those who lived as women rewrote the rules of gender, so that Cohen-Portheim could write in absolute terms, 'No male is simply male, and no female simply female'.[130]

The experience of world war, which depleted societies of men and gave women unprecedented access to economic and other forms of independence, was one that shifted gender norms in unsettling ways: a 1918 article in *The Times* gave voice to fears that 'one ill-effect of the war would be the development of a definite third sex, something neither man nor woman'.[131] In this wider experience of gender disruption, the trans history of internment and PoW camps played an important but overlooked part. If we leave unchallenged the assumption that theatrical gender nonconformity and trans experience are mutually exclusive, we risk covering up one of the most significant strands of trans history that Europe has ever seen.

4

'A feminine soul confined by a masculine body'
The entangled history of gay and trans experience

The Japanese town of Edo overlooked a rocky cove on the south-eastern edge of the island of Honshu. For centuries, it was really little more than a fishing village. The construction of a castle in the mid-fifteenth century elevated its importance a little, as houses and businesses began to cluster around the household of the local feudal lord. But it was in 1603 that everything changed.

During the period 1603–1868, Japan was ruled by the Tokugawa shōgunate, a military government that enforced a strictly isolation-ist foreign policy. The Tokugawa government moved the shōgun's residence over 200 miles north-east, from the former capital of Kyoto to that fishing village – hence the Tokugawa period is also often known as the Edo period. Under their rule, Edo grew into a cramped and thriving city, its population increasing to over a million by the early eighteenth century.[1] Today, it is known as Tokyo, and is one of the most populous cities in the world.

The dramatic increase in Edo's population – particularly its male population – led to the development of a thriving sex indus-try.[2] The outskirts of the city became the *ukiyo*, or pleasure quar-ters: the name translates directly as 'floating world', referring to the carefree, weightless experience of tea, sake and sex that awaited visitors. The customers of the floating world included local urban men and women alongside *daimyo* (powerful feudal lords) and *samurai* (their military retainers). To the shōgunate, Japan's hundreds of daimyo posed a potential threat: many of them were very wealthy, and they commanded substantial local power bases. In order to keep a close eye on them and minimise their opportunities to build political or military opposition, the shōgunate required every daimyo to keep a house in Edo as well as on their own estates, and to live there in alternate years, performing bureaucratic duties such as tax-collecting during their stay.[3] The daimyo and their hundreds of samurai would shuttle to and from Edo each year, leaving their wives and concubines (who I'll talk more about later) behind in their countryside compound. Edo became, in the words of seventeenth-century poet Ihara Saikaku, a 'city of bachelors'.[4] Within the floating world, these men had access to sex with women (often peasants, seeking work or entering into indentureships in response to rural food poverty); with *onnagata* (AMAB actors who lived as female onstage and offstage, and also sometimes engaged in sex work); or with *wakashū*.[5] *Wakashū* were not women, but neither were they men. In fact, the question of their gender was inextricably bound up with the kind of sex – and the kind of partners – they had. They represent just one part of a history that forces us to dismantle any notions we have that 'gay' and 'trans' are clearly separate categories.

In Western culture, in fact, the very origin story of these two ideas is intertwined.

Have I a masculine beard and manly limbs and body?
Yes, I am confined by these: but I am and remain a woman.[6]

These lines appeared in Latin* in an 1864 book, *Inclusa* ('Enclosed') penned by the German lawyer Karl Heinrich Ulrichs. Ulrichs, who had previously described themself in a letter to their family as one of a 'race' of 'man-loving half-men', described their experience as that of having 'a feminine soul confined by a masculine

---

* I've edited the original translation by Hubert C. Kennedy slightly for clarity.

body'.[7] Their way of seeing themself was taken up in earnest by the sexologists of late-nineteenth- and early-twentieth-century Europe: a new field of quasi-medical, quasi-anthropological, quasi-sociological professionals who sought to study and diagnose various forms of queerness through a scientific lens. Richard von Krafft-Ebing (whose psychological case studies of trans women we've encountered before) wrote of 'men' who 'feel themselves to be females' and 'women' who 'feel themselves to be males'.[8] Havelock Ellis, his younger British counterpart, reported the words of one AMAB person: 'We are all women; that we do not deny'.[9] He believed that AFAB people who experienced a sense of maleness in the same way were likely to betray this on the outside: 'there are all sorts of instinctive gestures and habits which may suggest to female acquaintances the remark that such a person "ought to have been a man"'.[10]

For people living in Western Europe or the USA today, who are used to hearing trans people described as 'men trapped in women's bodies' or vice versa, these quotations read like textbook articulations of trans experience. For Ulrichs and their followers, however, they were something else. Ulrichs was motivated not primarily by a desire to explain their sense of gender, but by a desire to explain what it felt like to be a man who was attracted to other men. The term 'urning', which Ulrichs coined to refer to themself and other people like them, has been seen as an early articulation of gay identity – and Ulrichs, who lost their job and risked arrest by publishing under their own name, as the first modern gay rights activist. In Berlin, the Queer (Schwules) Museum is today housed on Karl-Heinrich-Ulrichs-Straße.

The model of queer attraction[*] that Ulrichs first articulated became known as 'inversion'. What had been inverted, in the

---

[*] I'm consciously referring to this attraction as 'queer', rather than as 'gay', 'homosexual' or 'same-sex': I'll talk more about my reasons for avoiding these terms shortly.

eyes of the sexologists and their contemporaries, was the natural direction of sexual desire: men were supposed to be attracted to women, and women to men. Desire for men, in the eyes of Ulrichs and many of those around them, was an intrinsically female thing. You couldn't *be* 100 per cent male and attracted to men: that just didn't compute, and so an AMAB person who *was* attracted to men became, in some essential way, female. The understanding of sexual and romantic attraction as an intrinsic part of gender – maleness necessitating attraction to women, femaleness necessitating attraction to men – was a longstanding ideology, but it was particularly bolstered in nineteenth-century Europe by the burgeoning Industrial Revolution. Particularly in middle-class households, this naturalised the division between strong, independent men who worked outside the home and passive, nurturing women who worked inside the home to raise children – fostering a sense that these gender stereotypes, their complementarity, and their mutual attraction were the natural order of things.[11] When American psychologists John Money and John and Joan Hampson outlined the concept of 'gender roles' in a 1955 scientific paper, they would reassert the idea that (hetero) sexuality was an intrinsic part of gender – to be a man included and necessitated being attracted to women, and vice versa – and therefore that sexuality could be taken into account when establishing the 'real' gender of an intersex child.[12]

Ulrichs, and later the sexologists, looked for evidence of this gendered experience in people who were attracted to the same gender as the one they were assigned at birth – and they found it. Ulrichs noted that AMAB people like themself had a 'feminine' gait and gestures.[13] Krafft-Ebing observed that 'men [who] are females in feeling . . . [eschew] smoking, drinking, and manly sports, and, on the contrary, [find] pleasure in adornment of person, art, *belles-lettres*, etc., even to the extent of giving [themself] entirely to the cultivation of the beautiful'; while 'women [who are] males . . . will have nothing to do with dolls . . . The *toilette* is neglected, and pleasure found in a coarse, boyish life.' 'Occasionally,' he noted with distaste, 'there may be attempts to smoke and drink.'[14] For these reasons, Ulrichs posited a biological explanation for inversion, legitimising their experience as 'natural' by pointing to recent embryological research that showed that embryos were initially not sexually differentiated: perhaps, Ulrichs suggested, the embryos of future inverts developed from this undifferentiated point in a mixed or contrary way, giving them the sex organs of one gender and the sex drive of another.[15] Krafft-Ebing agreed, devoting pages to identifying how inversion manifested itself not just in behaviour, but also in visible aspects of the body.[16]

Given that Ulrichs was primarily motivated by a desire to achieve freedom and tolerance for queer *relationships*, it's understandable that inversion has been seen not as an aspect of trans history, but as an aspect of gay history. But the truth is more complicated. Krafft-Ebing set out four 'degrees' of inversion, each of which caused people to experience their gender in a different way. In the first degree, the invert had a 'predominating homo-sexual instinct' but with 'traces of heterosexual': people of this degree had 'sexual feeling' for 'persons of the same sex', but their gendered behaviour didn't change ('Character and feeling . . . still correspond with the sex'), meaning their inversion was 'curable' ('he recognizes his impulse toward his own sex as an aberration, and finally seeks aid').[17] In the second degree, the invert had 'inclination only toward the same sex', leading them to undergo 'a deep change of character': for the AMAB invert, 'his feelings and inclination . . . become those of a female', and 'he also feels himself to be a woman during the sexual act', with 'desire only for passive sexual indulgence'.[18] In the third degree, 'The entire mental existence is altered to correspond with the abnormal sexual instinct', an experience Krafft-Ebing called 'effemination' for AMAB people and 'viraginity' for AFAB people: these are the 'men . . . feel themselves to be females' and 'women . . . feel themselves to be males', to the extent of the person profiled in the case study in the previous chapter, who, when discussing her love of performing female roles onstage, reported that from 'the age of twelve or thirteen, I had a definite feeling of preferring to be a young lady', and expressed a desire as an adult for gender reassignment surgery.[19] In the fourth degree, aspects of the physical body (though not the genitals) appeared at odds with the gender the invert was assigned at birth, and they experienced what we would now call body dysmorphia, 'the delusion of a transformation of sex': one case study 'felt . . . that [their] genitals were changed into those of a female', and 'felt the growth of [their] breasts'.[20]

In other words, inversion wasn't a synonym for homosexuality: it was a spectrum of gendered and sexual experience, ranging from what we would now call bisexuality to what we would now call trans identity.[21] In fact, the 'homo' in 'homosexuality', meaning 'same', makes it an inadequate translation for a model of queerness that framed sexual attraction as necessarily between *different* genders. What's more, every kind of inversion – even the 'curable' first degree – contained an element of cross-gendered experience.

In a way, this isn't surprising. To be sure, many people today don't experience any connection between their sexuality and their gender: in the words of non-binary writer and academic Ben Vincent, it's a distinction between 'who one wishes to go to bed *with*' and 'who one goes to bed *as*'.[22] Some of Ulrichs's contemporaries also objected: American maths professor James Mills Peirce argued that 'There is an error in the view that feminine love is that which is directed to a man, and masculine love that which is directed to a woman', while German writer and activist Adolf Brand argued for male homosexuality – particularly the desire of older men for younger men – as intrinsically virile.[23] But for others, inversion offered a valuable way to make sense of their experience. Some of the ideas about how inversion changed a person's gender are based on stereotypes – for example, when Krafft-Ebing wrote that the second-degree invert 'feels himself to be a woman during the sexual act', it seems pretty clear that he was equating 'woman' with 'enjoys being penetrated' – but if those inverts were socialised to believe that those stereotypes were real, seeing being penetrated as an intrinsically female thing, then this would still have affected their sense of gender. Inversion also offered many people who experienced queer attraction an explanation for the discomfort and lack of connection they felt with normative ideas of maleness and femaleness (something that, as I'll say more about later, still resonates with many gay, lesbian and bi people today).[24] As a result, the idea of inversion was embraced positively by many, persisting in Britain as the dominant way of understanding queer attraction even after Freud's work offered an alternative model that didn't connect sexuality with gender.[25]

It also paved the way for the understanding of trans experience as a legitimate phenomenon in its own right. When the German sexologist Magnus Hirschfeld wrote *Die Transvestiten* (*The Transvestites* – a term he used to refer to people we'd describe as transgender today) in 1910, he explicitly connected trans and gay experience, writing of the trans women he treated as patients: 'One can understand all too well that most of them wish they had been born female, a wish that is certainly expressed in great measure by homosexuals'.[26] The legacy of the idea of inversion meant that homosexuality and trans identity remained entangled for many years: sometimes it provided an excuse to deny trans people medical care on the basis that they were 'really just gay', other times it threw up barriers in the way of trans people whose transition wouldn't 'make them straight' in the eyes of society.[27] But ultimately, it equipped scientists, medics and politicians with the

conceptual tools they needed to recognise that some people identified as, and would prefer to live as, a gender different from the
one they were assigned at birth, and that this could be seen as a
legitimate medical need rather than a moral failing.[28] The history
of inversion, then, is trans history as well as gay history – both
because it framed sexuality as a form of gender identity, and
because it was in some ways the precursor to the political rights
and medical care that some trans people now have access to.

Inversion was a newly articulated theory in nineteenth-
century Europe. But the understanding of sexuality and gender
as entangled was much older, and much more global. In medieval Europe, sexuality was one factor used to assign a binary
gender to intersex people. In 1296, the Italian surgeon Lanfranco
da Milano argued anxiously that ambiguous genitalia should not
be surgically altered to resemble a clitoris 'if it becomes erect
upon touching a woman'; while a story circulated in seventeenth-century English books of marvels told of a person whose
body suddenly acquired male-coded sex characteristics while
'wantoning in Bed with a Maid', and who thereafter lived as a
man.[29] In medieval Christian discourse, what we would now
call same-sex activity was condemned primarily in gendered
terms: the main problem with it, for many writers, was that it
involved men behaving like women (being penetrated) or
women like men (penetrating or seducing women).[30] Later, in
seventeenth- and eighteenth-century England, 'molly houses'
provided a safe space for AMAB people not only to socialise
and have sex, but to use women's names and act out the process
of giving birth.[31] At the same time, in Peking (today's Beijing,
then the capital of Qing Dynasty China), *xianggong* – performers and sex workers, who were penetrated during anal sex with
older men – were trained to walk and talk in a feminine way
from a young age, wearing makeup and adopting a female identity as part of their role.[32] Also contemporaneous were a

significant number of people – often described as 'female husbands' – who lived as men while married to women in eighteenth- and nineteenth-century Britain and the USA, and whose male identities were bolstered by the apparent heterosexuality of their relationships.[33]

None of these histories can be clearly assigned to either 'gay/ lesbian' or 'trans' categories. Instead, they all demonstrate how sexuality has often been inextricable from the way people experience their gender, or from the way they're gendered by others. When I first started researching this and trying to explain it to people, I fretted that it sounded heteronormative and regressive: the historiographical equivalent of asking a gay couple, 'So who's the man and who's the woman?' I worried that it sounded misogynistic, too, in the way it often conflates femaleness with passivity and penetrability. But I realised that, whether or not it felt comfortable, I needed – as with all the other histories in this book – to take these sexual-gendered experiences on their own terms. If queer attraction and queer sex had gendered meanings in particular historical periods and cultures, I can't – no one should – just ignore that because it doesn't sit comfortably alongside the ideals I personally hold today.

We can and should treat these stories as gay, lesbian and bi history too: seeing them as trans histories doesn't take that away. But they fit equally well into trans history: the history of people disrupting gender, or living as a gender different from the one they were assumed to be at birth. In fact, they tell us about how sexuality and gender have often intersected in a way that complicates our attempts to tease out a separate narrative of trans history. They're important examples because they show us how easy it is to erase trans history by framing it as *just* lesbian or gay history, when the reality is that those categories overlap.

But more than that, history also shows us that sexual attraction and activity have worked to create new spaces for gender fluidity

– and to create new genders altogether. In this chapter, these are the stories I really want to tell.

Musicians in yellow and servants with topknots

The Persian philosopher Abū Ḥāmid Muḥammad al-Ghazālī was one of the most significant Islamic theologians of the eleventh century. In his book *Iḥyā' 'Ulūm al-Dīn* (*The Revival of the Religious Sciences*), he laid out guidance for Muslims that covered all areas of daily life, from religious practice to food, music and travel. Spanning forty chapters over four volumes, it was an immense and influential work: it became the third most frequently cited Islamic text of its age, second only to the Quran and the *hadith* (the record of the words and deeds of the Prophet Muhammad).[34]

Among the many subjects that al-Ghazālī addressed was appropriate clothing for different genders. Boys, he wrote, should wear only white. They should also avoid wearing variegated colours or silk – because these are associated with women, and with *mukhannathūn*.[35] In other early Islamic guidance on dress, mukhannathūn were distinguished by being permitted to wear yellow: a colour, according to the *hadith*, that the Prophet Muhammad explicitly prohibited for men but not for women.[36] Mukhannathūn, from this evidence, appear as a category of people who share permissions and characteristics with women, but aren't the same as women: a group of people, then, whose gender is woman-adjacent but ultimately neither male nor female.

The word mukhannathūn is derived from words indicating pliability, suppleness and softness: in this, it's not dissimilar to the word 'molly' (of 'molly houses'), which derives from the Latin *mollis*, meaning 'soft'.[37] It's not a neutral term, but a slur: the literary scholar Franklin Lewis translates it into modern English as 'fag'.[38] It's difficult, however, to come up with an English translation that isn't inappropriately gendered or equally pejorative: some historians translate it as 'effeminate', others as 'beardless boy' or 'youth', none of which really capture its significations. For this was not just a gendered category, but a sexual one: it referred to AMAB people who were seen to behave in a feminine way, to be attractive to men, and/or to be someone who was penetrated during anal sex with men (a bottom, in contemporary parlance).

Despite the pejorative force of the term used to refer to them, these people were not always a low-status group, and their femininity was not always understood as correlated with their sex life. Historian Everett Rowson has traced the stories of a loosely affiliated group of musicians in seventh-century Medina, one of the holy cities of Islam, located in the west of modern Saudi Arabia.[39] The group were hired separately and together to sing at events, and they drew praise for their cheeky wit, their physical attractiveness and their musical skill. Their de facto leader, a musician called Ṭuways, was known for their musical and rhythmic innovation as well as for their feminine appearance. One proverbial expression used them as the benchmark for skilful composition in a type of quantitative syllabic metre called *hazaj*: people could be described as 'better at *hazaj* than Ṭuways'.[40] Another used their gender as a benchmark: to be 'more effeminate than Ṭuways' became proverbial too.[41] To avoid using the slur mukhannathūn to refer to Ṭuways and people like them, I've chosen here to follow the lead of these seventh-century proverbs, and call them simply 'people like Ṭuways'.

Ṭuways and their fellow musicians presented in a feminine way: painting their hands with henna, styling their hair, wearing jewellery and feminine clothes.[42] Just as in al-Ghazālī's book four centuries later, they were often correlated with women: placed between men and women in events programmes, referred to by strangers with familiar nicknames (a kind of intimacy and lack of respect more associated with women than with men), and admitted to women's spaces. The latter indicates that they were not perceived as a sexual threat. Importantly, at this point in history, this wasn't because people like Ṭuways were seen as being attracted to men; instead, they were mainly seen as not experiencing sexual attraction at all. One story recounting how a group of people like Ṭuways reacted to a threat of castration depicts them referring to their penises as simply 'a spout for urine', and accepting the castration with a shrug: 'What would we do with an unused weapon, anyway?'[43] The gender of people like Ṭuways in seventh-century Medina, then, is perhaps better seen as entangled with asexuality than as entangled with homosexuality. However, whether or not they experienced sexual attraction, at least some of them – including Ṭuways – did marry and have children.[44]

The castration of this group of people like Ṭuways may not have taken place in reality, and the story of the conversation between them as they awaited the surgery was almost certainly invented for entertainment. But it's nonetheless revealing of how their gender was understood. Not only are the group presented as asexual, but their gender is associated with having no penis. 'With castration,' the character of Nasīm al-Saḥar exclaims, 'I have become a mukhannath in truth!', to which their companion Nawmat al-Ḍuḥā replies, 'Or rather we have become women in truth!' The implication here is that people like Ṭuways are best, or most 'truly', represented by having a body without a penis, and are very like women, but that they are not the same as women: they're a group of people who are neither men nor women, and whose gender is partly defined by their lack of sexual desire.

People like Ṭuways were far from universally liked in the seventh century – their music and cheeky wit was not suited to conservative tastes – and their growing reputation for being penetrated by men gradually led to greater stigmatisation.[45] At least one of Ṭuways's contemporaries, al-Dalāl, had a reputation for anal sex with men.[46] (They were also proverbially defined as effeminate: people could be 'more effeminate than al-Dalāl'.) This became gradually more associated with people like Ṭuways; by the ninth century, being penetrated by men was – along with lacking a beard – an intrinsic part of their gendered categorisation. They continued to be seen not as women, or as gay men, but as a separate gender. As historian Afsaneh Najmabadi points out, 'In nineteenth-century Iran, adult men who shaved their beards were called *amradnuma* (looking like an amrad [a Persian synonym for people like Ṭuways]) and not *zan'numa* (looking like a woman)'.[47]

The experience of people like Ṭuways – AMAB people whose gender is bound up with their perceived or actual sexual involvement with men, and specifically with their penetrated position – is one shared by groups of people in many different cultures, both historically and today. Historians often subsume these groups under the umbrella of 'homosexuality', or at best 'gender-based homosexuality' – a phrase that makes little sense when you stop to think about it, since if a person is gendered differently by their sexuality, the attraction between them and their partner is no longer one of 'sameness'.[48] The labels we give to people matter. In all cases, it's ethically important to try to represent the experience of people in the past accurately. In cases where people's genders and sexualities intersect, it's important to avoid erasing the multiple different queer aspects of their experience. And in the case of people who are gendered differently because of their penetrated sexual position, what makes these histories even more tricky to navigate is that the lines between agency and coercion, between self-expression and necessity, are often blurred. One historical group who present this problem are the *wakashū* of Tokugawa Japan.

The term wakashū had three related meanings: it could refer to a teenage boy or AMAB person; to a man's younger and/or less powerful AMAB partner; or to an AMAB sex worker and performer (a group who became increasingly numerous after AFAB actors were banned from the Japanese kabuki stage in 1629 due to fears that their attractiveness incited brawls).[49] In all cases, wakashū were easily recognisable. Hairstyle was a significant marker of gender in Japan in this period – it's often the only reliable way to ascertain the gender of a figure in a print or painting – and the hairstyle of the wakashū was unique: the crown of their head was shaved, and the long sections at the back and sides were looped together into a topknot.[50] They wore a type of kimono called a *furisode*, with long, swinging sleeves that hung down to at least their knees: this was female-coded attire, particularly associated with young, unmarried women.[51] In the many, often erotic, visual depictions of them that survive from the Tokugawa period, wakashū are thus easily distinguishable from men and women.

Just as in early modern Europe, clothing and hair in early modern Japan were hugely significant parts of what it meant to belong to a particular social group. To wear the clothing and hairstyle of a wakashū *was* to materially shift the way you were gendered by others.[52] It was also, just as importantly, to shift the way that your *age* was understood. Age in Tokugawa Japan is best seen as a social measurement, rather than a chronological or biological one: wakashū were younger than adults not primarily because they were born more recently (though many of them were) but because they presented their hair and clothing in a particular way and occupied a particular social space. In chronological years, wakashū could be as young as seven or as old as forty; in terms of their biological lifespan, they could be pre- or post-pubescent. But their *social* age was always poised at the point between child and adult.[53] This meant that people didn't just automatically become wakashū at a particular point in their life:

there was an element of choice about whether or not to become – or to make someone become – a wakashū by changing their hair and clothing.[54]

There were plenty of factors to take into account when making the choice about when to transition into, or out of, the category of wakashū, but significant among them was sex. One of the most crucial ways in which wakashū were distinguished from men and women was the way they fitted into the sexual value-system of Tokugawa Japan. The floating world offered sex with three gendered categories: men, women and wakashū.[55] Men of all ranks had sex with wakashū in the floating world as part of one-off transactions, while many samurai also employed whole retinues of wakashū as servants, choosing one or more of the most attractive among them for sex.[56] As I'll talk more about in a moment, the age gaps and unequal power dynamics in these sexual relationships meant many of them may well have been abusive by contemporary standards.

Sex between men wasn't against the law in Japan during this period, but it was frowned upon: men who slept together risked being regarded derisively as 'woman-haters'.[57] Sex between men and wakashū, however, was legitimate: men were expected to be attracted to both women and wakashū. The practice became known as shudō (an abbreviation of wakashūdō, meaning 'the way of wakashū'), and the association of shudō with high-ranking samurai helped to increase its social status. An entire genre of literature and art sprang up around shudō, in which the visual features that made wakashū different from men and women – their hair and clothing – were eroticised, seen as arousing markers of their sexual availability.[58] This emphasis on difference means that, again, we can't accurately interpret shudō as 'homosexuality': instead, it's better seen as sex between two different genders.[59]

Like al-Dalāl and others, wakashū were exclusively penetrated *by* the men they had sex with, rather than penetrating them.

While wakashū could also sleep with (and penetrate) women –
indeed, many of the plotlines of *shudō* literature revolved around
women 'stealing' attractive wakashū from their samurai lovers –
they were still often seen as the submissive, seduced partners in
these scenarios.[60] (Indeed, femaleness was less correlated with
sexual submission in Edo Japan than it was in other parts of the
world at this time.) In this sense, the gender of wakashū – again,
a gender distinct from that of men and women – was bound up
with their sexual practices, their appearance and their age.[61]

The sexual appeal of wakashū, and the economic benefits that
this appeal offered, led to further disruption of gender. Wakashū
were all assigned male at birth, but AFAB people, within and
outside the sex industry, also wanted access to their world, and
their customers. Consequently, by the early nineteenth century,
they began to present as wakashū too, adopting the topknot hairstyle, and pairing it with men's *haori* (jackets) in order to emphasise
that they wanted to be gendered differently from women.[62] Here
again, then, the desire to satisfy particular sexual desires led to the
creation of new, disruptive gendered practices. The emergence of
these wakashū intensified the non-binary gender of the entire
category – making it, for example, impossible to tell from visual
depictions what gender a wakashū had been assigned at birth.[63]

Wakashū were a historically specific gender, and in the second
half of the nineteenth century, a new regime in Japan led them to
fade from existence. In 1868, the Tokugawa shōgunate fell. With
the end of military dictatorship came the restoration of the
Emperor as overall ruler of Japan. The fifteen-year-old Prince
Mutsuhito set about a programme of reform and what he saw
(due to the increasing globalising and colonial influences of
Europe and the USA) as modernisation, bringing Japanese
customs closer to those of Europe. New regulations mandated
short, cropped, European-style hair for all AMAB people, signalling the end of the wakashū topknot. Gender was reframed as

binary and defined by the genitals; age, similarly, was newly tied to chronology and biology. People adopting clothing or hairstyles associated with a gender other than the one they were assigned at birth were censured and, in some areas, criminalised. Sex between men, and between older and younger partners, also faced greater regulation.[64] All of these factors made it impossible for wakashū to exist as they had done.

It's easy to romanticise lost genders like wakashū – and to be sure, the new regulations and ideologies closed off one expressive and sexual outlet for people who didn't feel comfortable living as men or women. But wakashū were never just a free, uninhibited expression of non-binary gender, or of sexual desire. Some wakashū were prepubescent, making some of these relationships look like child abuse to contemporary eyes. Even where the age gap was less severe, the power dynamics between wakashū and their male partners were decidedly unequal. According to popular discourse, the wakashū was expected to be romantically devoted to their partner, but they couldn't expect the same devotion in return: the man was simply out to satisfy his lust. Wakashū were portrayed as allowing men to penetrate them not because they wanted to be penetrated, but because they either loved their partner or wanted his money: these factors would lead them to reluctantly endure the pain and discomfort of being penetrated.[65] Obviously, some will genuinely have enjoyed the sex, but the fact that their pain and reluctance was assumed and yet disregarded gives us a good idea of the power dynamics and lack of enthusiastic consent that must often have characterised their sex lives.

The fact that so many wakashū were sex workers also complicates how we understand their agency concerning their gender and sexuality. Commercial sex with wakashū was seen as more pleasurable than sex with a wakashū who was also your romantic partner, and there were plenty of ways to access it.[66] As I've talked about, many wakashū worked in brothels; others were employed by samurai as a combination of servants and concubines; still others were employed by businesses such as shops, with sexual services forming part of their duties.[67] Wakashū employed by samurai were sometimes forbidden from having sexual relationships with anyone other than their employer-partner.[68] Some wakashū chose freely to do sex work; some chose, but in the context of growing poverty and famine in rural areas; some were hired out by their families (who could also control the hairstyle and dress that cemented and marked wakashū status). Complicating our understanding of their agency further is the fact that wakashū were predominantly younger than their male partners; if not always chronologically, then certainly socially. Although Tokugawa society didn't have the same concept of the 'age of consent' as many countries do today, the age gap will at the very least have skewed the power dynamics of their relationships further.[69]

The stories of wakashū and people like Ṭuways show us that histories of queer sexuality and gender aren't always comfortable. But unless we want to restrict our trans histories to upper-class people who are completely unbound by economic concerns – or to people whose sexual relationships are exclusively with people of the same age, class and race – we have to grapple with the question of whether the people whose stories we're telling disrupted gender freely of their own accord, or did it because they felt they had to. As I've emphasised throughout this book, it's often impossible to draw the line between internal motivation ('this is how I identify', 'this is what makes me feel comfortable') and external motivation ('I need to do this to access the opportunities I want, to sleep with who I want, or to survive'). Like any big group of people, motivations and experiences will have varied widely: we shouldn't dismiss all of these stories because some of them were coerced into disrupting gender. And we shouldn't forget that, no matter what the motivation, the existence of wakashū and people like Ṭuways created spaces where genders outside of the binary *could* exist in the medieval and early modern world.

Horn, leather and wood

While the daimyo and samurai of Tokugawa Japan were away in Edo, their wives and concubines remained behind in their rural compounds. Sometimes in groups of up to twenty, they were confined to their estate and forbidden from having sex with people other than their lord or partner.[70] Even when the daimyo was present, they remained mostly isolated from the outside world.[71] But this isn't a story of men enjoying the pleasures of the floating world while women and other AFAB people meekly awaited their return. Visual sources from the period tell us a very different story. As their male partners slept with women and wakashū, the wives and concubines are shown in prints and paintings masturbating, sleeping with male servants, seducing travelling salesmen – and having sex with each other.

Japanese erotic prints are awash with dildos. AFAB people are shown alone or together using *harigata*: dildos made from wood, leather or horn, sometimes hollow, equipped with a waist strap for use with a partner or an ankle strap for use alone.[72] Often there is lube: cream or oil held in a suggestive shell-shaped dish. Sometimes the dildo is double-headed for joint use; sometimes it is rigged up to an impressive, if implausible, pulley system to enable hands-free masturbation.[73] Dildos are represented as standard components of a dressing-table, and pedlars are shown marketing phalli of varying shapes and sizes to their excited customers.[74]

The prints also often have dialogue, giving us more insight into these imagined scenarios. In one 1801 print by the artist

Chokyosai Eiri, part of an album titled *Fumi No Kiyogaki* (which translates as both *Neat Version of a Love Letter* and *Pure Drawings of Female Beauty*), two people express their arousal and excitement. One wears a large dildo strapped around their waist, and holds a shell-shaped container of lube; the other strokes the dildo in anticipation. The captions detail their conversation. The person wearing the dildo says, 'Seeing as we're going to do it like this, I'll put lots of the cream [lube] on it. So really make yourself come. Without the cream this big one would not go in.' Their partner replies, 'Hurry up and put it in. I want to come. I want to come five or six times without stopping.'[75]

Eiri's print is representative of a genre of erotic pictures called *shunga*, a term that translates directly as 'spring pictures'; but they were also called *warai-e*, 'laughing pictures'.[76] As the name suggests, they were sold as much for entertainment as for erotic purposes.[77] They were read alone and communally by adults of all ages and genders; given as wedding gifts; kept as a superstitious charm to prevent fire or ensure a samurai's safe return from war.[78] Readers could buy them in shops, on roadside stalls, or from travelling pedlars, or borrow them from commercial libraries that made regular visits to homes; booksellers didn't keep them in back rooms or under the counter, but displayed them openly alongside non-erotic works.[79] Though the Japanese government banned erotic books in 1722, visual prints and paintings were exempt, and even the book ban was only sporadically enforced. The relative political and cultural isolation of Tokugawa Japan allowed shunga and erotic books to flourish, unaffected by the sensitive moral and religious norms that kept a tighter lid on erotic publications in Europe.[80]

The images of dildos that we see in shunga are clearly, in part, responses to male fantasy. When men thought about what their partners got up to when they weren't around, it served their egos and their libidos to imagine that those partners were desperately missing having sex with them, and might need to seek alternative sexual outlets – but not to imagine that they were able to replace them completely. Any lesbian will tell you that dildos aren't the only option for sex between women or AFAB people, just as anyone with a clitoris will tell you there are plenty of ways to masturbate that don't require a penis or a penis-substitute. But to imagine people enjoying sex together without even needing something that *resembled* a penis would have been pretty threatening to patriarchal ideology, and to the self-image of individual men – that is, if it even occurred to them as a possibility. In shunga, AFAB people are very rarely depicted masturbating or having sex together without the aid of a dildo, or another penis-substitute such as vegetables, wooden spoons or penetrating fingers; and when they do use dildos, they often comment on how the experience couldn't possibly match up to the 'real thing'.[81] Masturbation is represented as something people would only do when they can't have sex with a man.[82] The dominance of dildos in shunga, then, is partly evidence of the artists' lack of imagination, of the systemic misogyny of the period, and of an awareness of what their male audience wanted to see.[83]

Few women are conclusively known to have been shunga artists. There are some exceptions – one of the most well known being Katsushika Ōi, daughter of the renowned artist Katsushika Hokusai – but the majority of known names are male. What we do know, however, is that women bought and read (or looked at) shunga. European and American visitors to Japan, who were used to far greater censorship of erotic content and particular concern for delicate female readers, were scandalised by the openness with which Japanese men and women not only admitted to having shunga, but shared them with guests. American book dealer and journalist Francis Hall, who lived in Japan from 1859–66, wrote in his diary:

Shopping in the streets [of Yokohama], I stopped at a store where was a man, wife, and wife's sister in attendance. I was about to go when the old gentleman reached to the top of a case of drawers and took down ten boxes carefully wrapped up. He undid them and out of each box took three books full of vile pictures executed in the best style of Japanese art, accompanied with letter press. We were alone in the room, the man, wife and myself. He opened the books at the pictures, and the wife sat down with us and began to 'tell me' what beautiful books they were. This was done apparently without a thought of anything low or degrading commensurate with the transaction. The official that comes into your house will pull perhaps an indecent print from his pocket. I have known this to be done.[84]

Hall's shock at the wife's enjoyment of shunga would not have been shared by his Japanese contemporaries. Japanese books openly discussed the need for women to be sexually satisfied to ensure their physical and mental health.[85] Women were regular customers of travelling booksellers and book-lenders: indeed, as the people who worked at home, they were often alone when the book-lender came to call, and would be the first to receive and open an order of shunga.[86] Some shunga took the form of erotic parodies of women's romances and self-help books, suggesting an explicitly female audience.[87] Since book-lenders travelled to even the remotest areas, shunga was accessible to all women, and not just those based in larger towns or cities.[88] If women purchased a book, they were likely to circulate it among their family and friends.

Those shunga books and prints which made it to Europe did not enjoy such wide circulation. When the Victoria and Albert Museum in London was offered a shunga print in 1931 – the same print of two people with a dildo that I described earlier

– they accepted the print only on the condition that it could be stored along with 'several similar volumes, which are kept locked up in our safe, with a notice that they are to be issued only to serious students of Japanese Ethnography and Art at the discretion of the Keeper of the Department and with his personal authority'. The print was also omitted from the public catalogue, meaning that it could only be found by someone who already knew it was there – and who seemed to the departmental curator to be the right sort of person.[89] It took decades for the collection to be opened up, and for shunga to reach the mixed-gender, socially diverse audience it had enjoyed in Japan.

Depictions of people using dildos, then, were – in Japan at least – not just for male eyes. What's more, we know they weren't inaccurate. Dildos were genuinely popular in Tokugawa Japan. They have been recovered in archaeological digs at daimyo compounds – one 1999 excavation revealed six wooden dildos – and contemporary advertisements show a variety of phallic options.[90] Historian Anne Walthall has called attention to a sex manual probably written by a late-seventeenth-century nun, which advocates masturbation with dildos, as well as sex using a double-headed one.[91] There is also some evidence to suggest that sex workers used dildos with AFAB clients.[92] And of course, there's no reason to assume that they weren't used by AMAB people too.

This dildo history has been highlighted by Japanese women as evidence of the long history of lesbian relationships in Japan.[93] This is, without a doubt, one of the things that makes it significant. But it's also worth thinking about what dildos do to gender. A dildo can, after all, be seen as a prosthetic penis. For some AFAB people who use one, it's not gendered at all; it's simply a gender-neutral toy they can use to enjoy a particular kind of sex. For others, it becomes a female penis when it's being used by a woman, or a non-binary penis when used by a non-binary person. For still others, it shifts their sense of gender when they're using it, or helps to affirm their own sense of masculinity or maleness – something many trans men experience through their use of prosthetics today.[94] The same can be true of people who are penetrated by dildos, alone or with a partner.

What this means is that dildos and other sexual prosthetics are tools (if you'll pardon the pun) that disrupt gender in myriad different ways. Their history is a place where sexuality and gender collide and intersect – and, consequently, a place where lesbian, gay and trans history overlap. We can't tell the story of dildos without dealing with that overlap, or without confronting the fact that much of our evidence has been shaped by the male gaze and by patriarchal assumptions about what counts as 'proper' sex. But we absolutely should tell it, because both the sexual and the gendered experiences it reveals are radical. And because – as a nineteenth-century Japanese woman told a scandalised Francis Hall – the pictures are really quite beautiful.

Bad publicity and bad history

It's important that we, as historians or as queer people, don't treat gender and sexuality as two things that *used to be* entangled but have *now* been teased apart. There can be a tendency in white queer circles to frame this as a narrative of 'progress' in which we've moved from an outdated past where all queer relationships had to have 'a man and a woman', to a liberated present in which sexuality has been unhooked from gender and queer relationships are characterised by sameness and mutuality. But that narrative doesn't represent everybody's experience.[95] If we frame the entanglement of gender and sexuality as a relic of an unenlightened past, we erase the experiences of many people – often, disproportionately, working-class people and people of colour.[96] There are plenty of examples of individuals, groups and cultures for whom it's not accurate to talk about 'gender' and 'sexuality' as separate concepts or experiences.[97] Ethnographer David Valentine has worked and spoken at length with Black and Latinx people in New York who understand themselves primarily as gay rather than as trans.[98] Afsaneh Najmabadi spoke to a group of trans people in Iran for whom the idea of a trans woman being a lesbian (i.e. transitioning to live as female, and being attracted to women) didn't make any sense: for them, trans people are inherently heterosexual, and transition is something you do in part to be able to live as one half of a straight couple.[99] Social scientist Deborah P. Amory has interviewed groups of *mashoga*, people living in a city (unnamed for their safety) on the coast of East Africa, who wear a mixture of male-coded and female-coded clothing, use female names, and often work in professions associ-ated with women. They describe their femininity as primarily motivated by attracting men; they are penetrated during sex, and their AMAB partners are seen as straightforwardly male (though in their native Swahili, all pronouns are gender-neutral).[100]

Valentine has also traced the process by which gender and sexuality were unlinked in white European and American queer thought during the second half of the twentieth century, and what it reveals is a process of white, middle-class gay and lesbian people sacrificing trans and gender-nonconforming people in pursuit of perceived respectability. Many of the rights and protec-tions that gay and lesbian people enjoy now were gained through a process of emphasising that they were 'just like everybody else'. This meant silencing, rejecting or excluding trans people along-side feminine gay men and masculine lesbians – groups who were disproportionately working-class – all of whom were perceived to undermine that aim.[101] The Daughters of Bilitis, an American lesbian activist group founded in 1955, described butch lesbians as 'the worst publicity we can get': it didn't matter whether those lesbians saw *themselves* as masculine, or whether they saw them-selves as expanding what it meant to be feminine, as long as mainstream society still saw them as gender-nonconforming.[102] It's important, therefore, for all of us to be critical of *why* we see a separation between gender and sexuality now, and how we got to this point.[103]

Even within the course of an individual's life, the line between 'who one wishes to go to bed *with*' and 'who one goes to bed *as*' may become more or less blurry. Some trans people who *do* understand gender and sexuality as distinct categories of experi-ence can be surprised when their sexuality changes as they transi-tion. They might realise their sexuality was always more about being attracted to difference than it was about being attracted to a particular gender; or they might notice that feeling differently about their body affects what they want to do with it and who they want to do it with. Other trans people are motivated to tran-sition in part by factors relating to sexuality, such as wanting to feel more comfortable in sexual situations.[104]

Indeed, the very existence of trans people shows up the absurd-ity of the way we think about sexuality in the contemporary Western world. What does it *mean* to say you're attracted to men or women, when from a trans-affirming perspective, those groups can have any type of body? What does it say about our under-standing of gender if trans men who have consensual sex with women, but don't tell those women they're not cis men, risk prosecution for 'gender fraud'?[105] Do bodies, presentation or lived experience matter most in terms of attraction, or is that different for everyone? Where do non-binary people fit into our existing categories of sexuality? Is gender really the most helpful way to categorise the people we're attracted to, or is it time for a new model: one that reflects the fact that knowing someone's gender doesn't always tell you much at all about who they are?[106]

Border wars

At this point, you might be wondering: where on earth are all the butches?

While butch lesbian history certainly intersects with some of the stories I've told or mentioned in this chapter – particularly the eighteenth- and nineteenth-century 'female husbands', and the nineteenth- and twentieth-century inverts – there's a reason I've been cautious about positioning butch stories as stories of the past. There's a pernicious narrative in anti-trans discourse that says the availability of trans identities today is causing butch identities to become extinct. As attitudes towards trans people have improved, the story goes, so transition has become a way to erase gender nonconformity from existence: if someone is threatening patriarchal ideology by being a gender-nonconforming woman, they can be made to transition, thus lining them neatly up with gender stereotypes once again. As a result, we're told, people who would in the past have identified as butch are now being pressured into identifying as male or non-binary instead: they're transitioning in droves, and writing a particular type of womanhood out of existence.[107] Consequently, some anti-trans campaigners argue, we should restrict access to social and medical transition, and persuade AFAB trans people that they'd really be better off living as butch women instead.

Writing a rebuttal to this transphobic narrative is tricky, because the truth is nuanced and complicated. It is simultaneously true that some of the people in the past who've lived as butch women might (if alive today) have preferred to live as non-binary people or trans men, *and* that some of them would still have preferred to live as women. It's true that some lesbians have used, and continue to use, male names and he/him pronouns while identifying as women, *and* that knowledge of this fact sometimes leads to the (inadvertent or deliberate) erasure of trans men's history. It's true that some butches today see butchness as a type of womanhood, *and* that some see it as a different gendered category.[108] It's true that butches share some aspects of their experience with all women, *and* that they have some distinct experiences that the majority of women don't share. It's true that butches can be cis or trans women, *and* that the gendered experience of these two groups – particularly how they experience the misgendering that often comes along with butch presentation – is not always identical.[109] It's true that the version of history that says, 'People who used to identify as butch now identify as trans' is oversimplistic – in fact, trans and butch experience have long coexisted, and have been easier or harder options for individuals depending on multiple factors including race and class – *and* that some people alive today have chosen to transition after realising that living as a butch woman wasn't right for them, and have found this a viable option because of greater tolerance towards trans people and easier access to medical transition.[110] It's true that this might mean there are fewer people who identify as butch in our contemporary world than in the twentieth century, *and* that many butch women continue to exist, being women while disrupting normative notions of what womanhood should be.[111] It's true that some butch women see shifts around butch identity as a loss; that some have responded to this loss by attempting to police trans identities; *and* that the vast majority of butches, whether they're grieving that loss or not, are vocally trans-affirming and recognise that trans people and butches share many of the same oppressions.

History is a space that's often fiercely contested between butch and trans people: not for nothing does writer and academic Jules Gill-Peterson call it 'the trans-masculine-butch-lesbian border wars'.[112] As with real-life border wars, though, I'd argue that the solution is not to vigorously defend our respective territories, but to work together to dissolve the borders – and to admit more people to the land we hold in common. There are many people in history whose experience both lesbians and trans people can relate to: Anne Lister is a case in point. There are also people who've been claimed as lesbian and trans, but who might be better described by other terms: Stephen, the protagonist of Radclyffe Hall's 1928 novel *The Well of Loneliness* − who is attracted to women, and has 'never felt like a woman' − is arguably best described as an invert in the novel's historical context (Havelock Ellis, author of the sexological text *Sexual Inversion*, even penned the preface of the first edition).[113] And there are people whose gender and sexuality are locked together in an unbreakable feedback loop, like the ones in this chapter. Only by recognising all of these facts can we avoid the (sometimes literal) casualties of this border conflict, and rewrite the historical map. Just as the floating world of Edo was created out of nothing − building a space on the margins for queer sexual and gendered experience − so putting an end to the border wars might enable us to create a new, shared space in which all of these people, and their many-layered sexual-gendered experiences, get to thrive.

5

'I am both man and woman'

Defiant bodies in early America and beyond

Seventeenth-century Warraskoyack, Virginia, was a place where everyone knew each other's business. An English colonial settlement on Powhatan land, on the marshy eastern coast of today's USA, Warraskoyack had a population of around thirty people: mostly a mixture of plantation workers, their families and their indentured servants. In 1623, this included twenty-nine white and four Black people. The community lived and worked together, worshipped together, and were united by their sometimes difficult quest to maintain possession of their stolen land. So when a sex scandal erupted in the winter of early 1629, there was no hope of privacy for the people involved: it quickly became the whole community's concern.

The couple accused of 'fornication' were a maid in the household of plantation manager Richard Bennett, who we know only as 'great Bess', and an indentured servant employed by Robert Eyros and John Tyos, who the community knew as Thomas Hall. Bess, whatever their role in the affair may have been, is a marginal figure in the official records; the investigation quickly began to focus around Hall. Specifically, the community became preoccupied with determining whether Hall was a man, a woman, or both. By the time Hall's case reached the general court in nearby Jamestown, on 25 March 1629, the witnesses – 20-year-old Francis England and 29-year-old John Atkins – could testify that Hall's gender had been weighed in on or investigated by a staggering twelve local people: England and Atkins themselves, Nicholas (whose surname is omitted), Roger Rodes, Mr Stacy, Alice Long, Dorothy Rodes, Barbara Hall, John Tyos, Captain Nathaniel Bass, and the unnamed wives of Allen Kinaston and Ambrose Griffen. Around one third of the Warraskoyack population had directly involved themselves in the task of establishing whether the person they knew as Thomas was 'man or woman'.

What did Hall have to say about all this? The legal records tell us that Captain Bass, a high-status local land owner who represented Warraskoyack on the Governor's Council and in the House of Burgesses, 'examined the said Hall . . . whether [they] were man or woman'. 'The said Hall,' we are told, 'replied [they were] both'.[1]

Hall, who had been born in Newcastle-upon-Tyne, told the court that they had been 'often told' they were 'christened by the name of Thomasine'. Until the age of twelve, they lived as female in Newcastle, 'clothed in women's apparel', before being sent to live with an aunt in London for the next ten years. But when their brother was 'pressed' into military service, Thomas(ine) followed suit: cutting their hair, they 'changed [their] apparel into the fashion of a man' to fight on the 'Isle of Ree' – probably the Île de Ré, an island off the west coast of France whose control was contested between French Catholics and Protestants in the 1620s. On returning to Plymouth, Thomas(ine) lived as female again, earning a living through lacemaking and other needlework, before emigrating in 1627. They seem to have lived as male and as female at different times in Warraskoyack: John Atkins, their current employer, told the court that they were 'as he thought a man and woman'; their former employer John Tyos was convinced they were a woman, while others believed them to be a man. In answer to one enquiry about why they wore women's clothing, Thomas(ine) had replied, intriguingly, 'I go in women's apparel to get a bit for my Cat'. This curious phrase refers not to expeditions seeking pet food, but probably to the French slang '*pour avoir une bite pour mon chat*': translated colloquially, this means 'to get a cock for my pussy', a display of courtroom bravery that gives us a tantalising glimpse of Thomas(ine)'s defiance.[2] Their gender nonconformity, then, served them economically – enabling them to shift from a soldier to a lacemaker to a servant, depending on where work could be found – and possibly sexually, though it's unclear whether they were referring here to sex work, sex for pleasure, or both.

The court, having heard this story and the testimony of the witnesses, made a decision. 'It was thereupon at this Court ordered,' the records state, 'that it shall be published in the plantation where the said Hall liveth that [they are] a man and a woman, [so] that all the inhabitants there may take notice thereof'. Thomas(ine), meanwhile, was henceforth to wear a mixture of male-coded and female-coded clothing at all times: '[they] shall go Clothed in man's apparel, only [their] head to be attired in a coif and cross-cloth', female-coded headwear, 'with an apron before [them]'.

This decision – to enshrine in case law Thomas(ine)'s status as 'a man and a woman', rather than forcing them to live as one binary gender or the other – was unprecedented. While its consequences for Thomas(ine) were far from uniformly positive, thwarting their previously fluid expression and marking them out as other within the local community to which they were bound by their indentureship, the case is still remarkable for its validation of a gender other than male or female – and for Thomas(ine)'s own self-identification as 'both' male and female, articulating an identity outside of the gender binary in 1629.[3]

But this is not just a story about self-identification. Thomas(ine)'s status as 'man and woman' was not simply taken on trust by the court, or by the people of Warraskoyack. Francis England, John Atkins and the other locals they named were not just gossiping about Hall: they were undressing them against their will. Thomas(ine) Hall's story is not a straightforward story of early non-binary resistance. It's a complicated story of sexual assault, community-sanctioned violence and invasive examinations. It's a story that exemplifies the fraught relationship between trans history and the body.

What emerges from the legal records is a community who sought to prove the 'truth' of Thomas(ine)'s gender by inspecting their genitals repeatedly and violently. After the initial report that Thomas(ine) and Bess had committed fornication, Hall had been, according to Francis England's witness testimony, 'put in man's apparel': as someone who could have sex with a woman, they were assumed to be a man. Along with local man Roger Rodes, England was dissatisfied with the ambiguity this created. 'Thou hast been reported to be a woman, and now thou art proved to be a man,' Rodes said to Hall. 'I will see what thou carriest.' Together, Francis and Roger 'laid hands upon the said Hall' and 'threw [them] on [their] back'. Francis 'felt the said Hall and pulled out [their] members': that is, their genitals. On the basis of this, they concluded that Thomas(ine) 'was a perfect man'. Shortly afterwards, Hall was in the house of Nicholas Eyros, relative of their employer Robert, and was assaulted again: this time by a group of three women, Alice Long, Dorothy Rodes and Barbara Hall. Alice, Dorothy and Barbara had heard Mr Stacy report that Thomas(ine) was 'a man and woman'; based on their own investigations, however, they pronounced Thomas(ine) a 'man'. But John Tyos, their current employer, maintained the contrary, and 'swore the said Hall was a woman'.

Captain Bass sought to resolve the issue by asking Hall 'whether [they] were man or woman'. Hall's response was that they were 'both', but 'had not the use of the man's part'. Here the manuscript of the legal records is damaged, obscuring Hall's full description of their body – but we know that on the basis of it,

Bass decided Thomas(ine) was a woman, and 'commanded' that they 'be put in woman's apparel'.

But Bass's conclusion did not satisfy the Warraskoyack community. 'The aforesaid searchers,' Francis England told the court, 'were not fully resolved, but stood in doubt of what they had formerly affirmed' – that is, having previously been convinced from their own examinations that Thomas(ine) was a man, they were confounded by Bass's conclusion that they were a woman. A few nights later, Alice, Dorothy and Barbara came upon Thomas(ine) asleep – now in the house of their new employer, John Atkins. Inspecting Thomas(ine)'s genitals while they slept, and deciding again that they were a man, they called Atkins 'to see the proof thereof'. But as Atkins approached, Thomas(ine) stirred as if about to wake, and Atkins fled without seeing their body. A few days later, Atkins and the three women were joined by two others, known from the records only as 'the wife of Allen Kinaston and the wife of Ambrose Griffen', and *again* 'searched' Thomas(ine), concluding that they were 'a man'.

Yet even after this, John Atkins still wasn't sure. Looking at Thomas(ine)'s genitals, Atkins asked them, 'Is this all you've got?' Thomas(ine) replied, 'No,' and described another aspect of their anatomy. Commanded by their employer to 'lie on [their] back and show the same', Thomas(ine) was inspected once more by the five women, who declared – for the fifth time! – that they were a man. Atkins commanded them to switch back to men's clothing, and took his story to Bass. At this point, having proved impossible to resolve within the Warraskoyack community, the case was passed to the Jamestown court. It was they who concluded, on the basis of all of this 'evidence' coupled with Thomas(ine)'s own narrative, that they were indeed 'a man and a woman' and should be treated as such.

The repeated sexual assaults that Thomas(ine) Hall endured – inflicted by men and women alike, and endorsed by their own

BEFORE WE WERE TRANS

employer – demonstrate that their body was central to how the Warraskoyack community determined whether they were a man or a woman. But that community *could not agree on what Thomas(ine)'s body actually meant.* The exact appearance of their genitals is unknowable today: the manuscript of the legal records, worn away in parts beyond legibility, grants them the privacy that – owing to their status as a queer person and an indentured servant – they were never allotted in their lifetime.[4] I've chosen not to repeat many of the fragments of bodily description in the manuscript here, as a way of avoiding subjecting Thomas(ine)'s genitals to invasive scrutiny yet again. But it seems clear that their body was ambiguous: that it didn't completely match the appearance of bodies labelled as 'men' in its contemporary society, or of bodies labelled as 'women'. This raises the question: is Thomas(ine) Hall part of trans history, or intersex history?

The spectrum of sex

The fraught and overlapping relationship between intersex and trans history complicates a huge number of stories of gender disruption, even those occurring as recently as the twentieth century. Intersex* is an umbrella category that includes every

---

* The term 'intersex' was coined in 1915 by the German-American zoologist and geneticist Richard Goldschmidt, who used it to refer to moths that combined 'male' and 'female' sex characteristics. The word was later transferred to descriptions of human beings, and has been embraced by official bodies such as the World Health Organization and United Nations alongside activist groups. Since 2006, however, intersex traits have been widely known by the medical community as 'disorders of sex development', or DSD. As the intersex activist and scholar Georgiann Davis outlines in her book *Contesting Intersex: The Dubious Diagnosis*, this terminology was partly born of lobbying by intersex activists, who were keen to move beyond the othering practice of classifying people as different types of 'hermaphrodite' and 'pseudohermaphrodite', and wanted a term that made no reference to genitals. But by pathologising intersex traits as inherently 'disordered',

person whose body doesn't match up with what is socially considered 'male' or 'female' sex.[5] While we're taught to think of 'sex' as something stable and coherent, dividing humanity into two clear biological categories – women with XX chromosomes, a vulva, uterus and ovaries, and higher levels of oestrogen; men with XY chromosomes, a penis and testes, and higher levels of testosterone – it's more accurate to think of it as a spectrum with a broadly bimodal distribution.[6] Statistical estimates of the prevalence of intersex traits vary widely, but it may include around 1 in 100 people, a prevalence that underlines the inaccuracy of binary understandings of sex.[7] Intersex traits might be visibly obvious through the genitalia, as Thomas(ine) Hall's was, but are more often invisible: the category includes, for example, people with androgen insensitivity syndrome (who may have XY chromosomes, internal testes, and genitalia that looks what we'd call 'female' from the outside), and people with Klinefelter syndrome (who have XXY chromosomes, lower levels of testosterone and genitalia interpreted as 'male'), as well as many other variations in primary and secondary sex characteristics.

It's worth saying a bit about how I'm using the word 'sex' here. As I've talked about before, 'sex' in the early modern period – and indeed until as late as the mid-twentieth century – referred to the nature of men, women and everybody else in both a biological and a social sense. More recently, it's become split off

---

rather than just different – and by suggesting that intersex people had a problem with their *development*, having somehow failed to fulfil their true male or female potential – the new DSD terminology reinforced the authority of doctors to classify, and often to non-consensually surgically modify, intersex bodies. As a result, the terminology of DSD is controversial within intersex communities. Consequently, I've chosen to use the term 'intersex' here – while recognising that, just as when we talk about trans history, applying any label to people from the past is a difficult balancing act between recording the terminology used in that place and time, avoiding perpetuating past violence by repeating slurs, and valuing the connection that people today feel with people in history.

from 'gender' in popular discourse, so 'sex' is used to indicate the biological differences between bodies, and 'gender' the social aspects of how we understand men, women and the rest of us. But this simple distinction fails to acknowledge the ways that (as I've mentioned already, and as I'll say more about later) sex has always been, and continues to be, a social as well as a biological idea. Bodies matter to our experience and our identities, but the *way* they matter is socially determined in a variety of ways. So while I'm using 'sex' in this chapter to refer to the way we think about the body as gendered, I'm never suggesting that what we think of as 'sex' can be reduced to objective biological fact.[*]

For endosex people (people who aren't intersex), learning that the binary way we're socialised to think about sex is inaccurate can be disconcerting, and often leads people to discriminatory behaviour. In the period when Thomas(ine) Hall was alive, intersex people were often seen as monstrous, and in many cases as portents from God intended to show humanity the error of its ways. One anonymous pamphlet described two babies born on 25 July 1615 in the south-east of England, and claims they were sent by God 'to check . . . our vicious condition . . . and to punish the sins of some particular parents'.[8] Two of the babies were twins: one twin was an emaciated girl, and the other 'neither a Brother nor a Sister, but Both'.[9] In this pamphlet, as is common in texts of this period, the intersex baby is also described as disabled in several ways: their arm, for example, is 'without bones' and has 'two fingers only'. Ideas about normative bodies, and the desire to pathologise them, stigmatise them and/or force them to conform, continue to cause physical and psychological harm to disabled and intersex people alike today.[10] Dying shortly after

* Similarly, while some use the words 'male' and 'female' to refer to bodies and 'man' and 'woman' to refer to social groups, I don't use them like this because it reifies a distinction between the bodily and the social that doesn't really exist. So 'male' in this book is just the adjectival form of 'man', and 'female' of 'woman'.

birth, the twins were buried in the village of Preston, today part of the Kent town of Faversham.

It's hard to know exactly how true the story of these twins really is. Medieval and early modern accounts of intersex babies very often blur the boundaries between real and supernatural. Sometimes they have body parts associated with animals, such as eagles' talons.[11] Sometimes their bodies are maps of symbolism, pointing to the many sins of their community or world: a baby born in 1512 in Ravenna, Italy, was said to have a 'horn', which 'did signify pride and ambition'; 'wings', signifying 'inconstancy and lightness'; no arms, signifying that people weren't doing enough 'good works', and 'two Sexes', signifying the sexual transgressions ('Sodomy, and beastly filthiness') that were supposedly prevalent in Italy.[12] Some narratives of intersex people are little more than tragic lists of the ways in which they were murdered: 'cast into the sea', 'carried unto the River', 'shot to death with Arrows', 'consigned to a certain Desert Island'.[13] As these murders, and the conflation with human–animal hybrids, suggest, underlying many of these ideas was a sense that intersex people are less than human.[14]

As with Thomas(inc) Hall's body, I've omitted many of the invasive details of these intersex babies' bodies that were printed in the original texts. Doctors of the period, however, were keen – and felt thoroughly entitled – to scrutinise intersex bodies closely, while texts about the lives of individual intersex people invited the ordinary reading public to take up this scrutiny too.[15] Indeed, medical professionals have a long history of perpetrating violence against intersex people – sometimes in the name of investigative curiosity, sometimes as part of efforts to make their bodies conform to ideas of what men's or women's bodies 'should' look like. Despite the efforts of intersex activists, this persists today, with intersex children across the world subjected to medically unnecessary surgeries.[16] Many doctors' reasons for these interventions have as much to do with male and female gender roles as they do with the idea that there are only two sexes – and in fact, these ideas have never been clearly separable.

When we look at this history, what we see is a world that is never content just to let intersex people *be*. Intersex bodies have always been made to stand for more than they are: for God's judgement, for the supernatural or monstrous, for threats to the patriarchal order. People whose intersex traits are obvious have rarely been able to fly under the radar. While trans history is often hidden behind ambiguous motivations for gender-nonconforming behaviour, intersex history is often violently laid bare before an invasive medical, religious or literary gaze.

Why does it matter whether people like Thomas(ine) Hall are intersex or trans history? In many ways, they fit comfortably into both categories: their body was read as 'both man and woman', *and* they lived, intermittently, as a gender different from the one they were assigned at birth. When they told Captain Bass that they were 'both', it seems likely that they were referring both to their body *and* to the way they lived, dressed and worked. Given that trans and intersex people face many similar oppressions today, as victims of systems that (in most countries) still force people to be assigned one of two genders at birth and stigmatise anyone who tries to move away from their birth assignment, should it not be a simple matter to acknowledge that our history often overlaps?

The problem is that trans and intersex people don't just share a history of oppression: we also share a history of appropriation. Trans people have appropriated intersex traits and identities to validate our genders or access medical treatment, and we continue to do so – often without thinking about the impact of our actions, or how we can give back to intersex communities by advancing their struggle for human rights. Sometimes, in fact, the language used by trans people has played right into the hands of those who want to subject intersex people to medical violence. In using intersex people for our own ends, trans people risk being no better than the medieval and early modern commentators who seized upon them to comment darkly on contemporary morals or to advance their own medical careers.

When we talk about the shared history of trans and intersex people, then – about the many people who disrupted gender in *both* their body *and* the social aspects of their life – historians and trans people need to make sure that we're validating both of these aspects of our ancestors' experience, and not emphasising one at the expense of the other. And we need to think about how the ideas that shaped their experience have contributed to *both* intersex *and* trans oppression today. Here more than ever, it's crucial to emphasise the multiplicity of people in the past.

Of course, medical and legal professionals have rarely been content simply to look at and interpret the bodies of trans and intersex people. Instead, they've often tried to change them, both hormonally and surgically. This is where the paths of trans and intersex history come closest together – and where the nature of our experiences, especially our agency and autonomy, most sharply diverge.

Today, intersex activists continue to campaign against the practice of surgically modifying intersex bodies at birth.[17] This practice – which many doctors would call 'normalisation', but many intersex people would call mutilation – dates back centuries. Long before the discovery of oestrogen and testosterone, the Italian surgeon Lanfranco da Milano (who we met in the previous chapter) recommended the removal of 'added flesh' around an intersex person's vulva 'with cutting instruments' in his 1296 book *Great Surgery*; while physician James Parsons recommended that surgeons 'snip', 'cut' or 'burn' away any parts that render an intersex person's vagina atypical in his 1741 book *A Mechanical*

BEFORE WE WERE TRANS

and Critical Enquiry into the Nature of Hermaphrodites.[18] Surgery like this is often medically unnecessary, and often – as scholar and activist Georgiann Davis has compellingly shown – motivated by assumptions about gender conformity (boys should be able to pee standing up, girls should be able to be penetrated during sex) and about what a 'normal' body looks like (whether an 'ambiguous' organ is considered a clitoris or a penis can depend simply on its length).[19] But it was through these non-consensual interventions on intersex people that the consensual treatments on which trans people today rely were developed. As Jules Gill-Peterson has shown in her careful, compassionate, politically resolute book *Histories of the Transgender Child*, which centres the experiences of trans and intersex children in the twentieth-century USA, experiments with changing intersex children's bodies through hormone treatment directly paved the way for the hormone replacement therapy many trans people access today.[20] The gap between the experiences of those children – who were stripped of agency and often didn't even know what was being done to them – and the experience of trans people today, who have been given the opportunity to change our bodies in the ways we want to precisely *by* the non-consensual treatment of these children, is stark.[21] This is a shared history, but it's a history whose outcome has been strikingly different for trans and intersex people.

Initially, though, as these medical techniques developed in the mid-twentieth century, trans people struggled to access them. As stories of surgical and hormonal interventions on intersex people gained wider attention, trans people realised the opportunities they presented, but found the door barred. The same doctors who were keen to change intersex bodies, which they saw as in need of 'correction', were reluctant to help trans people, whose problems they understood as psychological, not physical.[22] The treatments trans people wanted would only be available to them if they were found to be intersex. Faced with this barrier, some trans people chose what seemed a logical strategy. If the doctors needed them to be intersex – well, then, intersex they would be.

Becoming intersex

Among the many striking details of Roberta Cowell's autobiography, the cats are one of the things that stay with you. Cowell, before she transitioned, was a Spitfire pilot during the Second World War. Her plane was shot down over northern Germany in 1944, and she was imprisoned at the camp Stalag Luft I. The prisoners' meagre rations – which included bread laced with bits of broken glass by the local baker – were supplemented by Red Cross food parcels, but these didn't always arrive. 'At one period,' Cowell wrote in her 1954 memoir *Roberta Cowell's Story, By Herself*, 'we had no Red Cross parcels at all, and all the cats in camp vanished, never to return.' As if this image wasn't grim enough – for the cats and the prisoners – Cowell adds, 'Unfortunately we had no fuel either and so they had to be eaten raw, but there is very little that you cannot eat if you are hungry enough.'[23]

Cowell's experience during the war left her, unsurprisingly, with what appears clearly to the modern eye as PTSD. Following the war, she lived with her wife Diana, who she had married in 1941, and became a successful racing-car driver – but though 'Superficially, my life seemed full', it felt to Cowell 'pointless and empty'. The crisis point came when she experienced an intense flashback during the 1947 film *Mine Own Executioner*, in which a Spitfire pilot is shot down. 'I knew it was done with the aid of a studio mock-up of a Spitfire cockpit, with back-projection of the ground and the flak,' she recalls, 'but for a moment I was back again in the cockpit':

As the aircraft was hit and crashed in flames, I felt all the pent-up emotion released that I must have experienced when my own plane was shot down. But this time I was an observer, and was not armoured against emotion by my preoccupation with what I had to do. Now I felt the full impact of stark terror. Fear that I would be burnt alive, fear that I would be lynched by the soldiers, fear that I would be terribly injured by the crash.[24]

Frozen in her seat, it took her an hour to be able to leave the cinema.

Cowell's traumatic experience was the catalyst for her to explore, with the aid of therapy, the other reason she felt so 'restless and dissatisfied'. Her pattern of pursuing one ambition after another, never stopping to enjoy what she had achieved before rushing headlong in pursuit of the next goal, was, she reflected afterwards, 'a frantic effort to show the world at large how masculine and assertive I could be. It was an attempt to make up for what I knew, deep down inside me though not consciously: my nature was essentially feminine and in some way my world was out of joint.'[25]

What happened next, we know from other sources not published in Cowell's lifetime: most usefully, the experiences of surgeon and trans man Michael Dillon. Cowell sought gender reassignment surgery in the form of an orchiectomy (removal of the testes). As well as being affirming, this surgery would open the door to legal re-registration: by the mid-twentieth century, the only way for trans people to correct their birth certificates was to acquire a medical affidavit saying that the sex on their original birth certificate had been a mistake. Having an orchiectomy would allow Cowell to claim to a doctor that she had never had testes, and thus that this 'mistaken birth certificate' category applied to her. But in the face of medical opinion that overwhelmingly restricted access to medical transition to intersex people, Cowell struggled to get anyone to perform an orchiec-tomy. She and Dillon had struck up a friendship after she read his 1946 book *Self: A Study in Ethics and Endocrinology*, which argued that access to medical transition should be based on self-determi-nation rather than medical gatekeeping – and as a surgeon, he had the skills to give her what she needed. In 1951, he performed Cowell's orchiectomy. Following this – an option very few trans people had access to in mid-twentieth-century Britain unless, like Cowell, they knew the right people – she was able to be diagnosed as intersex, allowing her to re-register as a woman and access other medical treatment.[26]

But this is not how Cowell tells the story. According to her autobiography, she met Dillon just once for lunch. She is clearly sympathetic to him as a trans person, emphasising that 'He was as genuine a man as any I have met', but she doesn't present their relationship as close – and she certainly doesn't report him performing any surgery on her.[27] Instead, she goes to extraordi-nary lengths to present herself as intersex, and to claim that her physical transition began of its own accord before she accessed any medical treatment at all.

Cowell's autobiography is headed by a long quotation from 'Professor George Randegger, M.B.E., head of Rome's leading International Hospital'. Randegger validates her female identity ('From the hormonic, physical and psychological point of view, Miss Cowell is now absolutely a woman'), suggests that her phys-ical transition was spontaneous ('What is so extraordinary, making her case practically unique in medical literature, is that the changeover should come when she was an adult. It is not infre-quent at puberty'), and states that she began to have periods before she had gender reassignment surgery ('It is remarkable that menstruation began before any sort of operation had been performed.')[28] Cowell thus invokes medical authority from the very beginning in order to construct her identity as an intersex person. This narrative is embedded throughout her memoir. As a child, she recalls having 'a deep-rooted fear and hatred of monstrosities', such as a drawing of 'a two-headed cat' she recalls seeing in a picture book, which she attributes to 'to an instinctive knowledge of the abnormality of my own body'.[29] As a fat teenager, she loses weight but retains 'a large pelvis and feminoidal fat distribution'.[30] As an adult, a Harley Street doctor identifies her as having 'quite prominent feminine sex characteristics', including 'wide hips and narrow shoulders, pelvis female in type, hair distribution and skin female in type', and 'typically feminine' 'breast formation', concluding that 'There seemed to be some degree of hermaphroditism present'.[31] Examined by 'a specialist in glands', 'two gynaecologists, a professor of anatomy, two general practitioners, and another endocrinologist', she recalls being told that 'my body had begun to change [i.e. to feminise] quite a long time before I became aware of it, probably about ten years before they saw me', and that 'I had an abnormal – for a male – supply of female hormones'.[32] Following this, a specialist confirms that 'The patient is quite definitely not a man – she is undoubtedly a woman.'[33] Cowell justifies her subsequent decision to seek further surgery on the basis that, 'Having been assured that I was genetically a female, with female physical characteristics, there was only one possible course to follow, and that was to find out what could be done to make me an unequivocal member of the sex to which I would have belonged since birth, if I had not developed along the wrong lines.'[34] In using the language of improper development, she was echoing the contemporary understanding of intersex traits as a problem of underdevelopment; combined with the assemblage of medical specialists and tests, this helped her to construct a convincing intersex narrative for her contemporary readers.

Clearly, Cowell's thorough self-presentation as an intersex woman in her autobiography was strategic. Being diagnosed as intersex had allowed her to access the treatment she needed, and undermining this diagnosis would have risked her safety, her livelihood, her reputation and her continuing access to hormones – as well as potentially compromising Dillon's professional integrity (and outing him as trans) if his collusion in the process was revealed. Moreover, those contemporary doctors who *were* sympathetic to trans people understood their transness to have a genetic and/or hormonal origin similar, even identical, to the way they understood intersex traits.[35] But this is not a straightforward story of a trans person jumping through the necessary hoops to get what they need, or even of a trans person finding meaning in the argument that they were 'born this way' (Cowell did clearly find this helpful: as she says, 'Once I realised that my femininity had a *physical* basis I did not despise myself so much').[36] The problem is that Cowell doesn't just use her narrative of being intersex to validate her own female identity. She also uses it to throw other trans people – and, indeed, gay people and people of colour – under the bus.

From a young age, Cowell reports, she was 'horrified and repelled by homosexual overtures', and her 'loathing' extended to 'any boy who showed the slightest sign of being a "sissy"'.[37] As an adult, she retained an 'instinctive dislike of the "pansies"'.[38] Writing in a period where sex between men was still illegal, these repeated statements are crafted to win the sympathies of her 1950s audience by presenting her as thoroughly heterosexual and as never having been an 'effeminate' man. Living as a man, she abhorred gay men's approaches; living as a woman, 'The idea of kissing a girl was now almost as unthinkable as the idea of kissing a man would have been in my previous existence.'[39] This might well be an accurate record of her experience – but by choosing to appeal to public support in this way, she props up the homophobia of her contemporary society. Her 'instinctive dislike of the "pansies"' is justified by an anecdote that portrays gay men as unchivalrous, selfish and performative: 'One graceful creature with shoulders like a hock bottle was dancing with a girl. She stumbled and fell heavily. He made no effort of any sort to help her to her feet, but continued to dance by himself. "The show must go on," he explained.'[40] Later, she distinguishes the 'homosexuals' who approached her when she was living as male from the 'normal men' who were attracted to her as a woman.[41]

Cowell's understanding of sex, and of the meaning of intersex traits, is also racist and eugenicist. Citing the Russian philosopher P.D. Ouspensky, she writes that 'one of the chief signs of racial degeneration is a weakening of the distinguishing marks of the male and female' – reflecting the racist construction of the idea of 'sexual dimorphism' (rooted in the idea that white people's bodies were the most 'perfectly' divided into male and female) that I talked about in my introduction. Consequently, she concludes that since 'my secondary sex characteristics were poorly developed, and I had some female characteristics [. . .] It seemed to me that here was a strong moral argument for putting an end to my life.'[42] This for me was a hard passage to read, my sympathy for Cowell's suicidal feelings troubled and undercut by her eugenicist justification for them.

Cowell's treatment of trans women makes for similarly uncomfortable reading. She distinguishes herself sharply from her American contemporary Christine Jorgensen, insisting that 'our two situations were widely different'. Jorgensen, Cowell argues, 'had never been [intersex]': instead 'She was scientifically classified as a transvestite, a person with an irresistible urge to wear the clothing of the other sex.' Cowell presents Jorgensen's femaleness as purely external and therefore inauthentic; and she stresses that Jorgensen's 'change had apparently been induced entirely through artificial means, no spontaneous changes having taken place at all (as they did in my case).'[43] Although Jorgensen herself framed her transition in identical terms to Cowell – 'Nature made a mistake which I have corrected'[44] – for Cowell, they were categorically not the same.

Later in her narrative, Cowell reports meeting a 'transvestite' named Mary. It's difficult to describe her account as anything other than mean-spirited and transphobic. Mary calls Cowell to arrange a meeting, speaking in a 'funny little voice'. Deciding that the opportunity to see her 'wearing women's clothes' would be 'far too good to miss', Cowell heads off to the 'strange rendez-vous'. She immediately identifies Mary's femininity as uncon-vincing: 'From fifty yards away, and after dark at that, the figure could only have been that of a man'. Cowell describes her appearance with a mixture of ridicule and disgust: '[She] wore an off-white (very much off-white) coat of a fabric woven to simulate fur, lisle stockings, big black boots that looked like violin cases, and a head scarf with a tuft of straight, thinning hair escaping from the front. [Her] unmistakably masculine face was dabbed with white powder.'[45] Mary serves as a foil to emphasise Cowell's comparatively natural, unstudied femininity: while Mary is unable to 'pass' as a woman despite considerable effort, Cowell recalls frequently being called 'Miss' even before starting to present as female.[46] Like Christine Jorgensen and the 'pansies', Cowell sacrifices Mary in pursuit of public sympathy and valida-tion for her own female identity. She then uses Mary's case to distinguish the 'psychological' problems experienced by 'trans-vestites' from her own 'physical' problems, explaining the 'trans-vestite' as motivated by 'deep-seated homosexual tendencies' of the kind she has declared herself 'repelled' by, and as 'never hermaphroditic [i.e. intersex]'.[47] Cowell concludes by expressing hope that non-intersex people who want to transition – that is, people we now call trans – will be eliminated by modern science: 'As medical science reveals more of the secrets of the mind and of the body, perhaps a solution will be found to the problem of the transvestite.'[48]

Today Roberta Cowell is one of the most famous trans people in UK history. The similarity between her narrative and Christine Jorgensen's – both affluent, attractive white women who had fought in the Second World War and transitioned in the early 1950s – has led her to occupy a similarly iconic position in the lineage of trans history, and she is often cited as the first British trans woman to undergo gender reassignment surgery. But according to her own autobiography, she doesn't belong in narratives of trans history at all: she belongs in narratives of intersex history.

Consequently, Cowell's narrative of herself presents a thorny problem. The first problem is that she presents an edited version of the truth, omitting the surgery performed by Michael Dillon and claiming to have XX chromosomes – something that, while we can't verify it for certain, is unlikely to be true given that she had two children with her cis female wife. (Cowell notes the existence of her children in the opening sentence of her autobiography, never to refer to them again.) Researching trans history often involves untangling misinformation, but the ethical stakes are shifted when the misinformation comes from the trans person themself. Perhaps the right thing to do would be to simply accept Cowell's self-definition as an intersex woman?

In this case, I'm not sure that it is. The problem is that Cowell never stops at self-definition: she also wants to define everybody else. Gay men are repellent 'pansies'; people of colour 'degenerate'; trans women narcissists, fetishists and masochists who need to be 'cured'. Cowell repeated these claims in stronger language in a 1972 interview with The Sunday Times: 'I was a freak. I had an operation and I'm not a freak any more. I had female chromosome make-up, XX. The people who have followed me have often been those with male chromosomes, XY. So they've been normal people who've turned themselves into freaks by means of the operation.'[49] The suggestion that men with XX chromosomes and women with XY chromosomes are 'freaks' is deeply harmful to trans and intersex people alike, and Cowell's repeated insistence that her intersex body was 'corrected' by surgery is exactly the kind of rhetoric that was (and is) being used to legitimise non-consensual surgery on intersex people.[50] Her emphasis on her heterosexuality, femininity and conformity to gender roles both before and after transition also serves to prop up a medical system in which trans people who don't conform to gender stereotypes have long found it harder to access treatment. When gay trans man Lou Sullivan tried to access treatment in the USA during the 1970s, he faced repeated barriers, with one doctor claiming that they wanted to 'free the world of homosexuality by offering sex change surgery'.[51]

Roberta Cowell deserves sympathy, then, for the many ways in which she suffered: from PTSD, from depression, and indeed from transphobia after she came out publicly. But it's impossible to take her self-identification as intersex at face value without acknowledging the many different kinds of harm it perpetuated. She was both the victim and the oppressor in her transphobic and homophobic society.

In this, as someone who arguably appropriated an intersex identity, Cowell was not alone. Many other trans people in Europe and the USA used very similar intersex rhetoric to explain their identities, though usually without sustained attacks on other groups like those of Cowell.[52] In some cases, as with earlier histories like that of Thomas(ine) Hall, the use of this strategy renders the line between intersex and trans history so blurred that the categories, once again, start to overlap. One of the only people to have 'changed their sex' who Cowell treats sympathetically is Ewan Forbes-Sempill. As Cowell writes in her autobiography:

A recent instance of a public avowal of change of sex occurred in Scotland on September 12, 1952. An announcement in the

Aberdeen Press and Journal revealed that a Scottish . . . doctor, forty years of age, had been legally re-registered as a man. It showed remarkable courage, I thought, for the doctor to have taken this step.

There had been no surgery involved in the change, for none was needed; there had been, however, a series of male hormone treatments. As a child, the doctor had shown a strong dislike of frills and flounces, and had worn an Eton crop. Other comparatively masculine traits had been evident, such as an enthusiasm for hunting and fishing. But masculinisation could not have been at all 'freakish,' for the doctor had a large practice and was highly thought of by patients and neighbours. Now, after the change of sex, he has married. He is still in practice and is respected and loved by all.[53]

Cowell's sympathy and admiration for Forbes-Sempill are justified by his normative masculinity and by the fact that (as she implies) he was intersex: hormones, but no surgery, had been needed to effect his 'change of sex'. And certainly, as with Cowell, this is how Forbes-Sempill identified. A member of a Scottish noble family – his father John was 18th Lord Sempill and 9th Baronet of Craigievar – he identified as a boy from an early age and probably accessed hormone treatment in Europe while travelling with his mother on the pretence of a cultural tour.[54] As part of his social transition, he had his birth certificate 'corrected' on the basis that he was intersex, and placed a brief advert in the local paper to announce the change: 'Dr. E. Forbes-Sempill, Brux Lodge, Alford wishes to intimate that in future he will be known as Dr. Ewan Forbes-Sempill. All legal formalities have been completed.' When Ewan's elder brother died in 1965, his cousin John sued Ewan, arguing that he was not a real 'male heir' and should not be able to inherit the baronetcy of Craigievar; the court found in Ewan's favour, validating his intersex identity

further. He died in 1991; when the Craigievar estate was sold for
£1m in 2003, an article in the *Daily Telegraph* referred to him as
a 'hermaphrodite baronet', citing Ewan's claim that he was 'care-
lessly registered as a girl' at birth, and quoting the current Lord
Sempill as saying, 'As far as his predicament was concerned, we
always understood it was simply mistaken identification at birth.
No surgery was involved.'

But research into Forbes–Sempill's legal case muddies the
waters. The lawsuit was heard behind very closed doors, in a
solicitor's office rather than a courtroom, and when researcher
Zoë Playdon first tried to investigate it in 2004, she found that
the records of it had been deliberately suppressed.[55] In fact,
Playdon's work, along with the work of legal scholar Lesley-Anne
Barnes Macfarlane, has revealed that not all of the twelve medical
experts consulted in the case believed that Forbes–Sempill was
intersex; some believed he was more likely to be a trans man,
especially given that he had been taking testosterone for several
years, thus making it difficult to rely on the results of hormone
testing.[56] If they had concluded that he was a trans man, he might
well have lost the inheritance case: his male birth certificate
would have been voided, as there was legal precedent for denying
trans people the right to change their birth certificates on the
basis of self-identification.[57] It seems likely that Forbes–Sempill's
social capital, as a member of an aristocratic family, bought him
both the secrecy of the inheritance hearing and its outcome:
certainly, his testimony at the trial emphasises his normative
respectability and desire for a quiet life.[58] His history, once again,
becomes a place where intersex and trans histories overlap.

Forbes–Sempill's declaration that he was intersex was perhaps
not as straightforwardly harmful or appropriative as Cowell's. His
trans identity was formulated at an early age, in the 1920s and
1930s, when much of mainstream medical practice understood
transness to be a kind of intersex trait; and he isn't known to have

expressed the same homophobic, transphobic or racist sentiments as Cowell.[59] But his claim to be intersex did have an impact on others. As Playdon has pointed out, by describing himself as intersex when he came out in 1952, Forbes-Sempill avoided asking a court to re-register his birth on the basis of self-identification alone. It's possible – though not, of course, certain – that his aristocratic privilege might have enabled him to win such a case. This would have created a legal precedent of self-identification that would have changed the lives of countless trans people afterwards. It could certainly have affected the landmark judgement of the 1969–71 case Corbett v. Corbett, which codified in UK case law that it was impossible for non-intersex people to change the sex on their birth certificate; the legal team defending April Ashley, the trans woman involved in this case, were shown details of Forbes-Sempill's case only to be told they couldn't refer to it in court. They lost the case: a judgement that restricted trans rights in the UK until the Gender Recognition Act 2004.[60] In a sense, Ashley's loss – following a trial fraught with classism – closed the loophole that Ewan's win had created.[61] In fact, it was the problem that gender recognition posed for male primogeniture – the tradition by which aristocratic titles were inherited by the oldest male relative – that prevented the UK government from legalising it for so long.[62]

No trans person owes it to society to martyr themselves, or compromise their privacy, in order to benefit others. But we can recognise this while still acknowledging the effects that Forbes-Sempill's decisions and Cowell's prejudices had, and the extent to which their strategic identification as intersex people was enabled by their existing privileges as white people with the financial means to access private medicine (and, in Forbes-Sempill's case, legal representation). Forbes-Sempill's experience of being able to marry, succeed to a baronetcy and be 'loved by all' is in stark contrast to the case of a Scottish trans woman known only as X, who asked the Tayside Sheriff Court in 1957 to grant her a new birth certificate on the basis of self-identification. Despite the court acknowledging that 'any attempt to make [X] live as a male again would, in all likelihood, have serious consequences', they refused to grant her request. Had Forbes-Sempill tried to do the same in 1952, and succeeded due to his social capital, X's life may have been very different.[63]

Although much of the thinking around intersex and trans identities has shifted since Cowell and Forbes-Sempill transitioned, trans people do still instrumentalise the idea of intersex people to validate our identities. Sometimes we point to the existence of intersex people to help explain non-binary gender identities: if sex is a spectrum, we ask, surely it makes sense that gender is a spectrum too? At other times, we look for real or imagined intersex traits within ourselves to help explain our transness, or to reassure ourselves that it's real. As someone whose six-foot height and size-ten feet constantly marked me out as different when I was living as female, and who could sing the tenor part in my choir long before I started taking testosterone, I felt an unexpected pang of disappointment when my endocrinologist's report declared my blood tests to be 'entirely in line' with the gender I was assigned at birth. As I mentioned in my introduction, this is the dangerous flipside of the 'born this way' argument: it can lead us to think that trans identities are more valid, or *only* valid, if they have a proven biological cause.

Jordy Rosenberg's 2018 trans historical novel, *Confessions of the Fox*, plays with this aspect of the relationship between trans and intersex history in interesting and sometimes uncomfortable ways. *Confessions* reimagines the life of real eighteenth-century thief Jack Sheppard as a queer story that not only disrupts assumptions about historical people being cis and white until proven otherwise, but develops Sheppard's life into a compelling anti-capitalist, anti-incarceration and anti-colonialist narrative. Sheppard's story is preserved in a manuscript found by modern academic Dr Voth, who must also navigate the twin capitalist hellscapes of contemporary academia and corporate publishing, telling his own story through the footnotes to Sheppard's.

The novel tackles the tropes of trans narratives head-on, as both Rosenberg as writer and Voth as editor steadfastly resist the desires of eighteenth-century doctors and twenty-first-century publishers (and indeed, perhaps, twenty-first-century readers) to scrutinise or otherwise appropriate Sheppard's genitals. The manuscript describes Jack Sheppard as a 'human Chimera', but the page purporting to show a visual image of his 'chimeric' genitals has been removed — whether by Voth or by an unknown prior owner, it's never quite clear. Corresponding with the publisher for whom he is editing the manuscript, Voth faces repeated demands to provide the image: 'WE REQUIRE *SPECIFICITY* AS TO THE MEANING OF SEXUAL CHIMERA,' demands the publisher in threatening all-caps. 'READERS NEED TO BE ABLE TO VISUALIZE.' Voth insists that he literally does not have the image in question — 'As regards the missing page, I assure you there is no such thing' — but in the end, under threat of docked pay and legal action, gives up and Photoshops an image of a 'waterlogged slug' onto an image of an eighteenth-century manuscript page, reporting that the publisher 'motherfucking loved it'.[64] The whole exchange is a witty send-up of the obsession with trans people's genitals in both contemporary and historical culture. More powerfully, it exposes this obsession as futile and absurd: when the desire to see what's in a trans person's pants is finally fulfilled, it turns out to be just an empty signifier, just as knowing what a trans person's genitals really look like doesn't tell you anything about them (or about their gender). Sheppard's genitals are indeed a 'chimera' — partly in that they're a Photoshop mashup of two images, but also in that sex itself is a chimera, a composite and incoherent social and biological construct. And as Rosenberg shows, the body is never stable in any case: in fact, for Jack as for so many queer people, it is 'rewritten in the process of making love', reshaped and made differently meaningful by the touch of an affirming lover.[65]

But in suggesting that Sheppard's genitals are a 'human Chimera', Rosenberg is also suggesting that he may be intersex. Voth, as narrator, suggests the same.[66] Moreover, Voth hints at the same detail about himself, saying of his clitoris that 'what I have going on was outsized even before the T [testosterone, which can enlarge the clitoris]', and stating his desire to reclaim the word 'monster' (which, as I discussed above, was particularly associated with inter-sex people in early modern culture).[67] But the book never makes these hints explicit: indeed, it never uses the word 'intersex' at all.

What is going on here? Rosenberg has spoken about the diffi-culty of striking a balance between avoiding pandering to 'mainstream readers' spectacularising gaze' and 'communicat[ing] intimately with readers who I wanted to be able to write for': his references to Sheppard and Voth's genitals, he says, are for the latter, a way of centring trans readers that is also true to Voth's character.[68] But trans and intersex writer Bogi Takács has argued that by blurring the lines between trans and intersex history in its representation of Sheppard and Voth – using 'a wide variety of intersex-related examples and descriptions, but in a trans context', without ever referring directly to intersex people – the book suggests that 'trans people are . . . entitled to historical intersex narratives'. In other words, if we write about histories where the categories of trans and intersex overlap, but just treat them as trans history without explicitly mentioning the word 'intersex', we not only erase intersex history: we appropriate it. And just as with Cowell and Forbes-Sempill's histories, *Confessions* implies that Sheppard and Voth's intersex bodies serve to validate the reality of their trans identities.[69]

Liberating bodies

What, then, should we do with the intersections between inter-sex and trans history? There are many people in history who fit the criteria for both intersex and trans: their bodies didn't fit into a binary understanding of sex, *and* they lived as a gender different from the one they were assigned at birth. The instability of the concept of 'sex' only compounds this overlap. And there are also people in history whose self-identification as intersex, and/or whose treatment as intersex by the medical profession, mean we can't straightforwardly treat them as trans.

Just as with people like Anne Lister, who are important both to cis queer women and to trans people – but even more impor-tantly, given the continuing marginalisation of intersex people in contemporary society – historians need to tread carefully and responsibly when we talk about the histories of people who blur the boundaries between intersex and trans.[70] Whether we're interpreting textual or archaeological evidence, we need to explicitly name both groups of people to whom these histories are important, rather than granting one group the legitimacy and community of history at the expense of the other.[71] The visibility of non-binary people in contemporary culture is already threat-ening to eclipse intersex history even further: in August 2021, the discovery of the 1,000-year-old body of a person with Klinefelter syndrome, an intersex trait involving XXY chromosomes, was widely reported as being a 'non-binary Iron Age leader'.[72]

Trans people have responsibilities here too. We need to be aware of the harmful consequences for intersex people that can result from trans people using language like 'correcting' sex, even if that sometimes forces us to make difficult decisions about how to respect the self-identification of historical figures. We need to resist the idea that intersex variations are primarily legible or valuable in their capacity to 'validate' trans identities. We need to incorporate intersex activism into, or alongside, our trans activism – particularly around the issues of bodily autonomy and informed consent, which affect both groups so deeply.

The overlap between trans and intersex history is a symptom of a wider issue: the fact that the body is, and always has been, one of the factors that helps to construct our gender. Talking about this is risky, because it can threaten to play into the hands of anti-trans campaigners who believe that what makes a 'man' or a 'woman' is determined solely by bodily characteristics. Implicit in many of the claims that trans people are a 'new invention' is the idea that everyone in the past defined men and women based on penises and vulvas, and the disruption of this is a recent phenomenon or a symptom of our contemporary 'post-truth' society. But in fact, the relationship between gender and the body has *never* been simple, or separable from social ideologies. In an 1188 legal commentary, for example, the Italian canon lawyer Huguccio argued that an intersex person should be assigned male 'if he has a beard and always wants to engage in manly activities and not in those of women, and if he always seeks the company of men and not of women'.[73] Similarly, the sixteenth-century French surgeon Ambroise Paré saw 'genitalia' as just one among a range of factors by which a person could be judged male or female: these also included 'the face and by the hair, whether it is fine or coarse; whether the speech is virile or shrill; whether the teats are like those of men or of women; similarly whether the whole disposition of the body is robust or effeminate; whether they are bold or fearful, and other actions like those of males or of females.'[74] Medieval legal theorists from multiple strands of Islamic law defined men and women based on how they urinated, but also conceptualised men and women as 'protector and protected', and took this into account when judging the legal sex of intersex people.[75] Later, the designation of testosterone and oestrogen as 'male' and 'female' hormones resulted from an existing idea that men and women were essentially different (since in reality, the majority of people's bodies produce both hormones – a discovery that initially surprised scientists).[76]

We must also be aware that the idea of sexual dimorphism also has a racist history, formulated in eighteenth- and nineteenth-century European thought as a pseudoscientific basis for white supremacy. As Richard von Krafft-Ebing put it, in a representative view, 'the higher the anthropological development of the race, the stronger these contrasts between man and woman'.[77] We can see the origins of this in exoticised early modern accounts of the sexual difference of people of colour. The physician John Bulwer wrote of Native American people who 'have the generative parts of both Sexes' in Florida and Virginia – ironically the area where Thomas(ine) Hall, a white trans and intersex person, lived – while the Scottish lawyer and philosopher Henry Home, Lord Kames, explained the success of European colonial efforts in North America by claiming that Native American men 'are feeble in their organs of generation and have no ardour for the female sex'.[78]

While the body has an impact on how we understand gender and sex, then, how we *interpret* the body is – and always has been – a complicated, political, culturally specific process. It's useful here to return to the words of Shon Faye, which I quoted in my introduction, since she explains this so clearly: 'Our sexed bodies never exist outside social meanings: consequently, how we understand gender shapes how we understand sex ... The way we perceive and understand sex differences and emphasise their significance is so deeply gendered that it can be impossible to completely divorce the two.'[79] It's not that the body is irrelevant: it's that how we interpret the body, and what we do with that interpretation, is always about the gendered ideas that exist within our specific culture.

This history should lead us to question the obsession of contemporary transphobic discourse with the bodies and genitals of trans people. Numerous countries, including the UK, still require trans people seeking legal gender recognition to either undergo genital surgery or justify their decision not to.[80] Campaigns against trans women's right to enter women-only spaces frequently focus on their (real or imagined) bodily difference.[81] Sex 'verification testing' of women athletes focuses disproportionately on sex hormones over other physical advantages such as height or metabolism; and in a recent high-profile example, South African runner Caster Semenya endured invasive photographs of her 'private body parts' and was made to take hormonal contraceptives that 'caused significant weight gain, made her feel sick, and led to fevers and abdominal pain', analogous to other 'normalising' medical interventions on intersex people.[82] As a Black woman, Semenya is in any case at higher risk of suspicion regarding her gender. More widely, the contemporary transphobic practice of policing human bodies on the basis of sex – especially the focus on genitals as indicating someone's 'real' sex – has a racist history too, originating in fears that Black women, lesbians and sex workers were all 'hiding' their 'inferior or abnormal anatomic features in order to hide their deeper criminal natures'.[83] Relatedly, the avowed reasons behind this policing – to protect cis women – have their origins in the racist discourse that suggests white women are uniquely vulnerable and in need of protection; the same discourse that leads to the fatal over-policing of Black people, especially Black men and boys.[84]

Both the history of gender and bodies, and our contemporary need to develop more ethical ways of navigating the relationship between them, demand that we find new ways of knowing gender: ways that incorporate how our body affects our experience, but are not just about reducing everyone to their genitals. It's hard to find historical models for this, but not impossible. Eighteenth-century court records reveal one rare example of a historical trans and intersex person who becomes visible to historians in a way unrelated to their body: who enters the historical record not as someone transforming from one gender to another, or having their gender questioned, but simply as *being* neither male nor female. Mary Tom House was called before the Old Bailey court on 9 September 1767, indicted for stealing a linen shirt, a pair of silk stockings and a linen apron from Mary Haggett.[85] Mary Tom is recorded as a 'spinster', a female-gendered term, but a note in the court proceedings states, 'This prisoner was an hermaphrodite, so had the name of Tom, as a Christian name.' A further tantalising suggestion of possible queerness appears in the report by police constable John Glover that Mary Tom had given the stolen clothes 'to the woman that was in bed with [them]'. The inclusion of Mary Tom's story in the printed *Proceedings of the Old Bailey* demonstrates that it was thought to be of public interest, but no further attention is paid to their gender, or to their body; they are simply visible as someone living, stably, outside of binary gender. The fact that Mary Tom becomes visible in court records, however, means that their story does not have a happy ending: they were sentenced to be transported for seven years.[86] To find a truly humane example of how we might know gender and the body differently, we need to return to the twenty-first century, and to the literary world.

When anyone asks me to recommend a novel with a nonbinary protagonist, I recommend Sara Taylor's 2016 novel *The Lauras*. Both a coming-of-age tale and a queer love story, *The Lauras* is teenage Alex's narration of a road trip around the USA with their mother, in search of important places and people from her past. Alex doesn't have a gender: in their own words, they are a 'human-fucking-being'.[87] But importantly, this doesn't mean their body is absent from the novel: they're not simply an abstracted, genderless mind. They sweat, need the toilet, feel carsick, masturbate.[88] Taylor conceals the specificity of their body through all of these actions, carefully but never coyly – in fact, the obliqueness with which Alex describes masturbation ('I wanted to take my time with it and really luxuriate in the feeling, but I was so worked up I finished within a minute of beginning') rings more true both as a teenager's voice and as first-person internal narration than a more explicit description of body parts would have done. And in case the reader is struck by curiosity to 'know' Alex's gender by way of their body – in case we want to follow in the footsteps of the people who repeatedly undressed Thomas(ine) Hall in seventeenth-century Warraskoyack – Taylor confronts us brutally with the consequences of that desire. At a new school in Reno, Alex's 'refusal to pledge allegiance' to any gender draws curiosity and hostility, culminating in a panic-inducing scene in which they are ambushed in a dark bathroom.

It felt like I was stuck to the floor, like I'd never be able to overcome gravity enough to sit up again. The one on top of me shifted his weight down, and I felt cold air on my stomach as someone yanked up my shirt.

'No tits,' he said.

'That doesn't prove anything – half the sluts here are carpenters' dreams.'

'Yeah, but how many of them don't wear no bra?'

'I dunno. Just all the dykes and skanks, maybe? Move your ass – we came to get proof.'

The weight shifted up to my chest, and for a moment I couldn't breathe. My vision was weird, but as I blinked I saw that one of them was sitting back on his heels, camera phone out and at the ready. The third guy was straddling my shins, and as I tried to make sense of 'proof' he began fiddling with my belt, yanking down my jeans.

Suddenly I got it.

My thrashing only slowed them down a little as they tried to keep me pinned and get my clothes off at the same time. But my anger at being jumped had morphed into terror, hot and choking, underlaid like a baseline with the memory of hitch-hiking in Alabama, of having my head forced down. I started screaming then, and the guy sitting on my chest flailed, trying to cover my mouth, let go of my arm so he could do it and I clawed him across the face, gouging at his eyes.[89]

Alex's screaming brings them rescue, but they are traumatised by the assault: suppressing their emotions as a form of self-preservation, they remain 'scared . . . that what I wasn't feeling would all come out when I didn't expect it, when I couldn't handle it'.[90] The gang of students are framed by their references to 'sluts', 'dykes' and 'skanks' as casually but thoroughly misogynistic; the reference to 'hitchhiking in Alabama', when Alex was raped, positions this transphobic attack as clearly sexual assault. Any reader who previously desired to 'know' Alex's genitals is now forced to realise exactly what sort of person this desire aligns them with.

Crucially, however, Taylor does not leave Alex's story here: the experience of non-binary embodiment is not only one of trauma. Their relationship with an eighteen-year-old drag performer, Simon, comes to represent other, recuperative ways of knowing them. Simon enjoys dressing Alex up in outrageous outfits; importantly, as Alex says, 'he seemed to want to play with my genderlessness, rather than overwrite it with what he thought I should be'.[91] He delights in their capacity for ambiguity and transformation and, through his care for them, restores their body's capacity for desiring and being desired, transforming it from something that has been othered and invaded. He declines Alex's request for sex, refusing to take advantage of their vulnerability and desire to forget their assault, but 'got into the habit of leaning against me, putting his arm around me,' as Alex recalls warmly: 'kissing my neck in the long slow way that I'd longed for when I watched the teenagers on the beach in Florida, touching me in the warm, tingling ways that people reserve for lovers.'[92]

In her fierce protection of both Alex's privacy and their right to enjoy their body, Taylor too shows a kind of love for her protagonist. Alex's resilient genderlessness is akin to the real damaged manuscript of Thomas(ine) Hall's legal case, and the invented damaged manuscript of *Confessions of the Fox*. All of these allow trans people, and in the latter two cases intersex people, to be known to history in ways that include but are not limited to their bodies. We can only hope that Thomas(ine), and the other trans and intersex people whose stories I have told here, had the chance to learn what Jack Sheppard and Alex do: that the relationship between our bodies and our gendered experiences may be the root of so much oppression, but can also be a powerful source of joy.

6

'Because of the manifestation of Spirit'

Gender, spirituality and survival in
North America and South Asia

The river known in English as the Columbia rises in the Rocky Mountains, in the Ktunaxa (Kutenai) Nation, Canada. Flowing through rocky gorges and across vast plateaus, it crosses the border into the USA and flows into the Pacific at the port of Astoria in Oregon. At over 1,200 miles long, it is the largest river in the region. To traverse its entire length today, equipped with specialist hiking gear, would be an enormous feat of endurance; to do so in the first decade of the nineteenth century was even more remarkable. But two people from the Ktunaxa (Kutenai) Nation achieved just that. One of them was Kaúxuma núpika, and this extraordinary expedition was far from the only remarkable aspect of their story.

Kaúxuma núpika was born in the late eighteenth century, somewhere on the lower stretches of the Kootenay River, before it flows into the Columbia.[1] In 1808, as members of their local community would later recall to anthropologist Claude E. Schaeffer, a group of European fur traders arrived in the region, trapping otters and beavers in huge numbers to sell their skins within and outside of the American continent. When they left, Kaúxuma núpika went with them. Shortly afterwards, they married one of the traders: a man named Boisverd, servant to the fur trader and diarist David Thompson.[2] After spending a year with their husband, however, they left the Europeans again and returned home. On their return, they announced that they were

189

no longer a woman, but a man. Their new name, Kaúxuma núpika, translated as 'Gone to the Spirits' – a chosen name that made clear to everyone how their gender was entangled with their spiritual experience.[3] It's this kind of spiritual gendered self-hood that white trans people raised in largely secular societies are most liable to romanticise – and simultaneously, that we are often least able to understand.

A note on Freshwater—it is *not* a book about nonbinary/ trans identity through an Igbo lens, ffs. It is not about gender whatsoever and framing it as that is trying to force it over to a human/Western center. It is about embodiment as an ọgbanje.[4]

On 13 June 2021, the Nigerian writer Akwaeke Emezi aired their frustration on Twitter about the way readers were interpreting *Freshwater*, their award-winning semi-autobiographical debut novel. 'Readers can take whatever they want from the book, as usual,' they wrote, 'but let's be real about which texts get their centers acknowledged and respected, and which centers get shuf-fled around to make the work more palatable.' Books by white, Western writers, they pointed out, are far more likely to be inter-preted on the terms they've set than are books by non-Western writers of colour – meaning that many white readers of *Freshwater* have engaged (sometimes unwittingly, sometimes not) in acts of racist erasure. 'You cannot,' Emezi wrote, 'separate white supremacy/ colonialism/etc from reading a text centered in Igbo ontology, about an entity specific to Igbo reality, and then describing it as something else, without thinking about why you can't hold the indigenous center and what you might be erasing.'[5]

The protagonist of *Freshwater*, the Ada, is – like Emezi themself – an ọgbanje, an Igbo spirit born to a human mother.[6] The Ada shares some aspects of experience with non-binary people, but is not one; as Emezi put it in a later Twitter thread, 'the Ada was never human, even when she thought she was'.[7] Emezi has spoken in other contexts about how using the language and concepts of transness functioned as a 'gate', allowing them to access the concept of ọgbanje embodiment: 'It helped me think about things that language does not exist for.'[8] Similarly, the language of 'dysphoria' – often used by trans people to express their experience of embodiment – was, for them, a helpful way to articulate the experience of 'spirits who find themselves embodied in human form'.[9] But since they're not human, ọgbanje don't have a gender: fundamentally, 'gender is human and we are not'. At most, they may, in Emezi's words, '[use] flesh terms to contextualize things for the humans who can't think spiritfirst'.[10]

I first read *Freshwater* in May 2020, devouring it over one lockdown weekend on a camping chair in our sun-trap front yard. As with all the books chosen by my local queer book club, I took notes as I read, recording my thoughts in real time. Looking back at them now, I feel justifiably uncomfortable as I recognise in my own response the exact reading that Emezi called out on Twitter. Quoting the book's ọgbanje narrators, who describe themselves at the moment of the Ada's birth as 'trapped by this unfamiliar birthing, this abomination of the fleshly', I wrote, 'I mean I think a lot of trans people feel this way'.[11] When the Ada hit puberty and 'the hormones redid her body, remaking it without consent from us or the Ada', I wrote 'great evocation of transness'.[12] When the Ada tells her friends, before having top surgery, 'that she couldn't wait for when she could wear dresses again', and the ọgbanje reflect on how 'we saw ourself [with] dresses creeping up the thigh, gashing open at the front to show chest bone . . . Just like how having long hair weighing down our back made us want to wear buttons up to our throat, men's sleeves rolled up our biceps, handsome, handsome things', I exclaimed over how those desires resonated with my own: 'definitely non-binary experience!'[13]

I don't think I was wrong to feel a sense of recognition as I read the Ada's story; the very experience of reading fiction is about those points of contact between different realities, those moments when a character with whom you share very little articulates something that rings deeply true to you. But I *was* wrong to assume that what felt to me like the 'evocation of transness' was the *correct* reading, the one that Emezi had been aiming to achieve. As someone whose existence is primarily human rather than spiritual, I was so caught up in mapping my own trans experience onto the novel that I left no space for its own frame of reference. I approached the book gender-first, and as a result, I missed its urgent demands that I think spirit-first instead.

As Emezi's Twitter thread (and their many other assertions of their work's spiritual core) shows, I was far from alone in responding to *Freshwater* in this way. In fact, my response was a microcosm of the way white trans people, especially those of us without a faith, approach the intersections of gender and spirituality. Sometimes, as with ọgbanje, we misrepresent spiritual experiences as gendered because they look similar through a human lens. At other times, we simplify experiences that are both gendered *and* spiritual by flattening, erasing or failing to understand their spiritual dimension. It's these latter experiences whose histories I want to tell here.

It has become commonplace for groups like Indian hijras and Native American/First Nations Two-Spirit people, who cannot be accurately categorised by binary gender, to be namechecked as part of any argument for non-binary recognition. If 'other' cultures have non-binary genders, the argument goes, this proves that the Western gender binary is arbitrary. Some trans people have even been prompted to argue that they were not 'born into the wrong body', but 'born into the wrong culture'.[14] Anthropologists Evan B. Towle and Lynn M. Morgan have analysed how these arguments construct and deploy the figure of the 'transgender native': a figure simultaneously exoticised and romanticised, who is not 'a normal, fallible human being living within the gender constraints of his or her own society', but 'an appealing, exalted, transcendent being (often a hero or healer)'.[15] Writers and activists from groups commonly instrumentalised in this way have spoken out too. Two-Spirit Oji-nêhiyaw writer Joshua Whitehead, in the *kinanâskomitin* (acknowledgements) to his novel *Jonny Appleseed* – the story of a young Two-Spirit/ Indigiqueer cybersex worker – declares that the novel aims to show 'that Two-Spirit and queer Indigenous folx are not a "was", that we are not the ethnographic and romanticized notations of "revered mystic" or "shamanic", instead we are an *is* and a *coming*.'[16] Other Native American and First Nations writers have decried the practice of white trans people appropriating Two-Spirit identities: as Carrier First Nations two-spirited researcher* Michelle Cameron puts it, 'The term two-spirited has a *specific* cultural context, and removing it from that context simply because one likes the meaning of it is an act of colonization and must be resisted.'[17]

Exaltations of the 'transgender native' may employ spiritual language to underline their mysterious, powerful otherness – and/or to present them as part of a more authentic, liberated past, unsullied by grubby capitalist human concerns – but rarely do these vague gestures towards the spiritual actually engage with the complex spirituality of these genders in a meaningful way.[18] Non-binary writer Kate Bornstein, for example, opens the essay 'Transsexual Lesbian Playwright Tells All!' in her book *Gender Outlaw: On Men, Women, and the Rest of Us* by presenting trans history as inherently spiritual:

* As I noted in my introduction, although Cameron uses 'two-spirited' instead of 'Two-Spirit' to describe herself and others, the latter term was the one officially adopted at the 1990 Native American/First Nations Gay and Lesbian Conference.

My ancestors were performers. In life. The earliest shamanic rituals involved women and men exchanging genders. Old, old rituals. Top-notch performances. Life and death stuff. We're talking cross-cultural here. We're talking rising way way way above being a man or a woman. That's how my ancestors would fly. That's how my ancestors would talk with the goddesses and the gods. Old rituals.[19]

As Towle and Morgan point out, language like Bornstein's here – her references to 'rituals' and multiple gods – 'can perpetuate stereotypes about non-Western societies'.[20] What's striking, too, is the vagueness with which she refers to the spirituality of her 'ancestors'. They carried out 'shamanic rituals', but of what kind? They 'talk[ed] with the goddesses and the gods', but which gods were those?

On one level, Bornstein's lack of specificity is understandable: this piece was originally written as a talk for a queer writers' conference, and it's not fair to hold it to the same standards as an academic paper. In its vagueness and mystique, it effectively communicates a sense of the prestige and history of trans experience. But on another level, it's symptomatic of the way white trans people often engage only superficially with the intersections between gender and the spiritual – both in history, and in the present day.

In order to fully grasp many of the stories that are often framed as trans history, I realised as I reflected on Emezi's work, historians – especially white historians – need to work harder to understand their spiritual dimensions. Increasingly, historians are identifying the many ways in which religious life has provided opportunities for gender nonconformity or transness: for people living as male in monasteries (as Smaragdus of Alexandria did in the fifth century CE, for example) or for people joining religious orders that required castration (like the Galli, Roman followers of the goddess Cybele).[21] But the intersection of trans history and spirituality goes beyond this, encompassing people whose genders are themselves spiritual in nature. This is something that has been far less widely acknowledged, at least by white scholars working in secular contexts. We find it easy to gesture towards the spirituality of some non-binary genders, because it can (as I said earlier) be useful to us, adding a sense of status and authenticity to non-binary experience. But engaging with that spirituality more deeply often comes less naturally. For one thing, it takes work – both in the simple process of acquiring more knowledge, and (for those without a faith) in the more difficult process of thinking about gender as not solely concerned with the human self. For another, it might – as we come to understand more about it – emphasise the differences rather than the similarities between our gendered experiences, which might feel like it undermines the argument that non-binary genders from 'other' cultures can 'validate' our own. But even if it feels uncomfortable, this deeper engagement is necessary if we want to achieve the delicate balance of recognising the experiences they share with white Western trans people, while avoiding erasing their differences. As Cameron argues, while we might have some experiences in common, 'We are *not* all the same. Our diversity should be celebrated, honoured, and respected.'[22]

Gone to the spirits

Following their transformation into a man, Kaúxuma núpika became a prophet. It was this work that led them to traverse the length of the Columbia. As they travelled down the river to the sea, together with their wife (whose name sadly doesn't survive), they prophesied to those they met, foretelling the death, disease and destruction that would accompany European settler colonialism.

When Kaúxuma núpika and their wife arrived at Fort Astoria in 1811, they caused a sensation. That they did not belong to the local Coast Chinook Nation was obvious from their clothing: dressed in antelope and buffalo hides, probably embellished with colourful porcupine quillwork – quite different from the dress of the local people – they immediately stood out.[23] David Thompson described them as 'well dressed in leather, carrying a Bow and Quiver of Arrows'. He also noticed Kaúxuma núpika's 'conjuring stick', which was 'about 4½ feet in length': 'one side was painted black, with rude carved figures of Birds Animals and Insects filled with vermillion; the other side was painted red with carved figures in black'.

Thompson initially read Kaúxuma núpika as 'a young man', and it took him a while to recognise them as the person who had married his servant Boisverd. He noted that they had 'set [themself] up for a [prophet], and gradually had gained, by [their] shrewdness, some influence among the Natives as a dreamer, and expounder of dreams'.[24] However, their dire predictions of a forthcoming smallpox epidemic had not been popular: some local people had threatened to kill them as a result, leading Kaúxuma núpika to seek Thompson's protection.[25]

Impressed by the intrepid journey that Kaúxuma núpika and their wife had made, Thompson and several of his fellow traders decided to hire them as guides.[26] As they travelled inland, they met four local men who '[cast] their eyes with a stern look' on Kaúxuma. 'Is it true,' they asked Thompson, 'that the White men . . . have brought with them the Small Pox to destroy us, and two men of enormous size, who are on their way to us, overturning the Ground and burying all the Villages and Lodges underneath it; is this true, and are we all soon to die'? Thompson's reply, as he records it, is chilling in its reassuring disingenuousness: 'I told them not to be alarmed, for the white Men who had arrived had not brought the Small Pox, and the Natives were strong to live, and every evening were dancing and singing'. As scholar Suzanne Crawford O'Brien points out (in an account of Kaúxuma núpika's life that uniquely affirms their gender) the disastrous impact of smallpox epidemics on the Kutenai was still within living memory: in the first wave of disease, the population of the Kootenay river plateau had been almost halved.[27] It was probably as a result of these devastating memories that the locals who heard Kaúxuma núpika's prophecies were inclined to shoot the messenger. If Kaúxuma núpika had not 'been under our immediate care', Thompson noted, they 'should have been killed' by the locals as a result of their prophecies.[28]

This, however, was about to change. As the party travelled along, Kaúxuma núpika altered the tone of their predictions. Instead of foretelling death and destruction, they told the people they passed 'that gifts, consisting of goods and implements of all kinds, were forthwith to be poured in upon them; that the great white chief knew their wants, and was just about to supply them with everything their hearts could desire'. As the fur trader Alexander Ross recorded in his journal, Kaúxuma núpika and their wife were richly rewarded for these tidings, and by the time they reached Fort Okanogan (350 miles from Fort Astoria) they had been gifted as many as twenty-six horses, many bearing other treasures including robes and skins.[29]

After their journey with the traders was over, Kaúxuma núpika worked as a mediator, negotiating and translating between the Flathead, Blackfoot and Kutenai.[30] It was through this work that they were killed, probably at some point in the 1830s, by a company of Blackfoot warriors. Contemporary accounts of their death are brutal: they remained alive even after being shot several times, and only died once the Blackfoot cut open their chest and removed part of their heart.[31]

Our knowledge of Kaúxuma núpika's life today is filtered almost entirely through the accounts of white fur traders.

Schaeffer, as I mentioned above, did speak with some Kutenai people, but even his account of their words is filtered through his own judgements; and in any case, their recollections of how people responded to Kaúxuma núpika's gender ('some believed [they were] bereft of [their] senses') are likely to have been shaped by changing Native American/First Nations attitudes towards gender and sexual nonconformity brought about by colonial policies of forced assimilation.[32] Consequently, we mostly see their gender expression and motivations through a white, binary lens. It seems that most of the traders at Fort Astoria initially read them as a cis man, until Thompson revealed that he recognised Kaúxuma núpika as the former spouse of his servant Boisverd; thereafter, the traders treated them as a disguised woman, and rationalised their choice to present as male according to patriarchal assumptions. Apprentice fur trader Gabriel Franchère described Kaúxuma núpika's male presentation as one of personal safety, writing that they were 'dressed . . . up as a man, to travel with more security'; while Ross implicitly suggested that their intrepid travels and independence were enabled by male presentation, describing them and their wife in a romanticised tone as 'bold adventurous amazons'.[33] The accounts are also inflected by Christian moral ideology. Thompson, for example, suggested baselessly that Kaúxuma núpika was a sex worker, and that the resulting stigma had forced them to turn to prophecy to earn a living; while several traders commented archly on the contradictory nature of their prophecies, suggesting that they opportunistically switched from foretelling destruction to foretelling riches in order to reap the rewards granted to those who brought good tidings.[34] It's important to say that Kaúxuma núpika was hardly beyond moral reproach: they physically abused their first two wives, and (according to some accounts) only began to treat women better after their brother rebuked them.[35] But the portrayal of their prophecies as cynical inventions is an inaccurate picture that fails to take into account the extent to which both their predictions and their gender were embedded in the Kutenai spiritual world.

The problems we encounter when trying to tell Kaúxuma núpika's story, to see their experience from their own perspective, are far from unique. Historian Claudia Rogers has written of how, in the many places where historical Native American/First Nations voices are absent from the record, we might piece together accounts from their perspectives by thinking through what we know of their actions: if we know what someone *did*, can we perhaps move closer to grasping what they might have been thinking or feeling, and thus move beyond recapitulating the simplistic assumptions of white historians and contemporary observers?[36] With this in mind, we can start to appreciate the importance of spirituality to Kaúxuma núpika's life. The name they took when they started to live as a man, Gone to the Spirits, unmistakably highlights that they understood their gender as spiritual. Indeed, changes of gender in Kutenai culture, as in many other local nations, were usually the result of a dream or vision.[37] It was only after their transition – perhaps better referred to as a transformation – that they became a prophet, an occupation that required an intimate connection to the spirit world. Their ability to cross between genders, then, both reflected and intensified their power to cross other divides, including that between the human and the spiritual.[38] They acquired the power to heal: the Kutenai people who spoke to Schaeffer remembered them curing Chief David of an illness, and continued to attribute this, a century later, to their gendered transformation.[39] Even accounts of their death attest to their spiritual power. The Blackfoot recalled their supernatural levels of resilience; they also reported that their body lay undisturbed by wildlife after their death, while their spirit lingered on to sow discord among the warriors who killed them.[40]

The epic travels that Kaúxuma núpika subsequently under-took were a further form of border-crossing, and one that enabled them to share this spiritual power of prophecy. Their later work as an inter-tribal mediator can be seen in a similar light. Contrary to the fur traders' patriarchal and heteronorma-tive assumptions, in Kutenai society Kaúxuma núpika had no need to present as male in order to gain spiritual authority, to travel independently, or to have a female partner; in fact, they actually *lost* some aspects of social independence when they ceased to live as a woman.[41] The traders were also wrong to assume that their move from negative to positive prophecies was an opportunistic one: in fact, when viewed through a lens of Kutenai spirituality, they were two parts of a cohesive whole, a prophecy that the destruction of the known world would be followed by its renewal.[42]

Kaúxuma núpika's spiritual power, then, was enabled by their gender transformation. The reverse was also true: their gender transformation was inherently spiritual in nature. We can see them as part of the history of people who today describe them-selves by the inter-tribal term Two-Spirit.

Coined in the late 1980s, the term Two-Spirit was adopted formally in 1990 at the Native American/First Nations Gay and Lesbian Conference in Winnipeg.[43] The decision to adopt an inter-tribal term was motivated in part by a desire to publicly reject the often pejorative terms that had long been imposed by white scholars, and in part by a desire to create a Native American/First Nations-specific term rather than adopting Western vocab-ulary – both because this recapitulated a colonialist dynamic of classification, and because it was simply inaccurate. As Cherokee Two-Spirit writer Qwo-Li Driskill describes it, 'the term "Two-Spirit" is a word that resists colonial definitions of who we are. It is an expression of our sexual and gender identities as sover-eign from those of white GLBT movements'.[44]

While Two-Spirit is sometimes simplistically described as a synonym for gay/lesbian, trans, or non-binary, in fact none of those words are directly analogous. Although Two-Spirit as an umbrella term hasn't been universally embraced – some Native American/First Nations people feel, justifiably, that it homoge-nises a variety of diverse experiences and erases substantial inter-tribal differences, while others worry that it contributes to a romanticised and inaccurate portrayal of 'Native' acceptance of queer identities, akin to the 'transgender native' figure I described earlier – for many, the usefulness of having a term that underlines the specificity of their gendered and sexual experience outweighs its disadvantages.[45]

Since Two-Spirit is a newly coined and adopted term, much like the term trans, it's reasonable to be cautious about describing people in the past as 'Two-Spirit people'. Just as with trans history, however, I do think it's helpful to describe stories like Kaúxuma núpika's as 'Two-Spirit history': history that provides a point of connection and recognition for Two-Spirit people today, and which provides evidence that binary understandings of gender have never been accurate for capturing the totality of Native American/First Nations experience. Two-Spirit writer Kai Pyle has argued, in addition, that 'establish[ing] kin relations across time' is a specifically Indigenous way of thinking about history, akin to 'seven-generation' thinking (in Pyle's words, 'an ethics that requires us to think about our impacts and responsibilities in seven-generation increments', embedding a sense of care for and accountability to unborn generations in every decision we make).[46] In light of this, we might see talking about Two-Spirit histories as less anachronistic, and more a way of doing history that's appropriate to the cultures whose history it is.

Two-Spirit identities, in many ways, exemplify the complex and entangled nature of gender that I've set out in this book: they're a place where gender, sexuality, social role and spirituality intersect. Two-Spirit people don't fit neatly into a Western gender binary: in the words of Lakota activist Richard LaFontain, 'the masculine and feminine together are sometimes reflected so completely in the body of one person it's as if they have two spirits'.[47] This gendered difference – the fact that Two-Spirit people are neither men nor women – is often reflected in the way they dress and present themselves: we know Kaúxuma núpika dressed in a masculine way from the way the European fur traders universally read them as male at first glance. At the same time, Two-Spirit social roles are different from those of men and women: the work they do is often a mixture of tasks associated with men in their community and tasks associated with women,[*] and sometimes the first indicator of Two-Spirit identity is a child's inclination towards a particular kind of work.[48] Simultaneously, Two-Spirit sexuality is often queer: like Kaúxuma núpika, Two-Spirit people are more likely to be attracted to the same gender as the one they were assigned at birth. This last fact meant that, in a process that directly foreshadows the instrumentalisation of Two-Spirit people by white trans people today, nineteenth- and early-twentieth-century sexological texts often used the example of Two-Spirit people either as pathologising case studies, or to justify their arguments for the naturalness of homosexuality.[49]

Just as gender, social role and sexuality are inextricable here, so too is the spiritual dimension. As LaFontain's words (which I quoted above) show, the underlying *reason* for many people's Two-Spirit identities is a spiritual one: the incorporation of a

---

* Some anti-trans writers have argued that Two-Spirit identities only arise as a response to patriarchy: 'the evidence makes it clear that progressive tribes had no need for Two-Spirits, while ones with the harshest, most rigidly enforced sex roles required this social category as a way to deal with gay and gender-defiant men'. Arguments like this, though, display the racist assumption that white people can 'know' the gendered experience of Native American/First Nations people better than they can, as well as importing a Western form of patriarchal ideology to cultures where it doesn't apply.

male and a female spirit. Shoshone/Métis activist Michael
Owlfeather told researcher Sabine Lang that *tainna wa'ippe*
(Shoshone Two-Spirit people) 'didn't dress in women's clothes
just because of personal preference. It was because of the manifestation of Spirit. They had to do it.'[50] For some, the spiritual
aspect of the 'Two-Spirit' is a metaphor, but for others it's a literal
description of their experience.[51]

The spiritual power we saw in the life of Kaúxuma núpika is
supported by the words of many modern Two-Spirit writers and
activists. Carrie House, a Two-Spirit trans man of Diné (Navajo)
and Oneida Iroquois descent, describes him/herself as 'created'
and 'blessed' by the 'Holy People', including having 'the gift and
foresight to help others' from a young age.[52] Similarly, Lakota
people speaking to anthropologist Walter Williams told him
succinctly that the distinction between gay people and *winkte* (the
specific Lakota group who fit under the Two-Spirit umbrella)
was that 'Winkte is a gay with ceremonial powers'.[53]

Two-Spirit people of different nations have always experienced
and expressed this spirituality in different ways. In many cases,
their Two-Spirit identity is revealed to them in a dream or vision.[54]
Often, they have taken on specialised religious roles that – like
Kaúxuma núpika's prophecies and healing – reflect their ability to
cross otherwise impermeable borders. People of different nations
who fit under the Two-Spirit umbrella have their own, more
specific names. In the Crow Nation (located on the land also
known as Montana), for example, *boté* have a unique ability to
mediate between humans and the divine Sun.[55] Among the
Chumash and other tribes of the land known today as California,
'aqi have historically performed important roles around death and
burial, a liminal moment between one life and the next for which
their own gendered liminality equipped them.[56] *Hwame* of the
Mohave nation, and *tainna wa'ippe* of the Shoshone nation, are
healers or medicine people.[57] Lakota *winkte* have the power of

prophecy and the ability to bestow names on children that carry good luck.[58]

Importantly, many of these gendered experiences can't be fully understood without being rooted in the spiritual worldview of their culture. The constantly fluctuating gender of Diné (Navajo) *nádleehi*, for example – described by other Diné as 'responsible for all the wealth in the country', 'bring[ing] good luck and riches', and 'somehow, sacred and holy' – is best understood as a manifestation of *hozho*, the spiritual balance and harmony that is central to Diné religious belief.[59] It's crucial, then, to grasp the fact that the spirituality of Two-Spirit identities is, for many people, not just about people of particular genders being allocated corresponding religious roles: it's about their gender *itself* being wholly or partially spiritual in nature.

The violent suppression of Two-Spirit people by European colonisers was partly a response to their nonconforming gender expression, but it was also – in ways that haven't always been fully acknowledged – compounded by the spiritual nature of Two-Spirit identities, and the intimate involvement of Two-Spirit people in Native American/First Nations religious practices. European colonisation of the Americas was an inherently religious project. Early Puritan settlers saw their colonies as models of Christian faith and practice, exemplars for the rest of the world to follow; later, in the nineteenth century, the idea of 'manifest destiny' (the belief that white people had a divine mission to colonise the American continent) motivated European expansion into the west.[60] As a result, part of the colonisation process entailed attempts to forcibly Christianise Native American/First Nations people, which included suppressing their religious practices. In 1883, for example, the Commissioner of Indian Affairs, Hiram Price, issued a set of 'Rules for Indian Courts' that ordered the creation of a 'Court of Indian Offences' on every reservation. The court was to enforce rules against religious practices such as dances, feasts and 'practices of medicine men' (people who were, of course, often Two-Spirit). The punishment for these 'offences' was starvation – rations could be withheld for up to ten days following a first conviction, and for ten to thirty days following a second – or imprisonment.[61] While some Native Americans learned to use the rhetoric of the colonisers for their own benefit, asserting their right to religious freedom, this often met with resistance: religious freedom was largely seen as a principle only applicable to Christian worship.[62] In 1888, the church historian Philip Schaff wrote that the First Amendment of the US constitution – which included the decree that 'Congress shall make no law respecting an establishment of religion, or prohibiting the free exercise thereof' – 'presupposes Christian civilization and culture'.[63]

The rhetoric European colonisers used to describe Native American/First Nations religious practices was strikingly similar to the language they used to describe Two-Spirit people: both were seen as offences against Christian morality. One Methodist missionary described the Pawnee Ghost Dance in 1914 as a 'menace to the morals of our boys and girls'; William A. Jones, the US Commissioner of Indian Affairs from 1897–1905, claimed in 1902 that 'In many cases these dances and feasts are simply subterfuges to cover degrading acts to disguise immoral purposes'.[64] Two-Spirit people and their nonconforming gender expression, meanwhile, were seen by trader and coloniser Álvar Núñez Cabeza de Vaca in 1540 as 'a most brutish and beastly custom'; by artist Jacques le Moyne de Morgues in 1564 as 'odious' 'hermaphrodites'; by Spanish soldier Pedro Fages in 1775 as 'sodomites [who] permit the heathen to practice the execrable, unnatural abuse of their bodies'; by Office of Indian Affairs physician A.B. Holder in 1889 as 'the most debased' of all 'varieties of sexual perversion'; and by anthropologist Robert H. Lowie as 'perverts'.[65] (The majority of these morally charged judgements were directed at AMAB Two-Spirit people, because patriarchal ideology meant that AFAB people 'becoming more like men' were more likely to be celebrated, while AMAB people 'becoming more like women' were met with censure and often disgust.) It's clear from this pervasive sense of 'stamping out morality' that the suppression of Two-Spirit identities and the suppression of Native American/First Nations religion were two aspects of the same moral project.

Some colonisers even used the very existence of Two-Spirit people as a justification for settler colonialism, enslavement and genocide. Sixteenth-century Italian merchant-adventurer Girolamo Benzoni listed the idea that Native American/First Nations people were 'pathics' (bottoms in anal sex) who 'wear no beard' – a conclusion Europeans drew from their observations of Two-Spirit gender nonconformity – among the justifications for enslaving them. Similarly, this gender nonconformity (and the queer sexuality that, colonisers assumed, accompanied it) was used by several European commentators as evidence that Native American/First Nations people were less 'civilised' than Europeans, paving the way for claims that they were incapable of governing themselves, and/or were inherently racially inferior.[66] This focus on gender as a motivator for colonial practices shouldn't surprise us. As scholars of gender, sexuality and colonisation have shown, we can see settler colonialism as inherently gendered and sexualised, both in its often paternalistic nature, and in its focus on populating the land with settlers through sometimes coercive intermarriage and the eradication of indigenous family structures.[67]

The violence of the words with which European colonisers described Two-Spirit people was backed up with actions. Deborah Miranda, a writer with Esselen, Chumash, Jewish, French and Spanish heritage, has documented in horrifying detail the massacre of 'aqi in the area known today as California. On 23 September 1513, when a group of forty 'aqi were accused of 'sodomy', conquistador Vasco Nuñez de Balboa ordered their execution: they were eaten alive by mastiffs and greyhounds, enormous specially bred dogs who were trained to kill.[68] Those lucky enough to survive were forced to wear dress and perform work associated with the gender they were assigned at birth, both of which were clearly traumatic: Spanish priest Francisco Palóu described how one Two-Spirit person remained 'cast down and ashamed' for days after being separated from a group of women and forced to remove their apron, before fleeing as soon as they had the opportunity.[69] In other instances, Two-Spirit people were flogged, beaten, forced to repeat prayers in Spanish while kneeling on the ground, imprisoned in the stocks, or made to work while their movement was restricted by a *corma* (a wooden device that enclosed their feet and locked their legs together).[70] The torture they endured was not unique: in the late nineteenth century, Crow boté were similarly imprisoned, enslaved and forced to change their gender expression.[71] The gradual suppression of Two-Spirit people also, of course, led to the erosion of the religious practices in which they played an important part.

Miranda describes the 'extermination' of the 'aqi as 'gendercide' – a term that, like the term 'genocide', from which it is derived, doesn't just describe murder and physical violence, but also cultural erasure.[72] This erasure was enacted not just by forcing Two-Spirit people to change the way they dressed and worked, but through the broader project of re-educating Native American and First Nations children. In both the USA and Canada, the nineteenth century saw the introduction of residential schools that aimed to 'kill the Indian in the child' through forced assimilation.[73] Children were taught that their indigenous practices were inherently sinful, and this included suppressing the identities and expression of Two-Spirit children.[74] Survivors of residential schools recalled how all children were strictly segregated by gender, including separation of siblings: a boy caught talking to his sister could be punished by being forced to wear a dress as a form of humiliation.[75] One Two-Spirit survivor described the experience of being segregated with boys as akin to that of 'a woman in a man's prison'.[76] Two-Spirit children who wore clothes associated with a gender other than the one they were assigned at birth were punished; sometimes they were simply removed from school, never to return.[77] Phyllis Rogers, a Diné woman, recalled how her cousin, a nádleehi, initially managed to sleep in the girls' dormitory; but after being outed during a lice infestation, 'he was taken from school, and he never returned again. They would not tell us what happened to him, and we never saw him again.' The family never found out whether the young nádleehi survived.[78]

In 2015, the Canadian Truth and Reconciliation Commission released an extensive report detailing the systemic and individual violence committed in the country's residential schools. Out of six volumes, just one page makes mention of Two-Spirit people.[79] The USA has yet to undergo a similar process.

Called by the goddess

The status of Two-Spirit people as a group often cited as examples of non-binary gender in non-Western cultures – usually without due regard for the spiritual aspects of their experience – is shared by another group of people on the other side of the world, who also remain marginalised today. The origins of these people's spiritual power have been attributed to the ancient Hindu epic, the *Ramayana*.

Shortly after the Hindu deity Rama was married, he was forced into a fourteen-year exile by the machinations of his father's second wife. A weeping crowd followed him as he left the city of Ayodhya, accompanied by his wife Sita and his brother Lakshmana.

As he reached the riverside, he turned to his followers and told them kindly to return home: 'Men and women, please go back and perform your duties.'

Fourteen years later, when Rama returned, he was stunned to find a small crowd of followers awaiting him on the riverbank. When he asked what they were doing there, they told him that his previous command hadn't applied to them. They weren't 'men or women': they were hijras. In recognition of their devoted loyalty, Rama blessed the hijras, granting them the ability to confer divine blessing on others.[80]

Hijras – people living on the Indian subcontinent who present in a feminine way, often perform on the street, and frequently live in structured gharanas (lineage groups) made up of a guru (leader) and group of chelas (disciples) – are, like Two-Spirit people, often cited as examples of non-binary gender in non-Western cultures.[81] This isn't entirely inaccurate; hijras understand themselves, and are understood by their wider culture, as not men or women (though it's worth saying that, with the exception of Sanskrit, pronouns in most Indian languages are gender-neutral[82]). But only rarely do these casual references to hijras address the fact that many aspects of their identity and lived experience are rooted in religious belief and practice. The story from the *Ramayana* is disputed – many versions don't include it – but belief in the situation it seeks to explain, the ability of hijras to confer divine blessings, is very real. Hijras' infertility (sometimes a result of surgery, sometimes of intersex traits, sometimes of non-procreative sex with men) gives them the ability to confer – or to curse – the fertility of newly married people or of newborn babies. Consequently, they have long acquired much of their income by visiting households at these times to collect *badhai* (alms). Their visits are seen by the public as auspicious, bringing good luck and the blessings of the goddess Bahuchara Mata (though if not given badhai, hijras might threaten to curse the fertility of the baby or couple).[83]

As well as their *Ramayana* origin story, many Indian hijras express identification with Hindu figures who combine genders, including the deity Shiva (who can take the half-man/half-woman form of Ardhanarishvara); one of Shiva's representatives in the *Mahabharata*, Arjuna (a warrior who disguises himself as a eunuch dance teacher, Brihannala); and Shikhandi, another *Mahabharata* character who transformed into a man.[84] More than any other Hindu figure, however, hijras are affiliated with the goddess Bahuchara Mata. It is she who grants them their power to confer blessings; she to whom they pray for successful surgery; and she whom they worship above all others. Moreover, for many, it is she who 'calls' people to become hijras – underlining the fact that hijra identity, much like Two-Spirit identity, can be rooted in spirituality from its very beginnings.[85]

In addition to this, however – as anthropologist Gayatri Reddy found during her extensive ethnographic interviews with Hyderabad hijras in the early 2000s – many hijras combine Hindu and Muslim beliefs and practices. Worshipping the Hindu goddess Bahuchara Mata may be accompanied by observation of Islamic traditions including hajj (pilgrimage), daily prayers, and wearing a burqa. Notably, these represent a combination of male- and female-coded Islamic worship. The hijras that Reddy spoke to explained their Muslim identification partly with reference to surgery, which they associated with the Muslim practice of circumcision.[86] But their 'pluralistic' religious beliefs and practices also (as Reddy shows) reflect both the fact that Hindu, Jain and Muslim traditions commonly coexist in many parts of India, and the fact that both Islam and hijras occupy marginalised positions in India, particularly given the growing context of Hindu nationalism.

In Pakistan, many *khawaja siras* (an Urdu term that is used as the Pakistani equivalent of hijra) practise Sufism (Islamic mysticism) and are given privileged access to Sufi shrines.[87] When sociologist Amen Jaffer spoke to khawaja siras during the 2010s about their relationship to spirituality, many described themselves as *faqirs*: Sufi ascetics who renounce society, relationships and money in favour of their relationship with God.[88] This is a strategy that, Jaffer suggests, allows hijras to embrace and make sense of the social marginalisation they face; but it is also something deeply important to them, and deeply related to their gender. One khawaja sira explained that wearing women's clothes was an intrinsic part of faqir practice and renouncing worldly concerns:

> This world expects us to be men . . . anyone who steps out there with these women's clothes, defies the worldly . . . for us this is the life of the faqir . . . you relinquish yourself and your world and you become unaware of the world. We relinquish everything and the only thing we know is the presence of ourselves and of God.[89]

Individual hijras, of course, see their identity and experience as implicated in religious practice to different extents, and in different ways. This is particularly apparent in their relationships to sexuality. Some hijras see sex with men (whether paid or not) as an essential part of hijra identity, while others, for whom renunciation of sexuality (and often, surgery) is an aspect of religious asceticism, see the identity of hijra as inherently asexual.[90] These experiences are likely to shift and fluctuate within the lives of individual hijras, but they underline, nonetheless, that the gendered identity of hijras is bound up with sexuality as well as with spirituality.

To European observers from the eighteenth century onwards, the sexuality of hijras – and the perception that they were all engaged in sex work – was one of their most salient characteristics.[91] For this reason among several others, hijras share with

Two-Spirit people not just their spiritual gender identities, but their survival of attempts by European colonisers to eradicate them.

Historian Jessica Hinchy has meticulously traced the factors that led the British government of the Indian North-Western Provinces (NWP) to pass a law in 1871 called the Criminal Tribes Act.[92] Among the several targets of this law were people whom the British called 'eunuchs'[*], an ill-defined group encompassing a range of people assigned male at birth who presented in a feminine way and were perceived by the British (rightly or wrongly) to be having sex with men.[93] Under the law, police were required to draw up official registers of 'eunuchs' and, once registered, those on the register were forbidden from presenting as female in public or from performing, including the collection of badhai, which was one of their main sources of income. Children could also be forcibly removed from the households of registered people. The aim of the law was not simply to suppress or manage hijras and other gender-nonconforming people, or even to 'reform' them: according to nineteenth-century understandings of the body, anyone who was 'effeminate' (especially if they'd had genital surgery) would be physiologically incapable of doing hard or 'productive' work.[94] Instead, it aimed to eliminate them completely. In its own words, the goal of the Criminal Tribes Act was 'limiting and thus finally extinguishing the number of Eunuchs'.[95]

The precise targets of the law were vague. A 'eunuch' was defined as an 'impotent man', but this was an imprecise criterion that could hardly be judged at a glance. Consequently, it was decided that anyone whose appearance or dress was feminine and

* The colonial British term 'eunuch' here is not to be confused with the political (and sometimes religious) position of eunuch that existed in older societies including Byzantium, the Ottoman Empire and early modern China.

who appeared to have been assigned male at birth could be reasonably suspected of falling under the law.[96] This meant that feminine presentation accounted for the vast majority of convictions.[97] Arrests were likely accompanied by both physical and gendered violence from police in the streets. While most records of this are lost, there is evidence of some police officers forcibly cutting the hair of the feminine-presenting people they found, before selling their clothes and jewellery and dressing them in men's clothing against their will.[98]

The reasons for the NWP government's persecution of hijras and those like them were manifold. One, as I mentioned above, was that the government perceived a connection between feminine dress and 'sodomy', or other kinds of sex with men. They worried, moreover, that the sight of hijras' feminine presentation might corrupt men by encouraging them to want sex with hijras, effectively advertising 'immoral' sexual practices.[99] But the perceived or actual sexual behaviour of hijras was just one aspect of a broader sense that they were disruptive and 'ungovernable'. As itinerant street performers, hijras disrupted ideals of orderly public space. Their lineage-based households and adoption of children – along with their queer sexuality, whether they were asexual or slept with men – meant they existed outside of patriarchal family structures. All of these factors meant they threatened the government's attempts to know and contain their colonised population.[100]

The presence of children in hijra households was a particular preoccupation of the NWP government. This was framed as a matter of concern for the children's welfare because, in the government's eyes, hijra communities were sustained and augmented by the kidnap and forced castration of young boys.[101] In some histories of children's entry into hijra communities, the line between consent and coercion can be genuinely blurry, and it would be misleading to say that the government's 'kidnap' line was always wrong, but it was far from always right: people entered hijra households at a variety of ages and in a variety of contexts, and it's notable that, in Gayatri Reddy's interviews with hijras in Hyderabad, at least one person told her a false story of being kidnapped and forced into hijra life, under the assumption that it was what she wanted and expected to hear.[102] Moreover, the government's claim to be motivated by care is undermined by the fact that few records survive of what happened to the children who were removed from hijra households: it seems unclear that anyone really cared for their wellbeing once the box-ticking exercise of separating them from hijras had been completed, or that their feelings or agency were taken into account at any point in the process. (Indeed, colonial officials in India were quite happy to turn a blind eye to kidnap when they felt it was in the child's moral interests, such as kidnapping girls for forced marriage: it was their moral disapproval of hijras, not of kidnap, that motivated their actions here.[103]) In any case, the process of removing children fed directly into the government's larger aim of 'extinguishing' hijras by preventing them from passing on their beliefs and practices to the next generation.[104] And in this sense, it was a similar project to the residential schools that had such a devastating impact on Native American/First Nations communities: in both contexts, by targeting children, the colonial government was aiming to eliminate a way of life.

Two-Spirit people and hijras are not relics of the past. They continue to exist and thrive; to return to Joshua Whitehead's words, they are 'not a "was"', but 'an *is* and a *coming*'.[105] But stories of their past belong in any account of trans history. For one thing, their histories show us that genders other than male and female have always existed, and for another, underlining the historical existence of Two-Spirit people in particular is a politically important project because colonialist suppression led, in some cases, to the rejection of Two-Spirit people by their own communities. While many Native American/First Nations people have turned this around, re-embracing their Two-Spirit community members, Two-Spirit campaigners and their allies have highlighted that it remains a work in progress – which means that emphasising the extent to which Two-Spirit people are part of Native American/First Nations tradition remains crucial.

The rejection began as an act of self-protection. Those Chumash men and women who witnessed the terrible fate of the 'aqi, executed by Spanish dogs in 1513, responded by closing ranks: rounding up all the other 'aqi they could find, they brought them to the Spanish, 'spitting in their faces and crying out to our men to take revenge of them and rid them out of the world'.[106] Later, rejection of Two-Spirit people simply marked the success of colonial attempts to eradicate gender and sexual nonconformity. Residential schools and other forms of colonial governance indoctrinated Native American/First Nations communities with homophobia and transphobia, and erased memories of the important roles played by Two-Spirit people.[107] By the 1930s, Albert Sandoval, a Diné man, could tell the anthropologist Willard Hill that nádleehi were no longer respected in the way they had been; and that one young nádleehi, Kla, had been mocked by classmates until they 'put on . . . pants'.[108] Devastatingly, some young people even conflated the sexual abuse they suffered in residential schools with homosexuality, solidifying their opposition to all forms of queerness, and their sense that it was something imposed on their communities by white people.[109]

In India, the situation was more complex, but was still shaped by British ideologies and prejudices. Hijras, already marginalised by their class, did not fall from a position of respect to one of rejection in the same way – though some Indian men, around the time that the Criminal Tribes Act was passed, did use public denunciation of hijras in the newspapers as a way to fashion their respectable middle-class identities.[110] More recently, as movements for trans rights have become increasingly globalised – and as global HIV prevention programmes have demanded the classification of queer people into standardised (read: Western) categories – hijras and khawaja siras have been legally classified as trans in India and Pakistan respectively.[111] Though this has helped both groups to organise around demands for equality, to access funding and to build global solidarity, it has not been uniformly positive. India's Transgender Persons (Protection of Rights) Act grants gender recognition only to those with evidence of genital surgery. Conflating hijras and khawaja siras with trans people, meanwhile, leaves no room for aspects of their experience that might differ from dominant understandings of what it means to be trans: fluidity, belonging to multiple gendered categories, embracing or emphasising their visible difference from cis women.[112] The classification of hijras as trans has also stratified the spectrum of people who present in a feminine way, entrenching divisions into those who 'count' as hijras and those who don't, and encouraging border wars over what constitutes 'authentic' hijra identity.[113] Looking at hijra identities, past and present, on their own terms – including their spiritual dimension – can thus help us to recognise the way they disrupt contemporary Western categorisation as well as disrupting binary understandings of gender.

A tabernacle of flesh

I've focused on people from outside of Europe in this chapter, for two reasons: because I wanted to show how white appropriation and tokenisation of Two-Spirit and hijra identities often ignores their spiritual aspects, and because I wanted to show how colonialist imposition of Christian values and practices involved suppressing both indigenous spiritual practice *and* indigenous gendered experiences in a way that was often entangled.[114] It would be misleading, though, to say that the spirituality associated with white Western culture hasn't also given birth to new genders.

In Rhode Island in 1776 – around the same time as the first wave of smallpox was devastating Native American communities – an epidemic of typhus, then known as Columbus fever, swept through white settlements. One of its victims was a 23-year-old Quaker who had been christened Jemima Wilkinson. Jemima died from typhus, but their body arose from its deathbed possessed by the Spirit of God. The new being, known as the Public Universal Friend, was a genderless spirit in what a contemporary account called a 'tabernacle of flesh', comparing the Friend's body to a house of worship.[115]

The Friend became something of a religious celebrity in late-eighteenth- and early-nineteenth-century New England. As they travelled throughout the local area, their preaching – though none of its content was particularly theologically radical – drew huge crowds of Quakers.[116] Their genderless identity was reflected by a mixture of male- and female-coded clothing. Yale academic Ezra Stiles described them in his diary as wearing a 'light cloth cloak with a Cape like a Man's—Purple Gown, long sleeves to Wristbands—Man's shirt down to the Hands with Neckband—purple handkerchief or Neckcloth tied around the neck like a man's', and 'No Cap'; instead, they wore 'a Watch-Man's Hat' over 'Hair combed turned over & not long'.[117] Another, William Savery, described their combination of 'a loose gown' with other garments that were 'quite masculine', noting explicitly that this 'manifest[ed]' the fact the Friend was 'not supposed to be of either sex'.[118] Though some of these observers referred to the Friend as 'she', their followers avoided the use of gendered pronouns to describe them.[119]

Like Akwaeke Emezi and the other ọgbanje who I talked about earlier, the Friend was not a person, but a spirit; hence it's more accurate to speak about them as genderless than as non-binary. Nonetheless, as a white non-binary person – especially as a person with a Quaker background, though I have no faith now – their story means a lot to me. It tells me that the intersection of spirituality and gender disruption is a cross-cultural phenomenon. It reminds me that that thinking in spiritual terms can help us to move beyond the restrictive, binary gender categories that humans have created. And it embodies, too, the difficulties and aspirations at the heart of a book like this one. The Friend was a member of a settler colonialist community, and actively participated in the future of stolen land.[120] As a white person writing a global trans history, I've been constantly aware of the potential for my work to participate in this ongoing colonial process; constantly working to avoid falling into the pitfalls of appropriation, oversimplification and romanticisation that I highlighted earlier. The Friend's story – the way they represent hope and liberation in some ways, and oppression in others – is an essential reminder, for me, of the stakes of doing this kind of history. At the same time, though, they also remind me that to restrict ourselves to static, binary gender is to fall short of our potential – both as human beings, and as whatever else we might have the capacity to be.

Epilogue

Now we are trans

Sometimes, I feel that becoming a historian was like joining the police. Many arguments for dismantling our current police and criminal justice systems rest on the same central point: that however progressive and liberatory the values of individual officers, however anti-racist or pro-queer their personal politics might be, they are compromised by having sworn to uphold a system and a set of laws that are inherently oppressive. For Shon Faye, for example, in her wonderful book *The Transgender Issue*, 'Even if some aspects of day-to-day interaction between individual trans people and individual officers in local communities can be improved by greater awareness of trans issues within the police, *full reconciliation between trans liberation and policing is impossible*, because the police still function as the arm of a larger machine of criminal justice that cannot now and will never easily accommodate many trans people.'[1] Faye's views are shared by a great many anti-racist activists.[2] However much I sympathise with these arguments, I can't help but simultaneously think how painful they must be to read for people who share her politics but remain sincerely motivated by a desire to try to change the system from within.

I think what started to make me feel this way about history was memes. For several years now, queer people have deployed the spectre of 'historians' and 'academics' – faceless groups who are comically unable to see the obvious queerness of history – with great regularity on social media. 'Historians' are mocked for 'lov[ing] misgendering trans people in history'; smilingly repeating 'she cross-dressed as a man :)' in the face of evidence that an unnamed historical person 'literally lived as a guy for 50+ years!'; even depicted as Spongebob Squarepants shovelling records of trans history into a furnace.[3] In a 2019 tweet (since deleted), Twitter user Brooke wrote of 'carving "trans" into every bone of my body so when they find my skeleton in two hundred years they don't get too confused'. A reply parodied the response of an oblivious archaeologist: 'We must be careful not to jump to conclusions about what these ancient carvings could have meant; This individual could have had a passion for mass transit, transcontinental travel, or a combination of poor spelling and a love of trance music'.[4]

Every time I read jokes like this, I get a jolt of hurt and defensiveness: not *all* historians and academics are like that! I try so hard, every day, *not* to do the kind of history they're talking about! And yet I can hardly blame these people for talking and writing the way they do. The fact is that the discipline of history *is* set up to erase queer lives, and particularly trans lives.[5] We *are* expected to adhere to double standards of evidence, which encourage us to state with impunity that a historical figure was definitely cis, but to hedge with caveats the suggestion that they were maybe, possibly trans; to use phrases like 'cross-dresser' or 'impersonator' as if they're neutral, and to write lengthy defences of ourselves if we decide to avoid them; to expect backlash from colleagues and reviewers if we choose to use any pronouns for a historical figure other than those associated with the gender they were assigned at birth; to say, like the caricatured archaeologist above, 'We must be careful not to jump to conclusions', even when the evidence for trans experience is actually abundantly conclusive.[6] It hurts when people memeify the oblivious, transphobic 'historian', but it's also not unfair of them to do it. History, while it may not perpetuate physical harm, still repeatedly enacts violence against trans lives in the past and the present. And it's not the job of the communities we've hurt to give us the benefit of the doubt: it's *our* job to convince them that historians can be different.

In this book, I've identified new ways, and new places, to look for trans history. I've argued for the presence of trans experience in histories of gender-nonconforming fashion; histories of gender-nonconforming performance; and histories of people taking on a social role that isn't associated with the gender they were assigned at birth. I've shown that many trans histories are inextricable from histories of other experiences: the sexual, the intersex, the anti-patriarchal, the spiritual. I've argued both for acknowledging trans possibility in histories of widespread gender nonconformity that have previously been explained in other ways, and for understanding gendered histories on their own terms – including seeing them, where necessary, as *both* trans history *and* the history of other kinds of people and experiences.

In this last kind of history in particular, I've often been confronted by what writer and philosopher Hil Malatino (quoting fellow scholar Abram J. Lewis) calls the 'irreducible alterity' of people in the past: the fact that some histories of gender are *not* possible to map onto or relate to the way people experience gender today. Malatino characterises the acknowledgement of this 'irreducible alterity' as a form of care for those past people, an idea that speaks deeply to me.[7] It struck me, when I first read it, how different this framing of 'care' was from the arguments historians more commonly make against describing people in the past as trans: that it is presentist, that it is anachronistic, that it inappropriately fixes past people in modern categories. These arguments have rarely seemed to me to come from a place of *care for people in the past*; instead their priority seems to be history or historiographical methodology as an abstract, faux-objective entity. Still more rarely do they seem to acknowledge the concurrent urgency of *caring for people in the present*: the people who are living *now*, experiencing and articulating their gender in manifold ways and drawing strength from the histories of people who have done the same. Might it not be possible to find ways of recognising the essential difference of people in the past – people who disrupted gender before we were trans – while simultaneously holding space for the feelings of identification with them held by people in the present, the people who are trans now?

In *My Autobiography of Carson McCullers*, Jenn Shapland writes of how 'Queer histories often take the form of lists, of calling out and naming kindred spirits', but notes that 'This practice has largely gone out of vogue, as labelling a person's gender or sexual identity, past or present, is fraught with complexities'. While acknowledging these complexities, and the problems with what historian Laura Doan has called 'genealogical' approaches to queer histories, Shapland writes, 'There's a part of me, a defiant and somewhat juvenile part, that still wants the list'.[8] She follows this chapter not with a list of historical lesbians per se, but with a nod to it: a 'List of Carson's Possible Girlfriends'.[9]

I have never read a better, truer account of the experience of being a queer person writing queer history than Shapland's book. From the way that identification with historical figures can be a powerful trigger for self-realisation ('Within a week of finding [Carson's lesbian love letters], I would chop my hair short. Within a year I would be more or less comfortably calling myself a lesbian for the first time') to the unapologetic reclamation of a non-objective queer perspective ('[Josyanne] Savigneau's biography [of Carson McCullers] . . . positions me as a "partisan of homosexuality" seeking to "appropriate" Carson's story for my "cause". And perhaps I am.'), I felt consistently *seen* by it.[10] I was frustrated by the review it received in the *Observer*, in which Rachel Cooke mocked Shapland's 'tautologous' statement that 'For me, Carson's words are her words' (missing the point Shapland is making, that most previous biographers have *not* taken Carson at her word) and argued that 'her (over) identification with McCullers takes us nowhere that is very productive'.[11] What Cooke seemed to miss – what, in fact, she may have been simply unable to appreciate – is just how much it matters, for people who have persistently been told we have no history, when we find historical figures who *feel* like us. In zines and academic texts alike, trans and queer people have articulated this over and over again. Leslie Feinberg writes powerfully in hir 1996 book *Transgender Warriors* of how 'I grew up unable to find myself anywhere in history', but research-ing hir book provided Feinberg with 'examples of transgender in the leadership of social change'; hir goal in writing *Transgender Warriors* is that no young person will have to believe, as ze did, that 'the hatred I faced because of my gender expression was simply a by-product of human nature'.[12] CN Lester, in their 2017 book *Trans Like Me*, writes of finding 'the comfort of compan-ionship' in their teenage identification with Oscar Wilde, and of:

> What a tremendous gift it would have been, to have known that there were people in that history who might now be called trans, people who lived as the genders they *knew* that they were, regardless of what society had told them. To know that they had claimed their own lives with honesty and courage, and that maybe I could follow their lead and do the same.[13]

Hil Malatino describes turning to history 'desperate for some sense that other subjects had encountered and survived some of the transphobic, cissexist bullshit with which I was being repeat-edly confronted'; for 'a roadmap for another way of being'.[14] The editors of the diaries of Lou Sullivan – a writer, publisher and activist who fought for the rights of gay trans men – describe their encounter with his archive in terms of love: 'We opened his file folders with a careful, nervous touch; slow as with a new lover.

We were finding Sullivan just as – when looking for proof of a man like himself in library archives – he found [the trans man whose history he was to research,] Jack Garland.'[15] Mathilda, the queer Black narrator of Shola von Reinhold's stunning 2020 novel *LOTE*, describes a feeling of 'almost violent familiarity', 'probably not dissimilar to holy rapture', on encountering a photograph of the forgotten Black modernist poet Hermia Druitt (and when I read Mathilda's description of how she sought explanations for her identification with people from the past, including 'reincarnation' and 'a sort of celestial siblinghood', I gasped aloud with my own violent recognition).[16] In zir preface to the 2019 Non-Binary Leeds history zine *Trancestors* – a project to which I was proud to be asked to contribute – the zine's editor August echoes this, writing of how the zine was originally titled *respect ur elders*, and describing trans 'elders' as having 'paved the way to where we are now'; ze ends zir preface with 'Thank u, trancestors. We love u.'[17]

Comfort, desperation, love: this is the emotional register in which I, too, experience trans and queer history. Like Shapland, I came to identification with the queer past *before* I came to full articulation of my queer present: I knew that I felt deep hurt and anger about past injustices against queer men, and deep emotional identification with them, long before I realised that was one aspect of my trans experience. I have no doubt that my identification with them was what Cooke calls '(over) identification': to spend two days doing nothing but staring at the walls of my university room and angstily reading A.E. Housman because I'd just seen Tom Stoppard's *The Invention of Love* was, surely, to carry the discipline of 'history' beyond the bounds of all that was seemly and proper. But it's through such indecorous emotion that history has provided me with some of the most intensely important experiences of my life.

This is why it was so important to me to insist that the stories in this book are *trans history*. They are histories of gender not being binary, fixed, or tied to the body. They show there have always been people who disrupt these norms, and there have always been societies in which they aren't norms at all. These people might not be *like* me, and I might not be able to speak of them, even equivocally, as trans people, but they are people I can relate to nonetheless. In Malatino's words (discussing the artist Claude Cahun), they're a history that 'somehow slant rhymes with your present'; and in August's (discussing the Jewish gender categories of androgynos, tumtum, ay'lonit and saris), their experiences of life outside of today's gender binary provide 'Hope for self-definition describing my relationship with MY SELF, not with a binary we never asked for'.[18] These people, these stories are not part of trans history alone: it seems quite likely, for example, that Shapland and I might feel the same way about some of the same historical people, people who are part of both trans history and lesbian history. But I have faith that our communities are expansive enough to hold both of those meanings alongside each other; to recognise that one person's attachment to a history does not diminish our own.

The discipline of history isn't supposed to leave much room for emotion. We're supposed to be ruthlessly objective, dispassionately surveying the evidence (though I hope I've shown in this book that anyone who thinks they're doing this, at least where the history of gender is concerned, is kidding themselves). Both my background in literary scholarship and my personality make me a liability in this regard, and I'm glad. It's easy to assume that emotional engagement leads to bad history, to riding roughshod over the experiences of people in the past and having regard only for our own feelings. But for me, emotional connection to those past people is not just tolerable, it's *necessary*, because it's what leads us to *care* enough to take the time to know people in other times and cultures on their own gendered terms. It's what leads us to remember that these people are *people*, deserving of a humanising historiography that declines to display their bodies to the world and works determinedly to oppose the racist ideologies that have long tried to deny them humanity. In this sense I think identification and community with people of the past takes us somewhere very productive indeed. It's productive of solidarity; of care; of a new, trans-affirming, anti-racist, liberating way of doing history.

This is why trying to effect change from the inside is, for me – in this case at least – worth it. A trans gaze can be an incredibly productive historiographical tool. A trans gaze is what allows us to look at a case of historical gender nonconformity and remain open to the full spectrum of possibilities it represents.[19] A trans gaze is what allows us to read about an individual wearing a mixture of male- and female-coded clothing, and ask, 'But what did that *feel* like?' A trans gaze is what allows us to accept and take seriously the fact that a person's gender can be a spiritual or sexual experience, in a way we can't empathise with – or, indeed, that what looks like gender sometimes isn't at all – because we know first-hand how it feels when people don't take seriously how we articulate our selves. This is the gaze that I hope will continue to transform the way we think about the past.

The simple precept of *knowing people on their own terms* can transform more than history; it also has the power to liberate us in the present. I've shown throughout this book that the way we think about gender today is not natural or traditional but constructed and contingent; gender has *always* been open to disruption and challenge. This in itself is an important, potentially transformative realisation. But imagine if, alongside this, we could simply trust people to know their gendered selves – without prior assumptions, without constraining frameworks, without structures of assessment or judgement. When Faye argues that 'The liberation of trans people would improve the lives of everyone in our society'; when Feinberg argues that 'when [trans] lives are suppressed, *everyone* is denied an understanding of the rich diversity of sex and gender expression and experience that exist in human society'; this, I think, is key to what they mean.[20] People often ask me if I think we should aim for a future without gender, and while I usually feel a tinge of frustration at this kind of speculative enquiry (maybe we should, but we have gender *now*, so how do we pursue trans liberation in *this* society?), I always say that while the experience of having a gender is important to many people, there are lots of things about institutionalised, state-sanctioned gender that we could certainly do without. As Malatino puts it, 'There are genders and there is Gender and I believe we can have the former without the latter'.[21]

The other side of the coin from trusting people to know their own gendered selves is *seeing* them on their own terms: showing them the respect of knowing them in return. The truest articulation of what this means that I have ever read is, perhaps appropriately, in a book set hundreds of years in the future. In Ursula K. Le Guin's 1969 novel *The Left Hand of Darkness*, the narrator Genly Ai is a human emissary on the planet of Gethen. All Gethenians are both men and women; their bodies and genders crystallise as 'male' or 'female' (according to a binary human understanding) once a month, during their fertile period of *kemmer*, when the touch of someone they desire can prompt their body to shift in a particular direction. (The novel uses he/him pronouns as gender-neutral, a decision Le Guin later wrote of regretting, arguing for the use of they/them pronouns – 'let the pedants and pundits squeak and gibber in the streets' – or of invented a/un pronouns.[22]) At the novel's climax, Ai finds himself on a gruelling journey across the planet's northern ice sheet, accompanied by his Gethenian friend Estraven, who has saved his life by rescuing him from a labour camp. Ai has spent the novel wrestling with his discomfort about the Gethenian gender system, and being treated as a 'pervert' for his human body, which the

Gethenians perceive to be in a state of permanent *kemmer*. It is on the ice sheet with Estraven, huddled in a tent in the dark as the storm howls outside, that he finally confronts it for what it means:

> We were both silent for a little, and then he looked at me with a direct, gentle gaze. His face in the reddish light was as soft, as vulnerable, as remote as the face of a woman who looks at you out of her thoughts and does not speak.
>
> And I saw then again, and for good, what I had always been afraid to see, and had pretended not to see in him; that he was a woman as well as a man. Any need to explain the sources of that fear vanished with the fear; what I was left with was, at last, acceptance of him as he was. Until then I had rejected him, refused him his own reality. He had been quite right to say that he, the only person on Gethen who trusted me, was the only Gethenian I distrusted. For he was the only one who had entirely accepted me as a human being: who had liked me personally and given me entire personal loyalty, and who therefore had demanded of me an equal degree of recognition, of acceptance. I had not been willing to give it. I had been afraid to give it. I had not wanted to give my trust, my friendship to a man who was a woman, a woman who was a man.
>
> He explained, stiffly and simply, that he was in kemmer and had been trying to avoid me, insofar as one of us could avoid the other. 'I must not touch you,' he said, with extreme constraint; saying that he looked away.
>
> I said, 'I understand. I agree completely.'
>
> For it seemed to me, and I think to him, that it was from that sexual tension between us, admitted now and understood, but not assuaged, that the great and sudden assurance of friendship between us rose: a friendship so much needed by us both in our exile, and already so well proved in the days and nights of our bitter journey, that it might as well be called, now as

later, love. But it was from the difference between us, not from the affinities and likenesses, but from the difference, that that love came: and it was itself the bridge, the only bridge, across what divided us.[23]

This true and complete appreciation of the unfamiliar gendered experience of another: this is the future I want, both for our society and for our way of doing history. The same people who ask me whether I think we should have gender in the future – people at talks and training sessions I deliver: well-meaning cis people who are invested in a liberal idea of diversity, who want a positive and liberatory answer – also often ask what kind of future I see for trans rights. I never know how to answer this, because the truth is I'm afraid for our future a lot of the time. I'm afraid that it doesn't seem to matter how many individuals support trans rights, how big the majority on our side (and it is a majority), if a small but intensely vocal group of anti-trans activists have convinced governments and mainstream media outlets that our rights are inherently controversial and up for debate. I'm afraid of what that means for me, and I'm a hundred times more afraid of what it means for trans people of colour, working-class trans people, disabled trans people, trans people with none of the privileges I have.

What I do know is that the future I want is one that can't be separated from our history. History is a deeply flawed discipline in all the ways I've talked about here, and in our contemporary world, revisionist and inclusive histories are no safer from attack than trans rights are. But I haven't lost my belief in the ethical potential of history: its capacity to do good, to make a difference to our lives. When I imagine the future I want for trans people and for the world – for everyone oppressed by the way we think about gender right now – that future encompasses our history. I want a future where history provides sources of solidarity and community for people of all genders. I want a future where history is no longer brought out as a stick to beat us with, but provides a gloriously messy set of realities that show us the creativity of what human beings can do with gender. I want a future where we don't feel we always have to instrumentalise history as political activism, but can simply embrace it for the diverse human experiences it represents. I want a way of doing history that faces up to the inevitability that our task is not just intellectual, but emotional and political. I want a way of doing history that approaches *both* people in the past *and* people in the present with what August would call respect; what Malatino would call care; what Le Guin, and I with her, would call love.

Acknowledgements

First and foremost, this book would not exist if it weren't for my friend and editor Kate Craigie. Kate, I had no idea how you'd react when you asked if I wanted to write about trans history and I proposed the weird, difficult trans history book that had been preoccupying me for years. Your faith in and enthusiasm about this project is something I'll be forever grateful for. Thank you for your commitment to giving trans people a platform to tell trans stories, and your open-mindedness about what those stories might look like.

To my agent Holly Faulks, who stepped in halfway through the writing process to take this book on, thank you for your excitement about it, and for being willing to fight my corner. To Paula Akpan and Gem Soothill, huge thanks for your work in helping this book live up to its ethical and political principles. Any faults that remain in this (or any other) area are mine alone.

To all the trans writers and scholars I've cited here, heartfelt thanks for your rigorous and humane work; this book would not exist without you. Thanks also to those scholars who generously shared their unpublished work and thoughts with me: Dominic Janes, Francesca Mussi, and above all Claire Corkill. Claire, our conversations and work together about Knockaloe were absolutely foundational to my thinking about this book, and I can't thank you enough for that.

Beyond this, several academic colleagues and friends deserve particular thanks. Thank you to James Daybell, for taking the still-radical step of appointing a trans person to a project about gender, and for supporting me and my career so kindly and steadfastly since; and thank you to everyone else involved in the Gendering Interpretations project – especially Svante Norrhem, Emma Severinsson, Alice Power and Zorian Clayton – for all our conversations, which were invaluable in shaping my thinking about trans possibility and early modern gender-nonconforming fashion. Thank you to Dan Vo for sharing your inexhaustible knowledge of queer Asian history. Thank you to Kate Chedgzoy for supporting me so meaningfully as an early-career academic, for our conversations about the different things queer history can be and do, and for your wisdom about how to frame this book in academic contexts. Thank you to Claudine van Hensbergen for encouraging me to do this. Thank you to Jon Ward, for taking a chance when a colleague you barely knew asked if you wanted to collaborate about gender nonconformity, and for all our conversations since; thank you to everyone who's attended the gender nonconformity (un)conferences Jon and I have co-organised, for your conversations, ideas and queer joy. Thank you, above all, to the members of the shadowy organisation known only as The Book Club: every discussion we've had about trans history has strengthened this book immeasurably, and the politics that run through it have been shaped by your ethical commitments. I'm proud to be in a club with every one of you.

Heartfelt thanks too to the less shadowy, but no less illustrious, Queer Book Club Leeds: for your community and friendship, for loving *My Autobiography of Carson McCullers* as much as I did, and for being the best thing that's ever happened to me in Leeds. (Sorry for mentioning *The Well of Loneliness*; I still haven't read the whole thing though.) Elsewhere in my queer and activist communities, thanks also go to Quinn, August, Cheryl and Luna for conversations we've had about trans history that (though you may not have realised it) were pivotal in one way or another; to the Leeds Queer Film Festival organising committee for expanding my horizons, strengthening my politics and organising the only committee meetings I've ever actively looked forward to; to Nicola, Ray and Joe at The Bookish Type, for enriching my life with your books and providing a not-insignificant proportion of my bibliography; to Helen Graham, for Rainbow Plaques and for showing me the power of heritage as activism; and to the former York LGBT History Month committee, especially Ynda, for giving me space to work out what queer history really meant to me.

When I was a teenager, I promised myself that if I ever published a book, I'd dedicate it to my caring and inspirational English teacher, Mrs Kay. I thanked her in the acknowledgements of my first academic book, but it bears repeating here: Mrs Kay, I draw strength every time I write from your firm and sure belief in me. I doubt you'll read this – my name's changed since we last met, and this certainly isn't the book either of us expected me to write back then – but if you do, thank you.

To my friends – and especially to Gem, Joe, Susie, Harri, Lizzy, Hannah, Helen, Dan, Mike, Fern, Liz, Mary and John – thank you for your belief in me and this book; for our conversations, which informed it in small and huge ways; and for the love, support and laughter that sustained me as I threw myself into writing this book over the course of one lockdown year. I'm ridiculously lucky to have all of you. (Extra thanks to Mike for taking my author photo in your lovely garden!) Thank you also to my family: to my parents, for every book you ever bought and read me; to Siobhan, for helping me to see how important it was to be excited about what I was writing; to Rita, for your generosity and support of my career; and to Rob and Michaela for your companionship and laughter.

Thank you to Alex – for being my safest place, for the love and strength you give me every day, and for our life together. You're my favourite person and yours is my favourite gender.

My final thanks must go to the people who really made this book: the gender-nonconforming people of the past, named and unnamed, whose lives fill these pages. You have all my gratitude and all my love. I hope I've done you justice.

And to the people, trans or not, who find community and resonance in these stories today: thank you for being you. Keep going. Someday soon, people will look back and thank you too.

Bibliography

'1,000-Year-Old Remains in Finland May Be Non-Binary Iron Age Leader', the *Guardian*, 9 August 2021, <https://www.theguardian. com/world/2021/aug/09/1000-year-old-remains-in-finland-may-be-non-binary-viking-researchers-say> [accessed 5 October 2021]

Achebe, Nwando, *The Female King of Colonial Nigeria: Ahebi Ugbabe* (Bloomington: Indiana University Press, 2011)

Adams, Simon, *Leicester and the Court: Essays on Elizabethan Politics* (Manchester: Manchester University Press, 2002)

Agerholm, Harriet, '"Teenagers Becoming Transgender to be Cool" Article Slammed by Activists', the *Independent*, 18 April 2017, <https://www.independent.co.uk/news/world/americas/transgender-people-cool-article-daily-wire-criticism-response-twitter-a7687716.html> [accessed 16 March 2021]

Ainsworth, Claire, 'Sex Redefined', *Nature*, 518.7539 (2015), 288–291

Aishia, Samantha, 'Why Masculine Clothing Dominates the Gender-Neutral Fashion Game', *Fashion Industry Broadcast*, 4 May 2019, <https://fashionindustrybroadcast.com/2019/05/04/why-masculine-clothing-dominates-the-gender-neutral-fashion-game> [accessed 16 March 2021]

Aitkenhead, Decca, 'RuPaul: "Drag is a big f-you to male-dominated culture"', the *Guardian*, 3 March 2018, <https://www.theguardian. com/tv-and-radio/2018/mar/03/rupaul-drag-race-big-f-you-to-male-dominated-culture> [accessed 3 September 2021]

Alex, *Twitter*, 19 July 2021, <https://twitter.com/Axartsme/status/1417200818005098502> [accessed 1 October 2021]

Amadiume, Ifi, *Male Daughters, Female Husbands: Gender and Sex in an African Society* (London: Zed Books, 2015)

Amin, Kadji, 'Glands, Eugenics, and Rejuvenation in *Man into Woman*: A Biopolitical Genealogy of Transsexuality', *TSQ: Transgender Studies Quarterly*, 5.4 (2018), 589–605

Amory, Deborah P., 'Mashoga, Mabasha, and Magei: "Homosexuality" on the East African Coast', in Murray and Roscoe (eds.), *Boy-Wives and Female Husbands*, pp. 65–84

Ariosto, Ludovico, *Orlando Furioso in English Heroical Verse*, trans. by John Harington (London: By Richard Field, for John Norton and Simon Waterson, 1607)

Arvas, Abdulhamit, 'Early Modern Eunuchs and the Transing of Gender and Race', *Journal for Early Modern Cultural Studies*, 19.4 (2019), 116–136

Asanti, Ifalade Ta'shia, 'Living with Dual Spirits: Spirituality, Sexuality and Healing in the African Diaspora', *Journal of Bisexuality*, 10.1–2 (2010), 22–30

Baker, Catherine, 'Monstrous Regiment', *History Today*, 17 April 2018, <https://www.historytoday.com/history-matters/monstrous-regiment> [accessed 29 June 2021]

Balzer, Marjorie Mandelstam, 'Sacred Genders in Siberia: Shamans, Bear Festivals, and Androgyny', in Sabrina Petra Ramet (ed.), *Gender Reversals and Gender Cultures: Anthropological and Historical Perspectives* (London: Routledge, 1996), pp. 164–182

Barker, Meg-John, and Jules Scheele, *Sexuality: A Graphic Guide* (London: Icon Books, 2021)

Basset, Robert, *Curiosities: or The Cabinet of Nature* (London: Printed by N. and I. Okes, 1637)

Batelaan, Krystal, and Gamal Abdel-Shehid, 'On the Eurocentric Nature of Sex Testing: The Case of Caster Semenya', *Social Identities*, 27.2 (2020), 1–20

Bauer, Heike, *The Hirschfeld Archives* (Philadelphia: Temple University Press, 2017)

Beauchamp, Toby, *Going Stealth: Transgender Politics and U.S. Surveillance Practices* (Durham, N.C.: Duke University Press, 2018)

Belfanti, Carlo, 'The Civilization of Fashion', *Journal of Social History*, 43.2 (2009), 261–283

Bennett, Alan, *The History Boys* (London: Faber & Faber, 2004)

Bennett, Judith M., and Shannon McSheffrey, 'Early, Erotic and Alien: Women Dressed as Men in Late Medieval London', *History Workshop Journal*, 77.1 (2014), 1–25

Berry, Paul, 'Rethinking "Shunga": The Interpretation of Sexual Imagery of the Edo Period', *Archives of Asian Art* 54 (2004), 7–22

Bertelli, Pietro, *Diversarum Nationum Habitus* (Padua: [Pietro Bertelli], 1594)

binaohan, b., *decolonizing trans/gender 101* (Toronto: Biyuti Publishing, 2014)

Bittner, Robert, 'Hey, I Still Can't See Myself!: The Difficult Positioning of Two-Spirit Identities in YA Literature', *Bookbird*, 52.1 (2014), 11–22

Blackless, Melanie, Anthony Charuvastra, Amanda Derryck, Anne Fausto-Sterling, Karl Lauzanne and Ellen Leeb, 'How Sexually Dimorphic Are We? Review and Synthesis', *American Journal of Human Biology*, 12 (2000), 151–166

Bland, Lucy, and Laura Doan (eds.), *Sexology in Culture: Labelling Bodies and Desires* (Cambridge: Polity Press, 1998)

Bornoff, Nicholas, *Pink Samurai: The Pursuit and Politics of Sex in Japan* (London: Grafton, 1991)

Bornstein, Kate, *Gender Outlaw: On Men, Women, and the Rest of Us*, rev. edn. (New York: Vintage Books, 2016)

Bowen, Scarlet, '"The Real Soul of a Man in her Breast": Popular Opposition and British Nationalism in Memoirs of Female Soldiers, 1740–1750', *Eighteenth-Century Life*, 28.3 (2004), 20–44

British Museum, 'Fumi no kiyogaki 婦美の清書き (Neat Version of a Love Letter (or Pure Drawings of Female Beauty))', museum number 1972,0724,0.3, image 3, <https://www.britishmuseum.org/research/collection_online/collection_object_details.aspx?objectId=779979&partId=1> [accessed 16 July 2021]

—— 'Keichū nyo'etsu warai-dōgu 閨中女悦笑道具 (Sex Toys for Women's Pleasure in the Bedroom) / Tō: harigata 冬: 張形 (Winter: Dildo)', museum number 2012,3051.4, <https://www.britishmuseum.

org/research/collection_online/collection_object_details.aspx?objectI
d=3509620&partId=1&images=true> [accessed 16 July 2021]

Brownian, Carrie-Anne, 'Genderqueering the Dead', *4thWaveNow*, 12
January 2019, <https://4thwavenow.com/2019/01/12/gender-
queering-the-dead> [accessed 23 February 2021]

—— 'Transing the Dead: The Erasure of Gender-Defiant Role Models
from History', *4thWaveNow*, 31 October 2016, <https://4thwave-
now.com/2016/10/31/transing-the-dead-the-erasure-of-gender-
defiant-role-models-from-history> [accessed 23 February 2021]

Buckland, Rosina, *Shunga: Erotic Art in Japan* (London: British Museum,
2010)

Bulwer, John, *Anthropometamorphosis* (London: Printed by William
Hunt, 1653)

Burton, Jonathan, 'Western Encounters with Sex and Bodies in Non-
European Cultures, 1500–1750', in Sarah Toulalan and Kate Fisher
(eds.), *The Routledge History of Sex and the Body: 1500 to the Present*
(London: Routledge, 2013), pp. 495–510

Buruma, Ian, 'The "Indescribable Fragrance" of Youths', *New York
Review of Books*, 11 May 2017, <https://www.nybooks.com/articles
/2017/05/11/japanese-edo-indescribable-fragrance-youths>
[accessed 16 July 2021]

Butler, Judith, *Gender Trouble: Feminism and the Subversion of
Identity*, 10th anniversary edn. (New York and London:
Routledge, 1999)

Bychowski, Gabrielle M.W., Howard Chiang, Jack Halberstam,
Jacob Lau, Kathleen P. Long, Marcia Ochoa, C. Riley Snorton,
Leah DeVun and Zeb Tortorici, '"Trans*historicities": A
Roundtable Discussion', *TSQ: Transgender Studies Quarterly*, 5.4
(2018), 658–685

Cameron, Michelle, 'Two-Spirited Aboriginal People: Continuing
Cultural Appropriation by Non-Aboriginal Society', *Canadian
Woman Studies*, 24.2 (2005), 123–127

Camminga, B, 'Disregard and Danger: Chimamanda Ngozi Adichie
and the Voices of Trans (and Cis) African Feminists', *The Sociological
Review Monographs*, 68.4 (2020), 817–833

Capp, Bernard, 'Playgoers, Players and Cross-Dressing in Early Modern London: The Bridewell Evidence', *The Seventeenth Century*, 18.2 (2003), 159–171

Chambers, David, and Brian Pullan (eds.), *Venice: A Documentary History, 1450–1630* (Oxford: Blackwell, 1992)

Chess, Simone, 'Queer Residue: Boy Actors' Adult Careers in Early Modern England', *Journal for Early Modern Cultural Studies*, 19.4 (2019), 242–264

Children's Theatre Company, 'Not Your Punchline: The Need to Transform the Transphobic Panto Tradition', *OffBook*, 7 December 2020, <https://offbook.childrenstheatre.org/not-your-punchline-the-need-to-transform-the-transphobic-panto-tradition-6aa3f5efeb3a> [accessed 28 September 2021]

Clark, Anna, 'Anne Lister's Construction of Lesbian Identity', *Journal of the History of Sexuality*, 7.1 (1996), 23–50

Clark, Timothy, and C. Andrew Gerstle, 'What Was *Shunga*?', in Clark, Gerstle, Ishigami and Yano (eds.) *Shunga*, pp. 16–33

Clark, Timothy, C. Andrew Gerstle, Ishigami Aki and Akiko Yano (eds.), *Shunga: Sex and Pleasure in Japanese Art* (London: British Museum Press, 2013)

Clarke, John Henrik, 'African Warrior Queens', in Sertima (ed.), *Black Women in Antiquity*, pp. 123–134

Clarke, Paula C., 'The Business of Prostitution in Early Renaissance Venice', *Renaissance Quarterly*, 68.2 (2015), 419–464

Clover, Darlene E., and Kathy Sanford, 'Educating Epistemic Justice and Resistance Through the Feminist Museum Hack: Looking and Acting with Another Eye', *Museum International*, 72.1–2 (2020), 56–67

Cohen-Portheim, Paul, *Time Stood Still: My Internment in England, 1914–1918* (London: Duckworth, 1931)

Combahee River Collective, 'The Combahee River Collective Statement', in Barbara Smith (ed.), *Home Girls: A Black Feminist Anthology* (New Brunswick: Rutgers University Press, 2000), pp. 264–274

Cooke, Rachel, '*My Autobiography of Carson McCullers* Review – Identity Parade', the *Observer*, 2 May 2021, <https://www.

theguardian.com/books/2021/may/02/my-autobiography-of-carson-mccullers-review-identity-parade> [accessed 30 September 2021]

Corkill, Claire, 'Knockaloe First World War Internment Camp: A Virtual Museum and Archive' (unpublished doctoral thesis, University of York, 2013)

Cowan, Alexander, 'Gossip and Street Culture in Early Modern Venice', in Riitta Laitinen and Thomas Cohen (eds.), *Cultural History of Early Modern European Streets* (Leiden: Brill, 2009), pp. 119–140

Cowell, Roberta, *Roberta Cowell's Story, By Herself* (London: Heinemann, 1954)

Coyote, Ivan, *Rebent Sinner* (Vancouver: Arsenal Pulp Press, 2019)

Crenshaw, Kimberlé, 'Demarginalizing the Intersection of Race and Sex: A Black Feminist Critique of Antidiscrimination Doctrine, Feminist Theory and Antiracist Politics', *University of Chicago Legal Forum*, 1 (1989), 139–167

Crouthamel, Jason, '"Wir Brauchen Gauze Manner": Cross-Dressing, Kameradschaft und Homosexualität im Deutschen Heer wahrend des Ersten Weltkriegs' ['"We Need Complete Men": Cross-dressing, Comradeship and Homosexuality in the German Army during the First World War'], in Köhne, Lange and Vetter (eds.), *Mein Kamerad – die Diva*, pp. 65–75

Davis, Georgiann, *Contesting Intersex: The Dubious Diagnosis* (New York: New York University Press, 2015)

Davis, Jim, '"Slap On! Slap Ever!": Victorian Pantomime, Gender Variance, and Cross-Dressing', *New Theatre Quarterly*, 30.3 (2014), 218–230

Dekker, Rudolf M., and Lotte C. van Pol, *The Tradition of Female Transvestism in Early Modern Europe* (Basingstoke: Macmillan, 1989)

Detox . . ., *Twitter*, 23 January 2020, <https://twitter.com/The OnlyDetox/status/1220442901198536704> [accessed 28 September 2021]

DeVun, Leah, 'Erecting Sex: Hermaphrodites and the Medieval Science of Surgery', *Osiris*, 30.1 (2015), 17–37

—— *The Shape of Sex: Nonbinary Gender from Genesis to the Renaissance* (New York: Columbia University Press, 2021)

DeVun, Leah, and Zeb Tortorici, 'Trans, Time, and History', *TSQ: Transgender Studies Quarterly*, 5.4 (2018), 518–539

Diamond, Kelly-Anne, 'Hatshepsut: Transcending Gender in Ancient Egypt', *Gender & History*, 32.1 (2020), 168–188

Dinshaw, Carolyn, *Getting Medieval: Sexualities and Communities, Pre- and Postmodern* (Durham, N.C.: Duke University Press, 1999)

Doan, Laura, *Disturbing Practices: History, Sexuality, and Women's Experience of Modern War* (Chicago: University of Chicago Press, 2013)

Domenico, Hilde Di, and Isaline Pfefferlé, 'Where are the Women? Giving a Voice to Five Leading Female Professionals in Brussels' Cultural Scene', *Museum International*, 72.1–2 (2020), 10–17

Draskau, Jennifer Kewley, 'Prisoners in Petticoats: Drag Performance and its Effects in Great War Internment Camps in the Isle of Man', *Proceedings of the Isle of Man Natural History and Antiquarian Society*, 12.2 (2009), 187–204

Driskill, Qwo-Li, 'Stolen From Our Bodies: First Nations Two-Spirits /Queers and the Journey to a Sovereign Erotic', *Studies in American Indian Literatures*, 16.2 (2004), 50–64

Dugdale, William, *The Baronage of England* (London: Printed by Tho. Newcomb, for Abel Roper, John Martin, and Henry Herringman, 1675)

Dutta, Aniruddha, 'An Epistemology of Collusion: Hijras, Kothis and the Historical (Dis)continuity of Gender/Sexual Identities in Eastern India', *Gender & History*, 24.3 (2012), 825–849

—— 'Review: JESSICA HINCHY. *Governing Gender and Sexuality in Colonial India: The Hijra, c.1850–1900*', *Journal of British Studies*, 59.4 (2020), 950–952

Dworkin, Shari L., Amanda Lock and Cheryl Cooky, '(In)justice in Sport: The Treatment of South African Track Star Caster Semenya', *Feminist Studies*, 39.1 (2013), 40–69

Ekins, Richard, and Dave King, *The Transgender Phenomenon* (London: Sage, 2006)

Ellis, Havelock, *Studies in the Psychology of Sex, Vol. 1, Sexual Inversion* (London: The University Press, 1897)

Emezi, Akwaeke, *Dear Senthuran: A Black Spirit Memoir* (London: Faber & Faber, 2021)

—— *Freshwater* (London: Faber & Faber, 2018)

—— *Twitter*, 13 June 2021, <https://twitter.com/azemezi/status/1404113385915027457> [accessed 13 August 2021]

—— *Twitter*, 10 August 2021, <https://twitter.com/azemezi/status/1425237644292857858> [accessed 27 August 2021]

Emezi, Akwaeke, and Saidiya Hartman, 'Spiritfirst: Akwaeke Emezi with Saidiya Hartman', *New York Public Library*, 8 June 2021, <https://www.nypl.org/events/programs/2021/06/08/spiritfirst-akwaeke-emezi-saidiya-hartman> [accessed 13 August 2021]

Faderman, Lillian, *Odd Girls and Twilight Lovers: A History of Lesbian Life in Twentieth-Century America* (New York: Columbia University Press, 1991)

Faye, Shon, *The Transgender Issue: An Argument for Justice* (London: Penguin Books, 2021)

Feinberg, Leslie, *Transgender Liberation: A Movement Whose Time Has Come* (New York: World View Forum, 1992)

—— *Transgender Warriors: Making History from Joan of Arc to Dennis Rodman* (Boston: Beacon Press, 1996)

Ferraro, Joanne M., 'Making a Living: The Sex Trade in Early Modern Venice', *The American Historical Review*, 123.1 (2018), 30–59

Feu'u, Poiva Junior Ashleigh, 'A Comparative Study of Fa'afafine of Samoa and the Whakawahine of Aotearoa New Zealand', in *Representing Trans: Linguistic, Legal and Everyday Perspectives* (Wellington: Victoria University Press, 2017), pp. 171–203

Few, Martha, '"That Monster of Nature": Gender, Sexuality, and the Medicalization of a "Hermaphrodite" in Late Colonial Guatemala', *Ethnohistory*, 54.1 (2007), 159–176

Finkelpearl, P.J., 'Chamberlain, John (1553–1628), Letter Writer', *Oxford Dictionary of National Biography*, 23 September 2004, <https://www.oxforddnb.com/view/10.1093/ref:odnb/9780198614128.001.0001/odnb-9780198614128-e-5046> [accessed 16 March 2021]

Fisher, Will, *Materializing Gender in Early Modern English Literature and Culture* (Cambridge: Cambridge University Press, 2006)

Fitzgeffrey, Henry, *Satires* (London: Printed by Edw[ard] Allde, for Miles Patrich, 1617)

Fitzpatrick, Eilish, and Stella Maynard, 'Conversation with Jordy Rosenberg', *The Lifted Brow*, 11 November 2019, <https://www.theliftedbrow.com/liftedbrow/2019/11/11/a-conversation-with-jordy-rosenberg-by-eilish-fitzpatrick-and-stella-maynard> [accessed 18 February 2021]

Fontaine, Craig Charbonneau (ed.), *Speaking of Sagkeeng = Agadijindamin Sagkeeng* (Pine Falls, Manitoba: KaKineepahwitamawat Association, 2006)

Förster, Sascha, and Peter W. Marx, '"Das Kampfbereich war der Schauplatz der Damendarsteller": Spannungsverhaltnisse des Kölner Kriegstheaterarchivs' ['"The Battlefield was the Stage of the Female Impersonators": Tensions in the Cologne War Theatre Archives'], in Köhne, Lange and Vetter (eds.), *Mein Kamerad – die Diva*, pp. 77–89

Framke, Caroline, 'How RuPaul's Comments on Trans Women Led to a Drag Race Revolt — and a Rare Apology', *Vox*, 7 March 2018, <https://www.vox.com/culture/2018/3/6/17085244/rupaul-trans-women-drag-queens-interview-controversy> [accessed 19 February 2021]

'From the Archive, 13 May 1915: Anti-German Riots Spread', the *Guardian*, 13 May 2015, <https://www.theguardian.com/world/2015/may/13/anti-german-riots-lusitania-1915–first-world-war> [accessed 28 September 2021]

Füssel, Marian, 'Between Dissimulation and Sensation: Female Soldiers in Eighteenth-Century Warfare', *Journal for Eighteenth-Century Studies*, 41.4 (2018), 527–542

Gagliardo-Silver, Victoria, 'What I Mean When I Say I Want to Abolish the Police', the *Independent*, 1 June 2020, <https://www.independent.co.uk/voices/acab-abolish-police-george-floyd-protests-cops-a9543386.html> [accessed 1 October 2021]

Gamble, Joseph, 'Toward a Trans Philology', *Journal for Early Modern Cultural Studies*, 19.4 (2019), 26–44

Gerstle, C. Andrew, and Timothy Clark, 'Introduction', *Japan Review*, 26 (2013), 3–14

Gesink, Indira Falk, 'Intersex Bodies in Premodern Islamic Discourse: Complicating the Binary', *Journal of Middle East Women's Studies*, 14.2 (2018), 152–173

Gill-Peterson, Jules, *Histories of the Transgender Child* (Minneapolis: University of Minnesota Press, 2018)

Gilman, Sander L., 'Black Bodies, White Bodies: Toward an Iconography of Female Sexuality in Late Nineteenth-Century Art, Medicine, and Literature', *Critical Inquiry*, 12.1 (1985), 204–242

GIRES, 'The Gender Recognition Act Discussion (July 2019)', *GIRES*, 22 July 2019, <https://www.gires.org.uk/the-gender-recognition-act-discussion-july-2019> [accessed 19 February 2021]

Gods Handy-Worke in Wonders Miraculously Shewen Upon Two Women, Lately Delivered of Two Monsters (London: Printed [by George Purslowe] for I. W[right], 1615)

Gowing, Laura, 'Gender and the Language of Insult in Early Modern London', *History Workshop Journal*, 35 (1993), 1–21

Greer, Germaine, *The Whole Woman* (London: Doubleday, 1999)

Griffiths, David Andrew, 'Diagnosing Sex: Intersex Surgery and "Sex Change" in Britain 1930–1955', *Sexualities*, 21.3 (2018), 476–495

Gust, Onni, 'Colonialism and the Idea of "Sex" in Eighteenth-Century Enlightenment Thought', University of York, 3 November 2020

Haec-vir: or, The Womanish-Man (London: printed [at Eliot's Court Press] for I. T[rundle], 1620)

Haft, Alfred, 'Affirming the Life Erotic: Yoshida Hanbei's *Koshoku Kinmo Zui* (1686)', *Japan Review*, 26 (2013), 99–116

Hagemann, Karen, and Stefanie Schüler-Springorum, 'Preface', in Karen Hagemann and Stefanie Schüler-Springorum (eds.), *Home/Front: The Military, War, and Gender in Twentieth-Century Germany* (Oxford: Berg, 2002), pp. ix-xii

Halberstam, Jack, *Female Masculinity* (Durham, N.C.: Duke University Press, 1998)

Hall, Radclyffe, *The Well of Loneliness* (London: Virago, 1987)

Harrison, Wendy Cealey, 'The Shadow and the Substance: The Sex/ Gender Debate', in Kathy Davis, Mary Evans, and Judith Lorber (eds.), *Handbook of Gender and Women's Studies* (London: Sage, 2006), pp. 35–52

Hayakawa, Monta, 'Who Were the Audiences for Shunga?', *Japan Review*, 26 (2013), 17–36

Hayward, Maria, '"The Sign of Some Degree"?: The Financial, Social and Sartorial Significance of Male Headwear at the Courts of Henry VIII and Edward VI', *Costume: The Journal of the Costume Society*, 36 (2002), 1–17

Heintze, Beatrix, 'Written Sources and African History: A Plea for the Primary Source. The Angola Manuscript Collection of Fernão de Sousa', *History in Africa*, 9 (1982), 77–103

Hemmilä, Anita, 'Ancestors of Two-Spirits: Historical Depictions of Native North American Gender-Crossing Women through Critical Discourse Analysis', *Journal of Lesbian Studies*, 20.3–4 (2016), 408–426

Henderson, Kevin, 'J.K. Rowling and the White Supremacist History of "Biological Sex"', *The Abusable Past*, 28 July 2020, <https://www.radicalhistoryreview.org/abusablepast/j-k-rowling-and-the-white-supremacist-history-of-biological-sex> [accessed 22 February 2021]

Heyam, Kit, 'Gender Nonconformity and Military Internment: Curating the Knockaloe slides', *Critical Military Studies*, 6.3–4 (2019), 323–340

—— *The Reputation of Edward II, 1305–1697: A Literary Transformation of History* (Amsterdam: Amsterdam University Press, 2020)

Heywood, Linda M., *Njinga of Angola: Africa's Warrior Queen* (Cambridge, M.A., and London: Harvard University Press, 2017)

Hic Mulier: or, The Man-Woman (London: Printed [at Eliot's Court Press] for I. T[rundle], 1620)

Hill, Willard Williams, 'The Status of the Hermaphrodite and Transvestite in Navaho Culture', *American Anthropologist* 37.2 (1935), 273–279

Hillman, Betty Luther, '"The Most Profoundly Revolutionary Act a Homosexual Can Engage In": Drag and the Politics of Gender

Presentation in the San Francisco Gay Liberation Movement, 1964–1972', *Journal of the History of Sexuality*, 20.1 (2011), 153–181

Hinchy, Jessica, *Governing Gender and Sexuality in Colonial India: The Hijra, c.1850–1900* (Cambridge: Cambridge University Press, 2019)

Hines, Sally, 'Sex Wars and (Trans)Gender Panics: Identity and Body Politics in Contemporary UK Feminism', *The Sociological Review Monographs*, 68.4 (2020), 699–717

Hines, Sally, and Tam Sanger (eds.), *Transgender Identities: Towards a Social Analysis of Gender Diversity* (New York: Routledge, 2010)

Hirsch, Hadas, 'Clothing and Colours in Early Islam: Adornment (Aesthetics), Symbolism and Differentiation', *Anthropology of the Middle East*, 15.1 (2020), 99–114

Hirschfeld, Magnus, *The Sexual History of the World War*, trans. by A. Gaspar et al. (New York: Falstaff Press, 1937)

—— *Transvestites: The Erotic Drive to Cross Dress*, trans. by Michael A. Lombardi-Nash (Buffalo: Prometheus Books, 1991; first published 1910)

Hitchens, Peter, 'The Transgender Zealots Are Destroying Truth Itself', *Mail on Sunday*, 19 November 2017, <http://www.dailymail.co.uk/debate/article-5096679/PETER-HITCHENS-Transgender-zealots-destroying-truth.html> [accessed 25 March 2018]

Hockley, Allen, 'Review: Shunga: Function, Context, Methodology', *Monumenta Nipponica*, 55.2 (2000), 257–269 (p. 261)

—— '*Shunga: Sex and Pleasure in Japanese Art*, edited by Timothy Clark et al., and *Shunga: Sex and Humor in Japanese Art and Literature*, edited by C. Andrew Gerstle and Timothy Clark, and *Shunga: Erotic Art in Japan*, by Rosina Buckland (review)', *Monumenta Nipponica*, 69.1 (2014), 132–136

Holland, Peter, 'The Play of Eros: Paradoxes of Gender in English Pantomime', *New Theatre Quarterly*, 13.51 (1997), 195–204

hooks, bell, *Ain't I a Woman? Black Women and Feminism* (Boston: South End Press, 1981)

House, Carrie, 'Blessed by the Holy People', *Journal of Lesbian Studies*, 20.3–4 (2016), 324–341

Hufton, Olwen, 'Istruzione, Lavoro e Povertà' ['Education, Work and Poverty'], in Sara F. Matthews-Grieco (ed.), *Monaca, Moglie, Serva, Cortigiana: Vita e Immagine della Donne tra Rinascimento e Controriforma* [*Nun, Wife, Servant, Courtesan: The Lives and Images of Women between the Renaissance and Counter-Reformation*] (Florence: Morgana Edizioni, 2001), pp. 48–101

H U G I Y O, *Twitter*, 5 July 2020, <https://twitter.com/Hugoliine_/status/1279866585163988995> [accessed 1 October 2021]

Ihejirika, Chidera, 'Fuck Your Gender Norms: How Western Colonisation Brought Unwanted Binaries to Igbo Culture', *gal-dem*, 19 February 2020, <https://gal-dem.com/colonialism-nigeria-gender-norms-lgbtq-igbo/1/9> [accessed 29 June 2021]

Ikeda, Asato, 'Curating "A Third Gender: Beautiful Youths in Japanese Prints"', *TSQ: Transgender Studies Quarterly* 5.4 (2018), 638–648

Ikpo, David, 'Queer Participatory Visibility in Nigerian Nations', *Outing the Past Leeds*, <https://www.youtube.com/watch?v=BZafPQ887YU&list=PLvKomIEJxRSWbPhPmPo1C1tfs75WfZR_r&index=12> [accessed 29 June 2021]

incorrect patrochilles quotes, *Twitter*, 21 October 2019, <https://twitter.com/wrongptrchlls/status/1186375552548122624> [accessed 1 October 2021]

Ishida, Yoriko, 'Body and Gender Expressed by the Cross-Dressing of Hannah Snell in Eighteenth-Century Naval Culture in *The Female Soldier; Or, the Surprising Life and Adventures of Hannah Snell*', *IAFOR Journal of Literature & Librarianship*, 7.1 (2018), 77–92

isshehungry, *Instagram*, <https://www.instagram.com/isshehungry> [accessed 28 September 2021]

Jacques, Juliet, *Trans: A Memoir* (London: Verso, 2015)

—— *Variations* (London: Influx Press, 2021)

Jaffer, Amen, 'Spiritualising Marginality: Sufi Concepts and the Politics of Identity in Pakistan', *Society and Culture in South Asia*, 3.2 (2017), 175–197

Jahr, Christoph, '"Mr Goodhind, the Prima Donna of Ruhleben": Theater - und Geschlechterrollen im "Englanderlager Ruhleben" 1914–1918' ['"Mr Goodhind, the Prima Donna of Ruhleben": Theatre and Gender

Roles in the "English Prison Camp Ruhleben" 1914–1918'], in Köhne, Lange and Vetter (eds.), *Mein Kamerad – Die Diva*, pp. 91–99

James I, King of England, *Daemonologie in Form of a Dialogue, Divided into Three Books* (Edinburgh, Printed by Robert Walde-grave, printer to the Kings Majesty, 1597)

James, Andrea, 'I F*cking Hate @RuPaul', *BoingBoing*, 4 April 2014, <https://boingboing.net/2014/04/04/rupaul.html> [accessed 10 September 2021]

Janes, Dominic, 'The Varsity Drag: Gender, Sexuality and Cross-Dressing at the University of Cambridge, 1850–1950', *Journal of Social History*, forthcoming

Janin, Hunt, *The Pursuit of Learning in the Islamic World, 610–2003* (Jefferson: McFarland, 2005)

Jas, Ynda, 'Gender Beyond the Binary: Visualisation, Language and Conceptual Frameworks', *Ynda Jas*, 19 February 2021, <https://yndajas.co/articles/2021/02/19/gender-beyond-the-binary-visualisation-language-and-conceptual-frameworks> [accessed 22 February 2021]

—— 'Sexuality in a Non-Binary World: Redefining and Expanding the Linguistic Repertoire', *Journal of the International Network for Sexual Ethics and Politics*, 8 (2020), 71–92

Jefferson, Kevin, Torsten B. Neilands and Jae Sevelius, 'Transgender Women of Color: Discrimination and Depression Symptoms', *Ethnicity and Inequalities in Health and Social Care*, 6.4 (2013), 121–136

Johnston, Rich, 'A Very British Flavour of Transphobia to Consider', *Bleeding Cool*, 27 June 2020, <https://bleedingcool.com/pop-culture/very-british-transphobia> [accessed 28 September 2021]

Jones, Ann Rosalind, and Peter Stallybrass, *Renaissance Clothing and the Materials of Memory* (Cambridge: Cambridge University Press, 2000)

Jones, Zinnia, 'The Worst Assimilation of All: How Modern-Day Drag Hurts Trans Women and Achieves Little or Nothing of Value', *The Orbit*, 26 April 2014, <https://the-orbit.net/zinniajones/2014/04/the-worst-assimilation-of-all-how-modern-day-drag-hurts-trans-women-and-achieves-little-or-nothing-of-value> [accessed 3 September 2021]

Jordan, Patti, 'Gender Fluidity in Men's Fashion: From Shakespeare's Modern English to the New Millennium', *Critical Studies in Men's Fashion*, 4.2 (2017), 171–184

Journalists for Human Rights Indigenous Reporters Program, *Style Guide for Reporting on Indigenous People*, December 2017, <http://jhr. ca/wp-content/uploads/2017/12/JHR2017-Style-Book-Indigenous-People.pdf> [accessed 27 August 2021]

Joyce, Simon, 'Two Women Walk into a Theatre Bathroom: The Fanny and Stella Trials as Trans Narrative', *Victorian Review*, 44.1 (2018), 83–98

justannealien, *Instagram*, <https://www.instagram.com/justannealien> [accessed 28 September 2021]

Kames, Henry Home, Lord, *Sketches of the History of Man*, 4 vols. (Dublin: Printed for James Williams, 1774–75)

Kelly, Siobhan M., 'Multiplicity and Contradiction: A Literature Review of Trans★ Studies in Religion', *Journal of Feminist Studies in Religion*, 34.1 (2018), 7–23

Kennedy, Hubert C., 'The "Third Sex" Theory of Karl Heinrich Ulrichs', *Journal of Homosexuality*, 6.1/2 (1980/81), 103–111

Kim, Michelle, 'Drag Race Alumni Criticize RuPaul's "Conscious Exclusion" of Trans Queens', *them.*, 24 January 2020, <https://www.them.us/story/rupaul-drag-race-season-12-trans-queens-detox-carmen-carrera> [accessed 19 February 2021]

Köhne, Julia B., and Britte Lange, 'Mit Geschlechterrollen Spielen: Die Illusionsmaschine Damenimitation in Front- und Gefangenen-theatern des Ersten Weltkriegs' ['Playing with Gender Roles: The Illusion Machine of Female Impersonation in Front and Prison Camp Theatre of the First World War'], in Köhne, Lange and Vetter (eds.), *Mein Kamerad – die Diva*, pp. 25–41

Köhne, Julia B., Britte Lange and Anke Vetter (eds.), *Mein Kamerad – die Diva: Theater an der Front und in Gefangenenlagern des Ersten Weltkriegs* [*My Comrade, the Diva: Theatre at the Front and in Prison Camps of the First World War*] (München: Edition Text + Kritik, 2014)

Konadu, Kwasi, 'Naming and Framing a Crime Against Humanity: African Voices from the Transatlantic Slave System, ca. 1500–1900', in Trevor R. Getz (ed.), *African Voices of the Global Past: 1500 to the Present* (Boulder: Taylor & Francis, 2013), pp. 1–38

Koyama, Emi, 'Whose Feminism Is It Anyway? The Unspoken Racism of the Trans Inclusion Debate', *The Sociological Review Monographs*, 68.4 (2020), 735–744

Krafft-Ebing, Richard von, *Psychopathia Sexualis*, trans. by Franklin S. Klaf (New York: Stein & Day, 1965)

Lal, Vinay, 'Not This, Not That: The Hijras of India and the Cultural Politics of Sexuality', *Social Text*, 61 (1999), 119–140

Lang, Sabine, 'Native American Men-Women, Lesbians, Two-Spirits: Contemporary and Historical Perspectives', *Journal of Lesbian Studies*, 20.3–4 (2016), 299–323

Larson, Scott, '"Indescribable Being": Theological Performances of Genderlessness in the Society of the Publick Universal Friend, 1776–1819', *Early American Studies*, 12.3 (2014), 576–600

Lawner, Lynne, *Lives of the Courtesans: Portraits of the Renaissance* (New York: Rizzoli, 1987)

L'Estoile, Pierre de, *Registre-Journal du Règne de Henri III*, ed. by Madeleine Lazard and Gilbert Schrenck, 6 vols. (Genève: Droz, 1992)

Le Guin, Ursula K., 'Is Gender Necessary? Redux', in *Dancing at the Edge of the World: Thoughts on Words, Women, Places* (London: Gollancz, 1989), pp. 7–16

—— *The Left Hand of Darkness* (London: Gollancz, 2018)

Le Moyne de Morgues, Jacques, *Narrative of Le Moyne, an Artist Who Accompanied the French Expedition to Florida under Laudonniere, 1564*, trans. by Frederick B. Perkins (Boston: James R. Osgood, 1875)

Lehman, Peter, 'The Prosthetic Penis and the Trans Penis: Changing Representations of and Cultural Discourses About the Penis', *Studies in Gender and Sexuality*, 21.4 (2020), 285–290

Lester, CN, *Trans Like Me: Conversations for All of Us* (London: Virago, 2017)

Leupp, Gary P., 'Capitalism and Homosexuality in Eighteenth-Century Japan', *Historical Reflections/Réflexions Historiques*, 33.1 (2007), 135–152

—— 'The Floating World is Wide: Some Suggested Approaches to Researching Female Homosexuality in Tokugawa Japan', *Thamyris: Mythmaking from Past to Present*, 5 (1998), 1–40

Levitt, Heidi M., Francisco I. Surace, Emily E. Wheeler, Erik Maki, Darcy Alcántara, Melanie Cadet, Steven Cullipher, Sheila Desai, Gabriel Garza Sada, John Hite, Elena Kosterina, Sarah Krill, Charles Lui, Emily Manove, Ryan J. Martin and Courtney Ngai, 'Drag Gender: Experiences of Gender for Gay and Queer Men who Perform Drag', *Sex Roles*, 78 (2018), 367–384

Lewis, Franklin, 'Sexual Occidentation: The Politics of Conversion, Christian-Love and Boy-Love in 'Attār', *Iranian Studies*, 42.5 (2009), 693–723

Liddington, Jill, *Female Fortune: Land, Gender and Authority: The Anne Lister Diaries and Other Writings, 1833–36* (London: River Orams Press, 1998)

Lorde, Audre, 'The Master's Tools Will Never Dismantle the Master's House', in Reina Lewis and Sara Mills (eds.), *Feminist Postcolonial Theory: A Reader* (New York and Abingdon: Routledge, 2003), pp. 25–28

Macfarlane, Lesley-Anne Barnes, 'Gender Identity and Scottish Law: the Legal Response to Transsexuality', *Edinburgh Law Review*, 11.2 (2007), 162–186

MacLure, Maureen McVeigh, 'The Allure of Artifice: Titian's Half-Lengths and the Courtesan as Masquerader', *Rutgers Art Review*, 32 (2017), 19–39

Makepeace, Clare, *Captives of War: British Prisoners of War in Europe in the Second World War* (Cambridge: Cambridge University Press, 2017)

—— '"Pinky Smith Looks Gorgeous!" Female Impersonators and Male Bonding in Prisoner of War Camps for British Servicemen in Europe', in Robb and Pattinson (eds.), *Men, Masculinities and Male Culture*, 71–95

Malatino, Hil, *Trans Care* (Minneapolis: University of Minnesota Press, 2020)

Maltz, Robin, 'Real Butch: The Performance/Performativity of Male Impersonation, Drag Kings, Passing as Male, and Stone Butch Realness', *Journal of Gender Studies*, 7.3 (1998), 273–286

Manion, Jen, *Female Husbands: A Trans History* (Cambridge: Cambridge University Press, 2021)

Mann, Jenny C., 'How to Look at a Hermaphrodite in Early Modern England', *Studies in English Literature, 1500–1900*, 46.1 (2006), 67–91

Margari, Eleni, 'Hidden in Plain Sight: In Quest of Women and their Stories in Greek Museums', *Museum International*, 72.1–2 (2020), 118–129

Markowitz, Sally, 'Pelvic Politics: Sexual Dimorphism and Racial Difference', *Signs*, 26.2 (2001), 389–414

Martin, Ellis, and Zach Ozma (eds.), *We Both Laughed In Pleasure: The Selected Diaries of Lou Sullivan, 1961–1991* (New York: Nightboat Books, 2019)

Martin, Tristan K., and Deb Coolhart, '"Because Your Dysphoria Gets in the Way of You . . . It Affects Everything": The Mental, Physical, and Relational Aspects of Navigating Body Dysphoria and Sex for Trans Masculine People', *Sexual and Relationship Therapy* (2019), 1–18

Matić, Uroš, '(De)queering Hatshepsut: Binary Bind in Archaeology of Egypt and Kingship Beyond the Corporeal', *Journal of Archaeological Method and Theory*, 23.3 (2016), pp. 810–831

Mbah, Ndubueze L., 'Female Masculinities, Dissident Sexuality, and the Material Politics of Gender in Early Twentieth-Century Igboland', *Journal of Women's History*, 29.4 (2017), 35–60

McIlwaine, H.R. (ed.), *Minutes of the Council & General Court of Colonial Virginia, 1622–1632, 1670–1676, with Notes & Excerpts from Original Council & General Court Records, into 1683, Now Lost* (Richmond: The Colonial Press, Everett Waddey Co., 1924)

McKenney, Thomas Loraine, *Sketches of a Tour to the Lakes: Of the Character and Customs of the Chippeway Indians and of Incidents Connected with the Treaty of Fond du Lac* (Baltimore: Fielding Lucas Jr., 1827)

McLelland, Mark, 'Living More "Like Oneself"', *Journal of Bisexuality*, 3.3–4 (2003), 203–230

Mesch, Rachel, *Before Trans: Three Gender Stories from Nineteenth-Century France* (Stanford: Stanford University Press, 2020)

Middleton, Margaret, 'Queer Possibility', *Journal of Museum Education*, 45.4 (2020), 426–436

Middleton, Thomas, and Thomas Dekker, 'The Roaring Girl', in James Knowles (ed.), *The Roaring Girl and Other City Comedies* (Oxford: Oxford University Press, 2001)

Milano, Lanfranco da, 'Lanfranci Maioris', in *Cyrurgia Guidonis de Cauliaco: et Cyrurgia Bruni, Theodorici, Rogerij, Rolandij, Bertapalie, Lanfranci* (Venice, 1498)

Miller, Joseph C., 'Nzinga of Matamba in a New Perspective', *The Journal of African History*, 16.2 (1975), 201–216

Milloy, John S., *A National Crime: The Canadian Government and the Residential School System, 1879 to 1986* (Winnipeg: University of Manitoba Press, 1999)

Mills, Robert, *Seeing Sodomy in the Middle Ages* (Chicago: University of Chicago Press, 2015)

Miranda, Deborah A., 'Extermination of the Joyas: Gendercide in Spanish California', *GLQ: A Journal of Lesbian and Gay Studies*, 16.1–2 (2010), 253–284

Missouri Review, 'You Wouldn't Know Her From a Man: Male Impersonators of the Victorian Music Halls', *The Missouri Review*, 41.4 (2018), 83–93

Monumenta Missionaria Africa: África Ocidental (1622–1630), Coligida e Anotada pelo Padr António Brásio (Lisboa: Anência-Geral do Ultra, 1956)

Monumenta Missionaria Africa: África Ocidental (1651–1655), Coligida e Anotada pelo Padr António Brásio (Lisboa: Anência-Geral do Ultra, 1971)

Monumenta Missionaria Africa: África Ocidental (1656–1665), Coligida e Anotada pelo Padr António Brásio (Lisboa: Anência-Geral do Ultra, 1981)

Moreau, William E. (ed.), *The Writings of David Thompson, Volume 2: The Travels, 1848 Version, and Associated Texts* (Montreal: McGill-Queen's University Press, 2015)

Moretti, Laura, 'The Distribution and Circulation of Erotic Prints and Books in the Edo Period', in Clark, Gerstle, Ishigami and Yano (eds.), *Shunga*, pp. 300–317

Morgan, Cheryl Myfanwy, 'Trans Lives in Rome', in Ardel Haefele-Thomas (ed.), *Introduction to Transgender Studies* (New York: Harrington Park Press, 2019), pp. 372–377

Morgana, Luna, 'Mammy's Class War Part 1: Taste & Class', *GossipGrrrl*, 14 June 2021, <https://gossipgrrrl.substack.com/p/mammys-class-war-part-1> [accessed 28 September 2021]

—— 'Mammys Class War Part 2: The Working Classes are Revolting But We're Not the Most Bigoted', *GossipGrrrl*, 22 July 2021, <https://gossipgrrrl.substack.com/p/mammys-class-war-part-2> [accessed 28 September 2021]

Morgensen, Scott Lauria, 'Theorising Gender, Sexuality and Settler Colonialism: An Introduction', *Settler Colonial Studies*, 2.2 (2012), 2–22

Mori, Rie, 'Nanshoku Ōkagami ni Miru Dansei Fukushoku no Hyōgen: Wakashū no Furisode o Chūshin ni' ('The Expression of Male Clothes in *The Great Mirror of Male Love*: Focusing on the Wakashū Furisode'), *Bigaku*, 56.4 (2006), 41–54

Morland, Iain, 'Intersex', *TSQ: Transgender Studies Quarterly*, 1.1–2 (2014), 111–115

Mostow, Joshua S., 'The Gender of Wakashū and the Grammar of Desire', in Norman Bryson, Maribeth Graybill and Joshua S. Mostow (eds.), *Gender and Power in the Japanese Visual Field* (Honolulu: University of Hawaii Press, 2003), pp. 49–70

—— 'Utagawa *Shunga*, Kuki's "Chic" and the Construction of a National Erotics in Japan', in *Performing "Nation": Gender Politics in Literature, Theater, and the Visual Arts of China and Japan, 1880–1940*, ed. by Doris Croissant, Catherine Vance Yeh and Joshua S. Mostow (Leiden and Boston: Brill, 2008), pp. 383–424

—— 'Wakashū as a Third Gender and Gender Ambiguity Through the Edo Period', in Joshua S. Mostow, Asato Ikeda and Ryoko Matsuba (eds.), *A Third Gender: Beautiful Youths in Japanese Edo-Period Prints and Paintings (1600–1868)* (Toronto: Royal Ontario Museum, 2016), pp. 49–70

Mulholland, Paul, 'The Date of *The Roaring Girl*', *The Review of English Studies,* 28.109 (1977), pp. 18–31

Mulkerin, Tim, 'We Asked 3 Trans Drag Performers About the Present and Future of Drag. Here's What They Said', *Mic*, 9 February 2018, <https://www.mic.com/articles/187649/we-asked-3-trans-drag-performers-about-the-present-and-future-of-drag-heres-what-they-said#.wDSGK0Hzz> [accessed 3 September 2021]

Murphy, Amy Tooth, 'Butch on Butch: Historicising Butch Identity via Oral History', University of Plymouth, 10 March 2021

Murray, Stephen O., 'Gender-Mixing Roles, Gender-Crossing Roles, and the Sexuality of Transgendered Roles', *Reviews in Anthropology*, 31.4 (2002), 291–308

Murray, Stephen O., and Will Roscoe (eds.), *Boy-Wives and Female-Husbands: Studies in African Homosexualities* (New York: Palgrave Macmillan, 1998)

Najmabadi, Afsaneh, *Professing Selves: Transsexuality and Same-Sex Desire in Contemporary Iran* (Durham, N.C.: Duke University Press, 2013)

—— *Women with Mustaches and Men without Beards: Gender and Sexual Anxieties of Iranian Modernity* (Berkeley: University of California Press, 2005)

Niccols, Richard, *The Cuckoo* (London: Printed by F[elix] K[ingston], 1607)

Non-Binary Leeds, *Trancestors: A Non-Binary History Zine* (2019), <https://drive.google.com/drive/folders/1wiccteS1_mPn_cqYXkjaINTIE4be5ZYL> [accessed 30 September 2021]

Norton, Rictor, *Mother Clap's Molly House*, rev. edn. (Stroud: Chalford Press, 2006)

—— 'The Raid on Mother Clap's Molly House, 1776', *Homosexuality in Eighteenth-Century England: A Sourcebook*, <http://rictornorton.co.uk/eighteen/mother.htm> [accessed 5 July 2021]

Norton, Rictor (ed.), 'The Mollies Club, 1709–10', *Homosexuality in Eighteenth-Century England: A Sourcebook*, 1 December 1999, updated 16 June 2008, <http://www.rictornorton.co.uk/eighteen/nedward.htm> [accessed 16 July 2021]

Notehelfer, Fred G. (ed.), *Japan Through American Eyes: The Journal Of Francis Hall, 1859–1866* (Boulder: Westview Press, 2001)

O'Brien, Suzanne Crawford, 'Gone to the Spirits: A Transgender Prophet on the Columbia Plateau', *Theology & Sexuality*, 21.2 (2015), 125–143

O'Rourke, Chris, '"What a Pretty Man – or Girl!": Male Cross-Dressing Performances in Early British Cinema, 1898–1918', *Gender & History*, 32.1 (2020), 86–107

OED Online, 'cisgender, adj. and n.', 3rd edn., 2015, <https://www.oed.com/view/Entry/35015487> [accessed 16 March 2021]

—— 'gender, n.', 3rd edn., 2011, <https://www.oed.com/view/Entry/77468> [accessed 13 December 2021]

—— 'kinky, adj. and n.', 3rd edn., 2020 <https://www.oed.com/view/Entry/103575 > [accessed 23 September 2021]

Ogilby, John, *Africa* (London: Printed by Tho. Johnson for the author, 1670)

Old Bailey Proceedings Online, 14 June 1847, trial of John Sullivan (t18470614–1375), <http://www.oldbaileyonline.org>, version 6.0, 17 April 2011 [accessed 7 October 2021]

—— 9 September 1797, trial of Mary Tom House (t17670909–24), <http://www.oldbaileyonline.org> version 6.0, 17 April 2011 [accessed 7 October 2021]

Onstine, Suzanne, 'Gender and the Religion of Ancient Egypt', *Religion Compass*, 4.1 (2010), 1–11

Oram, Alison, 'Cross-Dressing and Transgender', in Harry Cocks and Matt Houlbrook (eds.), *Palgrave Advances in the Modern History of Sexuality* (Basingstoke: Palgrave Macmillan, 2006), pp. 256–285

Oyěwùmí, Oyèrónkẹ́, *The Invention of Women: Making an African Sense of Western Gender Discourses* (Minneapolis: University of Minnesota Press, 1997)

Pamment, Claire, 'Performing Piety in Pakistan's Transgender Rights Movement', *TSQ: Transgender Studies Quarterly*, 6.3 (2019), 297–314

Panayi, Panikos, '"Barbed Wire Disease" or a "Prison Camp Society": The Everyday Lives of German Internees on the Isle of Man, 1914–1919', in Panikos Panayi (ed.), *Germans as Minorities During the First World War: A Global Comparative Perspective* (Abingdon: Routledge, 2014), pp. 99–122

Pantoja, Selma, 'Njinga a Mbande: Power and War in 17th-Century Angola', *Oxford Research Encyclopedia of African History*, <https://oxfordre.com/africanhistory/view/10.1093/acrefore/9780190277734.001.0001/acrefore-9780190277734-e-326> [accessed 29 June 2021]

Parsons, James, *A Mechanical and Critical Enquiry into the Nature of Hermaphrodites* (London: Printed for J. Walthoe, 1741)

Pearce, Ruth, Sonja Erikainen and Ben Vincent, 'TERF Wars: An Introduction', *The Sociological Review Monographs*, 68.4 (2020), 677–698

Pember, Mary Annette, '"Two Spirit" Tradition Far From Ubiquitous Among Tribes', *Rewire News Group*, 13 October 2016, <https://rewirenewsgroup.com/article/2016/10/13/two-spirit-tradition-far-ubiquitous-among-tribes> [accessed 27 August 2021]

Pflugfelder, Gregory M., *Cartographies of Desire: Male–Male Sexuality in Japanese Discourse, 1600–1950* (Berkeley and London: University of California Press, 1999)

—— 'The Nation-State, the Age/Gender System, and the Reconstitution of Erotic Desire in Nineteenth-Century Japan', *The Journal of Asian Studies*, 71.4 (2012), 963–974

Piatowski, Peter, 'Where's the T? *RuPaul's Drag Race* and Transgender In/Exclusion', in Mike Perez, John C. Lamothe and Rachel Friedman (eds.), *Beyond Binaries: Trans Identities in Contemporary Culture* (Lanham: Lexington Books, 2021), pp. 69–81

Piętek, Robert, 'Constructing Angola's History Through Pictures – The Case of Queen Nzinga', *The Artistic Traditions of Non-European Cultures*, 6 (2018), 53–70

Playdon, Zoe, *The Hidden Case of Ewan Forbes: The Transgender Trial that Threatened to Upend the British Establishment* (London: Bloomsbury, 2021)

Pol, Lotte C. van, 'Antwerpen, Maria van (1719–1781)', *Huygens Institute for Dutch History*, <http://resources.huygens.knaw.nl/vrouwenlexicon/lemmata/data/Antwerpen> [accessed 29 June 2021]

Power, Miller, 'Non-Binary and Intersex Visibility and Erasure in Roman Archaeology', *Theoretical Roman Archaeology Journal*, 3.1 (2020), 1–19

Preciado, Paul B., *Testo Junkie: Sex, Drugs, and Biopolitics in the Pharmacopornographic Era*, trans. by Bruce Benderson (New York: Feminist Press, 2013)

Prosser, Jay, 'Transsexuals and the Transsexologists: Inversion and the Emergence of Transsexual Subjectivity', in Bland and Doan (eds.), *Sexology in Culture*, pp. 116–131

Prucha, Francis Paul, *Documents of United States Indian Policy*, 2nd edn. (Lincoln: University of Nebraska Press, 1990)

Pyle, Kai, 'Naming and Claiming: Recovering Ojibwe and Plains Cree Two-Spirit Language', *TSQ: Transgender Studies Quarterly*, 5.4 (2018), 574–588

Rachamimov, Iris, 'Camp Domesticity: Shifting Gender Boundaries in WWI Internment Camps', in Gilly Carr and Harold Mytum (eds.), *Cultural Heritage and Prisoners of War: Creativity Behind Barbed Wire* (New York: Routledge, 2012), pp. 291–305

—— 'The Disruptive Comforts of Drag: (Trans)Gender Performances among Prisoners of War in Russia, 1914–1920', *The American Historical Review*, 111.2 (2006), 362–382

—— '"Er War für die Gefangenen, Was Er Darstellte": Geschlectertransgressionen in Kriegsgefangenenlagern des Ersten Weltkriegs' ['"He Was, for the Prisoners, What He Imitated": Gender transgression in Military Prison Camps of the First World War'], in Köhne, Lange and Vetter (eds.), *Mein Kamerad – die Diva*, pp. 115–127

Rawson, K.J., 'Introduction: "An Inevitably Political Craft"', *TSQ: Transgender Studies Quarterly*, 2.4 (2015), 544–552

Redd, Danita R., 'Hatshepsut', in Sertima (ed.), *Black Women in Antiquity*, pp. 188–224

Reddy, Gayatri, *With Respect to Sex: Negotiating Hijra Identity in South India* (Chicago: University of Chicago Press, 2005)

Reinhold, Shola von, *LOTE* (London: Jacaranda Books Art Music, 2020)

Reis, Elizabeth, 'Impossible Hermaphrodites: Intersex in America, 1620–1960', *The Journal of American History*, 92.2 (2005), 411–441

Reiss, Matthias, 'Liebe, Sexualität und Männlichkeit in der Lagergesellschaft: Das Beispiel der Deutschen Kriegsgefangenen in den Vereinigten Staaten im Zweiten Weltkrieg' ['Love, Sexuality and Masculinity in the Prison Camp Society: The Example of German Prisoners of War in the United States during the Second World War'], presented at *Ninth Symposium of the Working Group for Interdisciplinary Men's and Gender studies* (Stuttgart, Germany), 15 December 2013, <https://www.fk12.tu-dortmund.de/cms/ISO/de /Lehr-und-Forschungsbereiche/soziologie_der_geschlechterver-haeltnisse/ Medienpool/AIM_2013_Tagung/Reiss_Liebe_Sexualitaet_ Maennlichkeit_in_der_Lagergesellschaft.pdf> [accessed 6 March 2018]

Repo, Jemima, 'The Biopolitical Birth of Gender: Social Control, Hermaphroditism, and the New Sexual Apparatus', *Alternatives: Global, Local, Political*, 38.3 (2013), 228–244

Riedel, Samantha, 'A Brief History of How Drag Queens Turned Against the Trans Community', *them.*, 10 March 2018, <https:// www.them.us/story/how-drag-queens-turned-against-the-trans-community> [accessed 3 September 2021]

Rifkin, Mark, 'Queering Indigenous Pasts, or Temporalities of Tradition and Settlement', in *The Oxford Handbook of Indigenous American Literature*, ed. by James Cox and Daniel Heath Justice (Oxford: Oxford University Press, 2014), pp. 137–151

Robb, Linsey, and Juliette Pattinson, 'Becoming Visible: Gendering the Study of Men at War', in Robb and Pattinson (eds.), *Men, Masculinities and Male Culture*, pp. 1–22

Robb, Linsey, and Juliette Pattinson (eds.), *Men, Masculinities and Male Culture in the Second World War* (Basingstoke: Palgrave Macmillan, 2017)

Robins, Gay, 'The Names of Hatshepsut as King', *The Journal of Egyptian Archaeology*, 85 (1999), 103–112

Rogers, Baker A., 'Drag As a Resource: Trans* and Nonbinary Individuals in the Southeastern United States', *Gender & Society*, 32.6 (2018), 889–910

Rogers, Claudia Jane, '"The People from Heaven"?: Reading Indigenous Responses to Europeans During Moments of Early Encounter in the Caribbean and Mesoamerica, 1492–c.1585' (unpublished doctoral thesis, University of Leeds, 2018)

Roscoe, Will, *Changing Ones: Third and Fourth Genders in Native North America* (New York: St Martin's Press, 1998)

Rosenberg, Jordy, *Confessions of the Fox* (London: Atlantic Books, 2018)

Rosenthal, Margaret F., *The Honest Courtesan: Veronica Franco, Citizen and Writer in Sixteenth-Century Venice* (University of Chicago Press, 2012)

Rosenthal, Margaret F., and Ann Rosalind Jones (eds.), *The Clothing of the Renaissance World: Europe, Asia, Africa, the Americas: Cesare Vecellio's Habiti Antichi et Moderni* (London: Thames & Hudson, 2008)

Row-Heyveld, Lindsey, '"Known and Feeling Sorrows": Disabled Knowledge and *King Lear*', *Early Theatre*, 22.2 (2019), 157–170

Rowson, Everett K., 'The Effeminates of Early Medina', *Journal of the American Oriental Society*, 111.4 (1991), 671–693

Rublack, Ulinka, 'Matter in the Material Renaissance', *Past & Present*, 219 (2013), 41–85

Rubright, Marjorie, 'Transgender Capacity in Thomas Dekker and Thomas Middleton's *The Roaring Girl* (1611)', *Journal for Early Modern Cultural Studies*, 19.4 (2019), 45–74

Rylan, Jules, 'Non-Binary Lesbians Have Always Existed', *Medium*, 16 October 2020, <https://radiantbutch.medium.com/non-binary-lesbians-have-always-existed-7db6b9e7e646> [accessed 10 March 2021]

Sajadi, Sahar, 'Deep in the Brain: Identity and Authenticity in Pediatric Gender Transition', *Cultural Anthropology*, 34.1 (2019), 103–129

Santore, Cathy, 'Julia Lombardo, "Somtuosa Meretrize": A Portrait by Property', *Renaissance Quarterly*, 41.1 (1988), 44–83

Sanz, Veronica, 'No Way Out of the Binary: A Critical History of the Scientific Production of Sex', *Signs: Journal of Women in Culture and Society*, 43.1 (2017), 1–27

Satenstein, Liana, 'Salvia Is the New Age Instagram Drag Star With a Fantastical Take on Reality', *Vogue*, 27 February 2018, <https://www.vogue.com/vogueworld/article/salvjiia-personality-on-insta-gram-to-know> [accessed 28 September 2021]

Sato, Yasuko, 'Early Modern Prostitutes, Concubines, and Mistresses (Review)', *Journal of Women's History*, 28.2 (2016), 156–165

Schaeffer, Claude E., 'The Kutenai Female Berdache: Courier, Guide, Prophetess, and Warrior', *Ethnohistory*, 12.3 (1965), 193–236

Schewe, Elizabeth, 'Serious Play: Drag, Transgender, and the Relationship Between Performance and Identity in the Life Writing of RuPaul and Kate Bornstein', *Biography*, 32.4 (2009), 670–695

Scott, Andrew G., *Emperors and Usurpers: An Historical Commentary on Cassius Dio's Roman History* (New York: Oxford University Press, 2018)

Seligmann, Raphael, 'With a Sword by Her Side and a Lute in Her Lap: Moll Cutpurse at the Fortune', in Thomasin LaMay (ed.), *Musical Voices of Early Modern Women: Many-Headed Melodies* (London: Routledge, 2017), pp. 187–209

Semerdijan, Elyse, '"Because he is so Tender and Pretty": Sexual Deviance and Heresy in Eighteenth-Century Aleppo', *Journal for the Study of Race, Nation and Culture*, 18.2 (2012), 175–199

Senelick, Laurence, *The Changing Room: Sex, Drag and Theatre* (London and New York: Routledge, 2000)

Serano, Julia, 'Autogynephilia: A Scientific Review, Feminist Analysis, and Alternative "Embodiment Fantasies" Model', *The Sociological Review Monographs*, 68.4 (2020), 763–778

Sertima, Ivan van (ed.), *Black Women in Antiquity* (London: Transaction Books, 1984)

Shakespeare, William, *Othello*, ed. by E.A.J. Honigmann and Ayanna Thompson (London: Bloomsbury Arden Shakespeare, 2016)

Shapiro, Eve, 'The Impact of Race on Gender Transformation in a Drag Troupe', in Sally Hines and Tam Sanger (eds.), *Transgender Identities: Towards a Social Analysis of Gender Diversity* (Abingdon and New York: Routledge, 2010), pp. 153–168

Shapland, Jenn, *My Autobiography of Carson McCullers* (Portland: Tin House Books, 2020)

Sheppard, Maia, and J.B. Mayo Jr., 'The Social Construction of Gender and Sexuality: Learning from Two Spirit Traditions', *The Social Studies*, 104.6 (2013), 259–270

Shi, Liang, 'Mirror Rubbing: A Critical Genealogy of Pre-Modern Chinese Female Same-Sex Eroticism', *Journal of Homosexuality*, 60.5 (2013), 750–772

Sigel, Lisa Z., '"Best Love": Female Impersonation in the Great War' *Sexualities*, 19.1–2 (2016), 98–118

Silva, Daniel F., '(Anti-)Colonial Assemblages: The History and Reformulations of Njinga Mbande', in Janell Hobson (ed.), *The Routledge Companion to Black Women's Cultural Histories* (London: Routledge, 2021), pp. 75–86

Simpson, Leanne Betasamosake, *As We Have Always Done: Indigenous Freedom through Radical Resistance* (Minneapolis: University of Minnesota Press, 2017)

Skidmore, Emily, 'Constructing the "Good Transsexual": Christine Jorgensen, Whiteness, and Heteronormativity in the Mid-Twentieth -Century Press', *Feminist Studies*, 37.2 (2011), 270–300

Smithers, Gregory D., 'Cherokee "Two Spirits": Gender, Ritual, and Spirituality in the Native South', *Early American Studies: An Interdisciplinary Journal*, 12.3 (2014), 626–651

Snorton, C. Riley, *Black On Both Sides: A Racial History of Trans Identity* (Minneapolis: University of Minnesota Press, 2017)

Sophie Labelle, cartoonist, *Twitter*, 1 May 2019, <https://twitter.com/assignedmale/status/1129052142910758913?lang=en> [accessed 28 September 2021]

Sperlin, O.B., 'Two Kootenay Women Masquerading as Men? Or Were They One?', *The Washington Historical Quarterly*, 21.2 (1930), 120–130

Splinter, Asa, 'Japan's Pre-Modern Images of Intersexuality' (unpublished master's thesis, Universiteit Leiden, 2019–2020)

[Star ver.Fall], *Twitter*, 21 February 2020, <https://twitter.com/StarSumiaki/status/1230997970339782656> [accessed 1 October 2021]

Statham, Edward Phillips (ed.), *A Jacobean Letter-Writer: The Life and Times of John Chamberlain* (London: K. Paul, Trench, Trubner & Co., 1920)

Stoughton, Thomas, *The Christians Sacrifice* (London: Printed by William Jones, 1622)

Straayer, Chris, 'Trans Men's Stealth Aesthetics: Navigating Penile Prosthetics and "Gender Fraud"', *Journal of Visual Culture*, 19.2 (2020), 255–271

Stryker, Susan, *Transgender History: The Roots of Today's Revolution* (Berkeley: Seal Press, 2017)

—— 'Transgender History, Homonormativity, and Disciplinarity', *Radical History Review*, 100 (2008), 145–157

Stryker, Susan, and Aren Z. Aizura (eds.), *The Transgender Studies Reader 2* (New York and London: Routledge, 2013)

Stubbes, Philip, *The Anatomy of Abuses* (London: [John Kingston for] Richard Jones, 1583)

Takács, Bogi, '[NOVEL] CONFESSIONS OF THE FOX BY JORDY ROSENBERG', *Bogi Reads the World*, <http://www.bogiread-stheworld.com/novel-confessions-of-the-fox-by-jordy-rosenberg> [accessed 26 April 2021]

Talbot, Steve, 'Spiritual Genocide: The Denial of American Indian Religious Freedom, from Conquest to 1934', *Wicazo Sa Review*, 21.2 (2006), 7–39

Talvacchia, Bette (ed.), *A Cultural History of Sexuality in the Renaissance* (London: Bloomsbury Academic, 2011)

Taylor, Ben, 'Zines by Non-Binary Leeds', *West Yorkshire Queer Stories*, 14 July 2019, <https://wyqs.co.uk/stories/zines-by-non-binary-leeds> [accessed 30 September 2021]

Taylor, Melanie A., '"The Masculine Soul Heaving in the Female Bosom": Theories of Inversion and *The Well of Loneliness*', *Journal of Gender Studies*, 7.3 (1998), 287–296

Taylor, Sara, *The Lauras* (London: Heinemann, 2016)

Tedlock, Barbara, *The Woman in the Shaman's Body: Reclaiming the Feminine in Religion and Medicine* (New York: Bantam Books, 2005)

Theis, Wolfgang, 'Grusswort', in Köhne, Lange and Vetter (eds.), *Mein Kamerad – die Diva*, p. 9

Thornton, John K., 'Legitimacy and Political Power: Queen Njinga, 1624–1663', *The Journal of African History*, 32.1 (1991), 25–40

Tinios, Ellis, 'Japanese Illustrated Erotic Books in the Context of Commercial Publishing, 1660–1868', *Japan Review*, 26 (2013), 83–96

Tobia, Jacob, *Sissy: A Coming-Of-Gender Story* (New York: G.P. Putnam's Sons, 2020)

Towle, Evan B., and Lynn M. Morgan, 'Romancing the Transgender Native: Rethinking the Use of the "Third Gender" Concept' in *The Transgender Studies Reader*, ed. by Susan Stryker and Stephen Whittle (New York: Routledge, 2006), pp. 666–684

traaaaaaannnnnnnnnns, *Twitter*, 24 September 2020, <https://twitter.com/traabot/status/1308947912026664960> [accessed 1 October 2021]

Transgender Trend, 'About Us', *Transgender Trend*, <https://www.transgendertrend.com/about_us> [accessed 25 March 2018]

Truth, Sojourner, 'Sojourner Truth, Speech at The Woman's Rights Convention Akron, Ohio, 1851', in Karlyn Kohrs Campbell (ed.), *Man Cannot Speak for Her: Key Texts of the Early Feminists*, 2 vols. (Westport: Greenwood, 1989), 2, 99–102

Truth and Reconciliation Commission of Canada, *Canada's Residential Schools, The Legacy: The Final Report of the Truth and Reconciliation Commission of Canada*, 6 vols. (Montreal: Published for the Truth and Reconciliation Commission by McGill-Queen's University Press, 2015), <https://ehprnh2mwo3.exactdn.com/wp-content/uploads/2021/01/Volume_5_Legacy_English_Web.pdf> [accessed 27 August 2021]

Turner, William, *A Compleat History of the Most Remarkable Providences* (London: Printed for John Dunton, 1697)

UK Government, 'Equality Act 2010', *legislation.gov.uk*, 2010 <https://www.legislation.gov.uk/ukpga/2010/15/contents> [accessed 16 March 2021]

Valentine, David, *Imagining Transgender: An Ethnography of a Category* (Durham, N.C.: Duke University Press, 2007)

Vetter, Anke, 'Einführung' ['Introduction'], in Köhne, Lange and Vetter (eds.), *Mein Kamerad – die Diva*, pp. 11–24 (p. 18)

Victoria & Albert Museum Archive, Nominal File 'Bowles, R.R.', MA/1/B2095

Vincent, Ben, *Transgender Health: A Practitioner's Guide to Binary and Non-Binary Trans Patient Care* (London: Jessica Kingsley Publishers, 2018)

Virginia General Court, 1622–29, Cases, with Minutes, ser. 8, vol. 15, Thomas Jefferson Papers, Library of Congress, <https://www.loc.gov/resource/mtj8.064_0002_0573/?sp=496> [accessed 27 April 2021]

Vitiello, Giovanni, 'The Dragon's Whim: Ming and Qing Homoerotic Tales from "The Cut Sleeve"', *T'oung Pao*, 78.4/5 (1992), 341–372

Vivo, Filippo de, 'Walking in Sixteenth-Century Venice: Mobilizing the Early Modern City', *I Tatti Studies in the Italian Renaissance*, 19.1 (2016), 115–141

Waiton, Stuart, 'Transgender Fetish is a Truly Shameful Modern Invention', *The Times*, 27 November 2017, <https://www.thetimes.co.uk/article/transgender-fetish-is-a-truly-shameful-modern-invention-g7036frog> [accessed 25 March 2018]

Walker, Robert, *The Female Soldier; Or, The Surprising Life and Adventures of Hannah Snell* (London: Printed for, and sold by R. Walker, 1750)

Walthall, Anne, 'Masturbation and Discourse on Female Sexual Practices in Early Modern Japan', *Gender & History*, 21.1 (2009), 1–18

Wanley, Nathaniel, *The Wonders of the Little World* (London: Printed for T. Basset . . ., R. Cheswel . . ., J. Wright . . ., and T. Sawbridge . . ., 1673)

Waters, Chris, 'Havelock Ellis, Sigmund Freud and the State: Discourses of Homosexual Identity in Interwar Britain', in Bland and Doan (eds.), *Sexology in Culture*, pp. 165–179

Weaver, Hilary, 'Drag Race Winner Sasha Velour Is Not Done Addressing Those RuPaul Comments', *Vanity Fair*, 15 March 2018, <https://www.vanityfair.com/style/2018/03/drag-race-winner-sasha-velour-addresses-rupaul-comments-at-nightgowns-show> [accessed 3 September 2021]

Weinberg, Albert Katz, *Manifest Destiny: A Study of Nationalist Expansionism in American History* (New York: AMS Press, 1979)

Welker, James, 'Toward a History of "Lesbian History" in Japan', *Culture, Theory and Critique*, 58.2 (2017), 147–165

Wells, Evelyn, *Hatshepsut* (Garden City: Doubleday, 1969)

Wenger, Tisa, 'Indian Dances and the Politics of Religious Freedom, 1870–1930', *Journal of the American Academy of Religion*, 79.4 (2011), 850–878

Westbrook, Laurel, 'Becoming Knowably Gendered: The Production of Transgender Possibilities and Constraints in the Mass and Alternative Press from 1990–2005 in the United States', in Hines and Sanger (eds.), *Transgender Identities*, pp. 43–63

Wheeler, Jo, 'Stench in Sixteenth-Century Venice', in *The City and the Senses: Urban Culture since 1500*, ed. by Alexander Cowan and Jill Steward (Aldershot: Ashgate, 2007), pp. 25–38

Wheelwright, Julie, '"Amazons And Military Maids": An Examination Of Female Military Heroines In British Literature And The Changing Construction Of Gender', *Women's Studies International Forum*, 10.5 (1987), 489–501

—— 'Snell, Hannah [alias James Gray] (1723–1792), Sexual Impostor', <https://www.oxforddnb.com/view/10.1093/ref:odnb/9780198614128.001.0001/odnb-9780198614128-e-25975> [accessed 29 June 2021]

Whitbread, Helena (ed.), *I Know My Own Heart: The Diaries of Anne Lister, 1791–1840* (New York: New York University Press, 1988)

—— *No Priest But Love: Excerpts from the Diaries of Anne Lister, 1824–1826* (Otley: Smith Settle, 1992)

Whitehead, Joshua, *Jonny Appleseed* (Vancouver: Arsenal Pulp Press, 2018)

Wichelns, Kathryn, 'From *The Scarlet Letter* to Stonewall: Reading the 1629 Thomas(ine) Hall Case, 1978–2009', *Early American Studies*, 12.3 (2014), 500–523

Wieser, Doris, 'Queen Njinga in a South-Atlantic Dialogue: Gender, Race and Identity', *Iberoamericana*, 17.66 (2017), 31–53

Wilchins, Riki Anne, *Read My Lips: Sexual Subversion and the End of Gender* (Ithaca: Firebrand, 1997)

Williams, Cristan, 'The Ontological Woman: A History of Deauthentication, Dehumanization, and Violence', *The Sociological Review Monographs*, 68.4 (2020), 718–734

Williams, Walter L., *The Spirit and the Flesh: Sexual Diversity in American Indian Culture* (Boston: Beacon Press, 1992)

Wimby, Dierdre, 'The Female Horuses and Great Wives of Kemet', in
Sertima (ed.), *Black Women in Antiquity*, pp. 36–48

Wright, Talen, Emily Jay Nicholls, Alison J. Rodger, Fiona M. Burns,
Peter Weatherburn, Roger Pebody, Leanne McCabe, Aedan Wolton,
Mitzy Gafos, and T. Charles Witzel, 'Accessing and Utilising Gender
-Affirming Healthcare in England and Wales: Trans and Non-Binary
People's Accounts of Navigating Gender Identity Clinics', *BMC
Health Services Research*, 21.609 (2021)

Young, Antonia, *Women Who Become Men: Albanian Sworn Virgins*
(Oxford: Berg, 1999)

Zabus, Chantal, and Samir Kumar Das, 'Hijras, Sangomas, and Their
Translects: Trans(lat)ing India and South Africa', *Interventions* (2020),
1–24

Notes

Introduction

1. *Old Bailey Proceedings Online*, 14 June 1847, trial of John Sullivan (t18470614–1375), <http://www.oldbaileyonline.org>, version 6.0, 17 April 2011 [accessed 7 October 2021].
2. Magnus Hirschfeld, *The Sexual History of the World War*, trans. by A. Gaspar et al. (New York: Falstaff Press, 1937), p. 148; see also Heike Bauer, *The Hirschfeld Archives* (Philadelphia: Temple University Press, 2017), p. 84.
3. Richard Ekins and Dave King, *The Transgender Phenomenon* (London: Sage, 2006), p. 82.
4. Laurel Westbrook, 'Becoming Knowably Gendered: The Production of Transgender Possibilities and Constraints in the Mass and Alternative Press from 1990–2005 in the United States', in Sally Hines and Tam Sanger (eds.), *Transgender Identities: Towards a Social Analysis of Gender Diversity* (New York: Routledge, 2010), pp. 43–63 (p. 46); Leslie Feinberg, *Transgender Liberation: A Movement Whose Time Has Come* (New York: World View Forum, 1992).
5. UK Government, 'Equality Act 2010', *legislation.gov.uk*, 2010 <https://www.legislation.gov.uk/ukpga/2010/15/contents> [accessed 16 March 2021].
6. 'cisgender, adj. and n.', *OED Online*, 3rd edn., 2015, <https://www.oed.com/view/Entry/35015487> [accessed 16 March 2021].

7. See Shon Faye, *The Transgender Issue: An Argument for Justice* (London: Penguin Books, 2021), p. xvi.

8. See Westbrook, 'Becoming Knowably Gendered', for a great overview of how new terminology, and articles aimed at teaching trans-related terminology and concepts, actually helped create new gendered possibilities in the 1990s and early 2000s.

9. Joseph Gamble, 'Toward a Trans Philology', *Journal for Early Modern Cultural Studies*, 19.4 (2019), 26–44 (pp. 27–30).

10. Ruth Pearce, Sonja Erikainen and Ben Vincent, 'TERF Wars: An Introduction', *The Sociological Review Monographs*, 68.4 (2020), 677–698 (p. 687); Leah DeVun and Zeb Tortorici, 'Trans, Time, and History', *TSQ: Transgender Studies Quarterly*, 5.4 (2018), 518–539 (p. 523).

11. For information on the scientific basis for thinking about sex as a spectrum, see Sally Hines, 'Sex Wars and (Trans)Gender Panics: Identity and Body Politics in Contemporary UK Feminism', *The Sociological Review Monographs*, 68.4 (2020), 699–717 (pp. 708–710).

12. Pearce et al., 'TERF Wars', p. 688; see also Wendy Cealey Harrison, 'The Shadow and the Substance: The Sex/Gender Debate', in Kathy Davis, Mary Evans, and Judith Lorber (eds.), *Handbook of Gender and Women's Studies* (London: Sage, 2006), pp. 35–52.

13. Faye, *The Transgender Issue*, p. 240.

14. See Jules Gill-Peterson, *Histories of the Transgender Child* (Minneapolis: University of Minnesota Press, 2018), pp. 97–127.

15. Susan Stryker, *Transgender History: The Roots of Today's Revolution* (Berkeley: Seal Press, 2017), p. 11. Stryker's book, first published in 2008, tells stories of trans history and activism in the USA from the nineteenth century onwards.

16. Susan Stryker and Aren Z. Aizura (eds.), *The Transgender Studies Reader 2* (New York and London: Routledge, 2013), p. 6.

17. 'gender, n.', *OED Online*, 3rd edn., 2011, <https://www.oed.com/view/Entry/77468> [accessed 13 December 2021]; William Shakespeare, *Othello*, ed. by E.A.J. Honigmann and Ayanna

Thompson (London: Bloomsbury Arden Shakespeare, 2016), 1.3.324.

18. Ynda Jas, a fabulous non-binary poet, musician and writer – and a good friend of mine – has written about this in their online article 'Gender Beyond the Binary: Visualisation, Language and Conceptual Frameworks' (*Ynda Jas*, 19 February 2021, <https:// yndajas.co/articles/2021/02/19/gender-beyond-the-binary-visu-alisation-language-and-conceptual-frameworks> [accessed 22 February 2021]). In the article they also discuss some new ways in which we might try to visualise gender, given the fact it's so personally contingent and specific.

19. See Emily Skidmore, 'Constructing the "Good Transsexual": Christine Jorgensen, Whiteness, and Heteronormativity in the Mid-Twentieth-Century Press', *Feminist Studies*, 37.2 (2011), 270–300.

20. Carolyn Dinshaw, *Getting Medieval: Sexualities and Communities, Pre- and Postmodern* (Durham, N.C.: Duke University Press, 1999), p. 21; Alan Bennett, *The History Boys* (London: Faber & Faber, 2004), p. 56.

21. Andrew G. Scott, *Emperors and Usurpers: An Historical Commentary on Cassius Dio's Roman History* (New York: Oxford University Press, 2018), pp. 128, 137–138.

22. See Gabrielle M.W. Bychowski, Howard Chiang, Jack Halberstam, Jacob Lau, Kathleen P. Long, Marcia Ochoa, C. Riley Snorton, Leah DeVun and Zeb Tortorici, '"Trans★historicities": A Roundtable Discussion', *TSQ: Transgender Studies Quarterly*, 5.4 (2018), 658–685 (p. 663). This is a brilliant discussion between a group of scholars of trans history. It's worth explaining the asterisk in the title 'Trans★historicities': here it's intended to communicate both histories of trans people ('trans historicities') and the concept of being 'transhistorical', as well as other words that might begin with 'trans' and intersect with gender (such as 'transnational'). In older sources, you might have seen the adjective 'trans' written with an asterisk on its own: 'trans★'. This was originally intended to indicate inclusion of non-binary and gender-nonconforming

people; in more recent years, though, activists have come to use the word 'trans' on its own to encompass all of those groups, and the asterisk has no longer felt necessary.

23. The curator Margaret Middleton points this out in her article 'Queer Possibility', *Journal of Museum Education*, 45.4 (2020), 426–436 (p. 431). Middleton's suggested approach to museum curation is similar, in many ways, to the way of doing history that I'm talking about in this book.

24. Jacob Tobia, *Sissy: A Coming-Of-Gender Story* (New York: G.P. Putnam's Sons, 2020), pp. 12–19.

25. Frustratingly, the most recent research on trans people's experiences of gender identity clinics in the UK notes that more research is needed into the experiences of trans people of colour – but there's substantial anecdotal evidence that they face additional barriers, particularly due to clinicians' Eurocentric and white-centric ideas of what constitutes normative male/female names and gender expression: see Talen Wright, Emily Jay Nicholls, Alison J. Rodger, Fiona M. Burns, Peter Weatherburn, Roger Pebody, Leanne McCabe, Aedan Wolton, Mitzy Gafos, and T. Charles Witzel, 'Accessing and Utilising Gender-Affirming Healthcare in England and Wales: Trans and Non-Binary People's Accounts of Navigating Gender Identity Clinics', *BMC Health Services Research*, 21.609 (2021).] For the healthcare experiences of trans women of colour in the US, see Kevin Jefferson, Torsten B. Neilands, and Jae Sevelius, 'Transgender Women of Color: Discrimination and Depression Symptoms', *Ethnicity and Inequalities in Health and Social Care*, 6.4 (2013), 121–136.

26. Tobia, *Sissy*, p. 14.

27. See Tobia, *Sissy*, pp. 16–17; Pearce et al., 'TERF Wars', p. 686.

28. Skidmore, 'Constructing the "Good Transsexual"', p. 271.

29. See Bychowski et al., 'Trans★ Historicities', p. 658; DeVun and Tortorici, 'Trans, Time, and History', pp. 518–519.

30. Bychowski et al., 'Trans★ Historicities', p. 677.

31. E.g. Kimberlé Crenshaw, 'Demarginalizing the Intersection of Race and Sex: A Black Feminist Critique of Antidiscrimination

Doctrine, Feminist Theory and Antiracist Politics', *University of Chicago Legal Forum*, 1 (1989), 139–167; Audre Lorde, 'The Master's Tools Will Never Dismantle the Master's House', in Reina Lewis and Sara Mills (eds.), *Feminist Postcolonial Theory: A Reader* (New York and Abingdon: Routledge, 2003), pp. 25–28; bell hooks, *Ain't I a Woman? Black Women and Feminism* (Boston: South End Press, 1981); B Camminga, 'Disregard and Danger: Chimamanda Ngozi Adichie and the Voices of Trans (and Cis) African Feminists', *The Sociological Review Monographs*, 68.4 (2020), 817–833; Emi Koyama, 'Whose Feminism Is It Anyway? The Unspoken Racism of the Trans Inclusion Debate', *The Sociological Review Monographs*, 68.4 (2020), 735–744.

32. Sojourner Truth, 'Sojourner Truth, Speech at The Woman's Rights Convention Akron, Ohio, 1851', in Karlyn Kohrs Campbell (ed.), *Man Cannot Speak for Her: Key Texts of the Early Feminists*, 2 vols. (Westport: Greenwood, 1989), 2, 99–102; see also Camminga, 'Disregard and Danger', p. 829.

33. Michelle Cameron, 'Two-Spirited Aboriginal People: Continuing Cultural Appropriation by Non-Aboriginal Society', *Canadian Woman Studies*, 24.2 (2005), 123–127 (p. 126); see also Kai Pyle, 'Naming and Claiming: Recovering Ojibwe and Plains Cree Two -Spirit Language', *TSQ: Transgender Studies Quarterly*, 5.4 (2018), 574–588 (p. 574). See also Poiva Junior Ashleigh Feu'u, 'A Comparative Study of Fa'afafine of Samoa and the Whakawahine of Aotearoa New Zealand', in *Representing Trans: Linguistic, Legal and Everyday Perspectives* (Wellington: Victoria University Press, 2017), pp. 171–203, on the value of these culturally specific genders for people in Samoa and Aotearoa/New Zealand.

34. Skidmore, 'Constructing the "Good Transsexual"'.

35. See Koyama, 'Whose Feminism', p. 738; Kevin Henderson, 'J.K. Rowling and the White Supremacist History of "Biological Sex"', *The Abusable Past*, 28 July 2020, <https://www.radicalhistoryreview.org/abusablepast/j-k-rowling-and-the-white-supremacist-history-of-biological-sex> [accessed 22 February 2021]; Camminga, 'Disregard and Danger', p. 827.

36. Combahee River Collective, 'The Combahee River Collective Statement', in Barbara Smith (ed.), *Home Girls: A Black Feminist Anthology* (New Brunswick: Rutgers University Press, 2000), pp. 264–274 (p. 267).

37. Cameron, 'Two-Spirited Aboriginal People', p. 125; emphasis added.

38. Koyama, 'Whose Feminism', p. 740; see also Leslie Feinberg, *Transgender Warriors: Making History from Joan of Arc to Dennis Rodman* (Boston: Beacon Press, 1996), pp. 112–119.

39. Camminga, 'Disregard and Danger', pp. 821–822; Bychowski et al., 'Trans★ Historicities', p. 662.

40. Henderson, 'J.K. Rowling and the White Supremacist History of "Biological Sex"'; Sander L. Gilman, 'Black Bodies, White Bodies: Toward an Iconography of Female Sexuality in Late Nineteenth-Century Art, Medicine, and Literature', *Critical Inquiry*, 12.1 (1985), 204–242; Sally Markowitz, 'Pelvic Politics: Sexual Dimorphism and Racial Difference', *Signs*, 26.2 (2001), 389–414; Pearce et al., 'TERF Wars', pp. 687–688.

41. Henderson, 'J.K. Rowling and the White Supremacist History of "Biological Sex"'.

42. See Gill-Peterson, *Histories of the Transgender Child*, p. 31, for more reflection on this issue.

43. Feinberg, *Transgender Warriors*, pp. 91–92.

44. Ivan Coyote, *Rebent Sinner* (Vancouver: Arsenal Pulp Press, 2019), p. 193.

45. Darlene E. Clover and Kathy Sanford have written about how this affects the narratives of history we're shown in museums: 'Educating Epistemic Justice and Resistance Through the *Feminist Museum Hack*: Looking and Acting with Another Eye', *Museum International*, 72.1–2 (2020), 56–67 (p. 58).

46. Middleton, 'Queer Possibility', p. 431.

47. Cultural managers Hilde Di Domenico and Isaline Pfefferlé point out that this accusation is frequently levelled at women: 'Where are the Women? Giving a Voice to Five Leading Female Professionals in Brussels' Cultural Scene', *Museum International*,

72.1–2 (2020), 10–17 (p. 16). See also Clover and Sanford, 'Educating Epistemic Justice', p. 60.

48. Middleton, 'Queer Possibility', pp. 433, 430; see also K.J. Rawson, 'Introduction: "An Inevitably Political Craft"', *TSQ: Transgender Studies Quarterly*, 2.4 (2015), 544–552 (p. 547); Dinshaw, *Getting Medieval*, p. 21; Lindsey Row-Heyveld, '"Known and Feeling Sorrows": Disabled Knowledge and *King Lear*', *Early Theatre*, 22.2 (2019), 157–170 (pp. 159–160).

49. Row-Heyveld, 'Known and Feeling Sorrows'.

50. Trans writer Juliet Jacques points this out in her own memoir: *Trans: A Memoir* (London: Verso, 2015), pp. 203–205. The fact that much of Jacques's most successful work has been memoir serves to prove her point – her fantastic new collection of short stories about trans history, *Variations* (London: Influx Press, 2021) gives me hope that, slowly, trans people are starting to get the chance to show what we can do outside of the memoir. See also Faye, *The Transgender Issue*, p. 15.

51. Stuart Waiton, 'Transgender Fetish is a Truly Shameful Modern Invention', *The Times*, 27 November 2017, <https://www.thetimes.co.uk/article/transgender-fetish-is-a-truly-shameful-modern-invention-g7036frog> [accessed 25 March 2018].

52. Peter Hitchens, 'The Transgender Zealots Are Destroying Truth Itself', *Mail on Sunday*, 19 November 2017, <http://www.dailymail.co.uk/debate/article-5096679/PETER-HITCHENS-Transgender-zealots-destroying-truth.html> [accessed 25 March 2018]; Harriet Agerholm, '"Teenagers Becoming Transgender to be Cool" Article Slammed by Activists', *Independent*, 18 April 2017, <https://www.independent.co.uk/news/world/americas/transgender-people-cool-article-daily-wire-criticism-response-twitter-a7687716.html> [accessed 16 March 2021]; Transgender Trend, 'About Us', *Transgender Trend*, <https://www.transgender-trend.com/about_us> [accessed 25 March 2018].

53. Carrie-Anne Brownian, 'Transing the Dead: The Erasure of Gender-Defiant Role Models from History', *4thWaveNow*, 31 October 2016, <https://4thwavenow.com/2016/10/31/transing

-the-dead-the-erasure-of-gender-defiant-role-models-from-history> [accessed 23 February 2021]. Be aware that the post, like many others on the site, contains transphobic views.

54. Pearce et al., 'TERF Wars', pp. 684–685; Cristan Williams, 'The Ontological Woman: A History of Deauthentication, Dehumanization, and Violence', *The Sociological Review Monographs*, 68.4 (2020), 718–734 (pp. 720–721); Toby Beauchamp, *Going Stealth: Transgender Politics and U.S. Surveillance Practices* (Durham, N.C.: Duke University Press, 2018), p. 32; CN Lester, *Trans Like Me: Conversations for All of Us* (London: Virago, 2017), pp. 118–119, 126–127.

55. Hil Malatino, *Trans Care* (Minneapolis: University of Minnesota Press, 2020), p. 14.

56. Tobia, *Sissy*, p. 222; see also Sahar Sajadi, 'Deep in the Brain: Identity and Authenticity in Pediatric Gender Transition', *Cultural Anthropology*, 34.1 (2019), 103–129 (pp. 111–113).

57. The social scientist Sahar Sajadi points out how politically useful the 'born this way' narrative is: 'Deep in the Brain', p. 117. See also Meg-John Barker and Jules Scheele, *Sexuality: A Graphic Guide* (London: Icon Books, 2021), p. 118.

58. Sajadi, 'Deep in the Brain', pp. 112–113.

59. Curator and art historian Eleni Margari takes a similar approach when looking for women's stories in museum collections: 'Hidden in Plain Sight: In Quest of Women and their Stories in Greek Museums', *Museum International*, 72.1–2 (2020), 118–129 (p. 128).

60. See e.g. Brownian, 'Transing the Dead'.

61. European Launch, 'Trans Historical: Gender Plurality before the Modern', University of York, 1/11/2021.

62. See Bychowski et al, 'Trans*historicities', pp. 658–659, 679: both Jack Halberstam and Gabrielle M.W. Bychowski discuss this 'politics of solidarity'.

63. Stryker, *Transgender History*, p. 1.

64. See b. binaohan, *decolonizing trans/gender 101* (Toronto: Biyuti Publishing, 2014).

Author's note

1. See also Marjorie Rubright, 'Transgender Capacity in Thomas Dekker and Thomas Middleton's *The Roaring Girl* (1611)', *Journal for Early Modern Cultural Studies*, 19.4 (2019), 45–74 (p. 52), who takes a similar decision for similar reasons.

Chapter 1

1. See Selma Pantoja, 'Njinga a Mbande: Power and War in 17th-Century Angola', *Oxford Research Encyclopedia of African History*, <https://oxfordre.com/africanhistory/view/10.1093/acrefore/9780190277734.001.0001/acrefore-9780190277734-e-326> [accessed 29 June 2021], p. 1, for more information on Luanda's establishment as a Portuguese fort.
2. Pantoja, 'Njinga a Mbande', pp. 2–3; Robert Piętek, 'Constructing Angola's History Through Pictures – The Case of Queen Nzinga', *The Artistic Traditions of Non-European Cultures*, 6 (2018), 53–70 (p. 62).
3. Piętek, 'Constructing Angola's History', p. 53; Pantoja, 'Njinga a Mbande', pp. 3–4.
4. Pantoja, 'Njinga a Mbande', p. 3.
5. Ibid., pp. 1–3.
6. Daniel F. Silva, '(Anti-)Colonial Assemblages: The History and Reformulations of Njinga Mbande', in Janell Hobson (ed.), *The Routledge Companion to Black Women's Cultural Histories* (London: Routledge, 2021), pp. 75–86 (p. 76).
7. Silva, '(Anti-)Colonial Assemblages', p. 77.
8. Ibid., p. 76.
9. Ibid., pp. 76–77.
10. Ibid., p. 77, n. 6.
11. One example of this is Carrie-Anne Brownian, 'Transing the Dead: The Erasure of Gender-Defiant Role Models From

History', *4thWaveNow*, <https://4thwavenow.com/2016/10/31/transing-the-dead-the-erasure-of-gender-defiant-role-models-from-history> [accessed 23 February 2021]. Be aware that this post, like many others on the site, contains transphobic views. See also Leslie Feinberg, *Transgender Warriors: Making History from Joan of Arc to Dennis Rodman* (Boston: Beacon Press, 1996), pp. 78, 83–87.

12. Ynda Jas, 'Sexuality in a Non-Binary World: Redefining and Expanding the Linguistic Repertoire', *Journal of the International Network for Sexual Ethics and Politics*, 8 (2020), 71–92 (p. 73).

13. Feinberg, *Transgender Warriors*, p. 14.

14. See Jen Manion, *Female Husbands: A Trans History* (Cambridge: Cambridge University Press, 2021), p. 266, for a real-life example of how this works.

15. See Feinberg, *Transgender Warriors*, pp. 83–87.

16. Jack Halberstam, *Female Masculinity* (Durham, N.C.: Duke University Press, 1998). Works that use 'female masculinity' to describe the people in this chapter include Kelly-Anne Diamond, 'Hatshepsut: Transcending Gender in Ancient Egypt', *Gender & History*, 32.1 (2020), 168–188; Ndubueze L. Mbah, 'Female Masculinities, Dissident Sexuality, and the Material Politics of Gender in Early Twentieth-Century Igboland', *Journal of Women's History*, 29.4 (2017), 35–60; Nwando Achebe, *The Female King of Colonial Nigeria: Ahebi Ugbabe* (Bloomington: Indiana University Press, 2011).

17. Danita R. Redd, 'Hatshepsut', in Ivan van Sertima (ed.), *Black Women in Antiquity* (London: Transaction Books, 1984), pp. 188–224 (p. 210).

18. Evelyn Wells, *Hatshepsut* (Garden City: Doubleday, 1969) pp. 185–186; Redd, 'Hatshepsut', p. 207.

19. Redd, 'Hatshepsut', p. 207; Gay Robins, 'The Names of Hatshepsut as King', *The Journal of Egyptian Archaeology*, 85 (1999), 103–112 (pp. 103, 111–112).

20. Diamond, 'Hatshepsut', p. 179.

21. Ibid., p. 173.

22. Redd, 'Hatshepsut', p. 219; Wells, *Hatshepsut*, p. 15, Fig. 8.

23. Uroš Matić, '(De)queering Hatshepsut: Binary Bind in Archaeology of Egypt and Kingship Beyond the Corporeal', *Journal of Archaeological Method and Theory*, 23.3 (2016), pp. 810–831 (p. 815); Diamond, 'Hatshepsut', pp. 176–177.

24. Wells, *Hatshepsut*, pp. 71, 77.

25. Ibid., pp. 78–79.

26. Ibid., pp. 141–144.

27. Ibid., p. 172.

28. Diamond, 'Hatshepsut', pp. 181–182.

29. Wells, *Hatshepsut*, p. 177.

30. Ibid., p. 186.

31. Ibid., pp. 193–194.

32. Ibid., p. 114.

33. Matić, '(De)queering Hatshepsut', p. 814.

34. Suzanne Onstine, 'Gender and the Religion of Ancient Egypt', *Religion Compass*, 4.1 (2010), 1–11 (p. 2); Diamond, 'Hatshepsut', pp. 178–179.

35. Onstine, 'Gender and the Religion of Ancient Egypt', p. 3; Matić, '(De)queering Hatshepsut', p. 814; Dierdre Wimby, 'The Female Horuses and Great Wives of Kemet', in Sertima (ed.), *Black Women in Antiquity*, pp. 36–48 (p. 36).

36. Diamond, 'Hatshepsut', pp. 168–169, 174; Matić, '(De)queering Hatshepsut', p. 814. Diamond also shows that several other rulers had also been depicted in non-binary ways.

37. Diamond, 'Hatshepsut', p. 174.

38. Matić, '(De)queering Hatshepsut', pp. 824–826; Diamond, 'Hatshepsut', pp. 175–176.

39. See Onstine, 'Gender and the Religion of Ancient Egypt', esp. pp. 1–2.

40. Wells, *Hatshepsut*, p. 265.

41. John Henrik Clarke, 'African Warrior Queens', in Sertima (ed.), *Black Women in Antiquity*, pp. 123–134 (pp. 124–125).

42. Ifi Amadiume, *Male Daughters, Female Husbands: Gender and Sex in an African Society* (London: Zed Books, 2015), p. 21.

43. Achebe, *Female King*, pp. 39–40.

44. Ibid., p. 13. For an alternative perspective on the queer possibility of marriages between AFAB people, see David Ikpo, 'Queer Participatory Visibility in Nigerian Nations', *Outing the Past Leeds*, <https://www.youtube.com/watch?v=BZafPQ887YU&list=PLvK0mIEJxRSWbPhPmPo1C1tfs75WfZR_r&index=12> [accessed 29 June 2021].

45. Amadiume, *Male Daughters*, pp. 42–43; 17; 89; 67

46. Ibid., pp. 123, 148.

47. Ibid., pp. 131–132.

48. Achebe, *Female King*, p. 89; Amadiume, *Male Daughters*, p. 119.

49. Ibid., pp. 98–99; Chidera Ihejirika, 'Fuck Your Gender Norms: How Western Colonisation Brought Unwanted Binaries to Igbo Culture', *gal-dem*, 19 February 2020, <https://gal-dem.com/colonialism-nigeria-gender-norms-lgbtq-igbo/1/9> [accessed 29 June 2021].

50. Ihejirika, 'Fuck Your Gender Norms'; Amadiume, *Male Daughters*, p. 148.

51. Mbah, 'Female Masculinities', pp. 35–36.

52. Ibid., p. 37.

53. Ibid., pp. 47–48.

54. Ibid., pp. 50–51.

55. Silva, '(Anti-)Colonial Assemblages', pp. 75–76.

56. Linda M. Heywood, *Njinga of Angola: Africa's Warrior Queen* (Cambridge, M.A., and London: Harvard University Press, 2017), p. 71.

57. Silva, '(Anti-)Colonial Assemblages', pp. 77–78.

58. Pantoja, 'Njinga a Mbande', pp. 6–7.

59. Silva, '(Anti-)Colonial Assemblages', p. 77.

60. Joseph C. Miller, 'Nzinga of Matamba in a New Perspective', *The Journal of African History*, 16.2 (1975), 201–216 (p. 202); John K. Thornton, 'Legitimacy and Political Power: Queen Njinga, 1624–1663', *The Journal of African History*, 32.1 (1991), 25–40; Silva, '(Anti-)Colonial Assemblages', p. 83; Pantoja, 'Njinga a Mbande', pp. 6–7.

61. Silva, '(Anti-)Colonial Assemblages', pp. 77–80; Heywood, *Njinga of Angola*, p. 59.
62. Thornton, 'Legitimacy and Political Power', pp. 38–39; Doris Wieser, 'Queen Njinga in a South-Atlantic Dialogue: Gender, Race and Identity', *Iberoamericana*, 17.66 (2017), 31–53 (p. 36).
63. Heywood, *Njinga of Angola*, p. 83; John Ogilby, *Africa* (London: Printed by Tho. Johnson for the author, 1670), sig. 3B6ᵛ.
64. Ogilby, *Africa*, sig. 3C1ʳ.
65. Wieser, 'Queen Njinga', p. 40.
66. Miller, 'Nzinga of Matamba', p. 208.
67. Miller, 'Nzinga of Matamba', pp. 208–210; Silva, '(Anti-)Colonial Assemblages', p. 78.
68. Miller, 'Nzinga of Matamba', p. 210; Silva, '(Anti-)Colonial Assemblages', p. 78.
69. *Monumenta Missionaria Africa: África Ocidental (1622–1630), Coligida e Anotada pelo Padr António Brásio* (Lisboa: Anência-Geral do Ultra, 1956), p. 366. Beatrix Heintze, 'Written Sources and African History: A Plea for the Primary Source. The Angola Manuscript Collection of Fernão de Sousa', *History in Africa*, 9 (1982), 77–103, gives a comprehensive list of letters about Njinga.
70. Pantoja, 'Njinga a Mbande', pp. 7–8.
71. Silva, '(Anti-)Colonial Assemblages', p. 78. For an example of a letter that shows the Portuguese using Njinga's sisters to manipulate them, see *Monumenta Missionaria Africa: África Ocidental (1656–1665), Coligida e Anotada pelo Padr António Brásio* (Lisboa: Anência-Geral do Ultra, 1981), p. 91.
72. Silva, '(Anti-)Colonial Assemblages', p. 78; Miller, 'Nzinga of Matamba', pp. 211–212; Pantoja, 'Njinga a Mbande', pp. 5, 10; *Monumenta Missionaria Africa: África Ocidental (1651–1655), Coligida e Anotada pelo Padr António Brásio* (Lisboa: Anência-Geral do Ultra, 1971), pp. 70–71.
73. Heywood, *Njinga of Angola*, pp. 193–201; Pantoja, 'Njinga a Mbande', p. 10.
74. Silva, '(Anti-)Colonial Assemblages', pp. 81–82; Wieser, 'Queen Njinga', p. 31.

75. Kwasi Konadu, 'Naming and Framing a Crime Against Humanity African Voices from the Transatlantic Slave System, ca. 1500–1900', in Trevor R. Getz (ed.), *African Voices of the Global Past: 1500 to the Present* (Boulder: Taylor & Francis, 2013), pp. 1–38 (p. 31).
76. *Monumenta Missionaria Africa: África Ocidental (1651–1655)*, vol. 11, pp. 524–528.
77. Konadu, 'Naming and Framing', p. 31.
78. Ibid., pp. 31–32; Pantoja, 'Njinga a Mbande', pp. 10–11.
79. Silva, '(Anti-)Colonial Assemblages', pp. 81–82.
80. Ibid., p. 82.
81. Thornton, 'Legitimacy and Political Power', p. 40.
82. Achebe, *Female King*, p. 37.
83. Achebe, 'Legitimacy and Political Power', pp. 59–61.
84. Achebe, *Female King*, pp. 53, 86–89.
85. Ibid., pp. 99–100, 89–90.
86. Ibid., pp. 99–103.
87. Ibid., p. 103.
88. Ibid., pp. 105–06.
89. Ibid., p. 39.
90. Ibid., pp. 105–106, 114–115
91. Ibid., pp. 103–104.
92. Ibid., p. 124.
93. Ibid., pp. 123–125.
94. Ibid., pp. 62, 64, 124.
95. Ibid., p. 136. For a full description of Ahebi's palace, see pp. 136–171.
96. Ibid., pp. 166, 147.
97. Ibid., pp. 148–149.
98. Ibid., pp. 172–184.
99. Ibid., pp. 172, 182.
100. Ibid., pp. 183–184.
101. Ibid., pp. 186–189.
102. Ibid., pp. 8, 89–90.
103. Ibid., pp. 90, 98–99, 120.
104. Ibid., pp. 77–86, 238 n. 28.

105. See Manion, *Female Husbands*, pp. 68–103; Rudolf M. Dekker and Lotte C. van Pol, *The Tradition of Female Transvestism in Early Modern Europe* (Basingstoke: Macmillan, 1989); Marian Füssel, 'Between Dissimulation and Sensation: Female Soldiers in Eighteenth-Century Warfare', *Journal for Eighteenth-Century Studies*, 41.4 (2018), 527–542; Scarlet Bowen, '"The Real Soul of a Man in her Breast": Popular Opposition and British Nationalism in Memoirs of Female Soldiers, 1740–1750', *Eighteenth-Century Life*, 28.3 (2004), 20–44.

106. Julie Wheelwright, '"Amazons And Military Maids": An Examination Of Female Military Heroines In British Literature And The Changing Construction Of Gender', *Women's Studies International Forum*, 10.5 (1987), 489–501 (p. 491, n. 2).

107. Julie Wheelwright, 'Snell, Hannah [alias James Gray] (1723–1792), Sexual Impostor', <https://www.oxforddnb.com/view/10.1093/ref:odnb/9780198614128.001.0001/odnb-9780198614128-e-25975> [accessed 29 June 2021]; Füssel, 'Between Dissimulation and Sensation', pp. 534–535.

108. Yoriko Ishida, 'Body and Gender Expressed by the Cross-Dressing of Hannah Snell in Eighteenth-Century Naval Culture in *The Female Soldier; Or, the Surprising Life and Adventures of Hannah Snell*', *IAFOR Journal of Literature & Librarianship*, 7.1 (2018), 77–92 (p. 82).

109. Ishida, 'Body and Gender', p. 80; Feinberg, *Transgender Warriors*, p. 14; see also Laurence Senelick, *The Changing Room: Sex, Drag and Theatre* (London and New York: Routledge, 2000), p. 302.

110. Bowen, 'The Real Soul of a Man in her Breast', p. 26.

111. For one example of an AFAB person who presented as male in a military context *and* asserted a male identity, see Lotte C. van Pol, 'Antwerpen, Maria van (1719–1781)', *Huygens Institute for Dutch History*, <http://resources.huygens.knaw.nl/vrouwenlexicon/lemmata/data/Antwerpen> [accessed 29 June 2021]; Dekker and Pol, *Tradition of Female Transvestism*, pp. 65–69.

112. Catherine Baker, 'Monstrous Regiment', *History Today*, 17/04/2018, <https://www.historytoday.com/history-matters/monstrous

-regiment> [accessed 29 June 2021]; Rachel Mesch, *Before Trans: Three Gender Stories from Nineteenth-Century France* (Stanford: Stanford University Press, 2020), p. 286.

113. Antonia Young, *Women Who Become Men: Albanian Sworn Virgins* (Oxford: Berg, 1999).

114. Stephen O. Murray, 'Gender-Mixing Roles, Gender-Crossing Roles, and the Sexuality of Transgendered Roles', *Reviews in Anthropology*, 31.4 (2002), 291–308 (pp. 293–294).

115. Poiva Junior Ashleigh Feu'u, 'A Comparative Study of Fa'afafine of Samoa and the Whakawahine of Aotearoa New Zealand', in *Representing Trans: Linguistic, Legal and Everyday Perspectives* (Wellington: Victoria University Press, 2017), pp. 171–203; Young, *Women Who Become Men*, pp. 111–122.

Chapter 2

1. Thomas Stoughton, *The Christians Sacrifice* (London: Printed by William Jones, 1622), sig. B1^r.

2. Stoughton, *Christians Sacrifice*, sig. Y4^r.

3. Ibid.

4. William Prynne, *The Unloveliness of Love-Locks* (London: Printed, 1628), sigs. A3^r-A3^v.

5. Carlo Belfanti, 'The Civilization of Fashion', *Journal of Social History*, 43.2 (2009), 261–283 (p. 263). Interestingly, hats and other headwear were considered to be particularly powerful indicators – see Maria Hayward's article '"The Sign of Some Degree"?: The Financial, Social and Sartorial Significance of Male Headwear at the Courts of Henry VIII and Edward VI', *Costume: The Journal of the Costume Society*, 36 (2002), 1–17.

6. Philip Stubbes, *The Anatomy of Abuses* (London: [John Kingston for] Richard Jones, 1583), sig. F5^v.

7. For more on how this worked in early modern thought, see Will Fisher, *Materializing Gender in Early Modern English Literature and Culture* (Cambridge: Cambridge University Press, 2006), especially

p. 13; and Bette Talvacchia (ed.), *A Cultural History of Sexuality in the Renaissance* (London: Bloomsbury Academic, 2011), p. 17.

8. Judith M. Bennett and Shannon McSheffrey, 'Early, Erotic and Alien: Women Dressed as Men in Late Medieval London', *History Workshop Journal*, 77.1 (2014), 1–25 (p. 4).

9. This example comes from Bennett and McSheffrey, 'Early, Erotic and Alien'. For a comparable example, see Lisa Z. Sigel, ' "Best Love": Female Impersonation in the Great War' *Sexualities*, 19.1–2 (2016), 98–118 (pp. 99, 100, 103).

10. I've written about this problem elsewhere, in my article 'Gender Nonconformity and Military Internment: Curating the Knockaloe slides', *Critical Military Studies*, 6.3–4 (2019), 323–. The curator Margaret Middleton also makes this point in her article 'Queer Possibility', *Journal of Museum Education*, 45.4 (2020), 426–436 (pp. 428–429).

11. See Samantha Aishia, 'Why Masculine Clothing Dominates the Gender-Neutral Fashion Game', *Fashion Industry Broadcast*, 4 May 2019, <https://fashionindustrybroadcast.com/2019/05/04/why-masculine-clothing-dominates-the-gender-neutral-fashion-game> [accessed 16 March 2021]; Bennett and McSheffrey, 'Early, Erotic and Alien', p. 5.

12. Simon Adams, *Leicester and the Court: Essays on Elizabethan Politics* (Manchester: Manchester University Press, 2002), p. 46. I've written about the threat posed by male favourites under kings who *were* attracted to men in my book *The Reputation of Edward II, 1305–1697: A Literary Transformation of History* (Amsterdam: Amsterdam University Press, 2020).

13. For a broader history of these fashion trends, see Patti Jordan, 'Gender Fluidity in Men's Fashion: From Shakespeare's Modern English to the New Millennium', *Critical Studies in Men's Fashion*, 4.2 (2017), 171–184.

14. Richard Niccols, *The Cuckoo* (London: Printed by F[elix] K[ingston], 1607), sig. B3^v.

15. *Haec-vir: or, The Womanish-Man* (London: printed [at Eliot's Court Press] for I. T[rundle], 1620), sigs. C1^r, C1^v.

16. Pierre de L'Estoile, *Registre-Journal du Règne de Henri III*, ed. by Madeleine Lazard and Gilbert Schrenck, 6 vols. (Genève: Droz, 1992), 2, 42; Laurence Senelick, *The Changing Room: Sex, Drag and Theatre* (London and New York: Routledge, 2000), pp. 163–164.

17. David Chambers and Brian Pullan (eds.), *Venice: A Documentary History, 1450–1630* (Oxford: Blackwell, 1992), pp. 124–125.

18. E.g. *Haec-Vir*, sigs. C2^r, C2^v; Niccols, *The Cuckoo*, sig. B3^v.

19. Ludovico Ariosto, *Orlando Furioso in English Heroical Verse*, trans. by John Harington (London: By Richard Field, for John Norton and Simon Waterson, 1607), sig. E3^v.

20. L'Estoile, *Registre-Journal*, 2, 42–43, 46, 185; Chambers and Pullan (eds.), *Venice: A Documentary History*, pp. 124–125; see also Ann Rosalind Jones and Peter Stallybrass, *Renaissance Clothing and the Materials of Memory* (Cambridge: Cambridge University Press, 2000), p. 79.

21. Jenn Shapland, *My Autobiography of Carson McCullers* (Portland: Tin House Books, 2020), p. 132.

22. Henry Fitzgeffrey, *Satires* (London: Printed by Edw[ard] Allde, for Miles Patrich, 1617), sig. F2^r.

23. Edward Phillips Statham (ed.), *A Jacobean Letter-Writer: The Life and Times of John Chamberlain* (London: K. Paul, Trench, Trubner & Co., 1920), p. 182.

24. James I, King of England, *Daemonologie in Form of a Dialogue, Divided into Three Books* (Edinburgh, Printed by Robert Waldegrave printer to the Kings Majesty, 1597), sigs. G2^r-G2^v.

25. P.J. Finkelpearl, 'Chamberlain, John (1553–1628), Letter Writer', *Oxford Dictionary of National Biography*, 23 September 2004, <https://www.oxforddnb.com/view/10.1093/ref:odnb/9780198614128.001.0001/odnb-9780198614128-e-5046> [accessed 16 March 2021].

26. *Hic Mulier: or, The Man-Woman* (London: Printed [at Eliot's Court Press] for I. T[rundle], 1620).

27. *Hic Mulier*, sigs. A4^r-A4^v.

28. Ibid., sigs. B2^v-B3^r.

29. Ibid., sig. B2^r.

30. Paula C. Clarke, 'The Business of Prostitution in Early Renaissance Venice', *Renaissance Quarterly*, 68.2 (2015), 419–464 (p. 427).

31. William Dugdale, *The Baronage of England* (London: Printed by Tho. Newcomb, for Abel Roper, John Martin, and Henry Herringman, 1675), sig. B4^r.

32. Bernard Capp, 'Playgoers, Players and Cross-Dressing in Early Modern London: The Bridewell Evidence', *The Seventeenth Century*, 18.2 (2003), 159–171 (p. 165).

33. *Hic Mulier*, sig. B2^t.

34. Bennett and McSheffrey, 'Early, Erotic and Alien', p. 2. For a fascinating look at the role played by accusations of gender nonconformity in sexualised insults and slander, see Laura Gowing, 'Gender and the Language of Insult in Early Modern London', *History Workshop Journal*, 35 (1993), 1–21 (the quote about 'wearing the breeches' is on p. 11).

35. Bennett and McSheffrey, 'Early, Erotic and Alien', 4; Ulinka Rublack, 'Matter in the Material Renaissance', *Past & Present*, 219 (2013), 41–85 (p. 55).

36. Cathy Santore, 'Julia Lombardo, "Somtusoa Meretrize": A Portrait by Property', *Renaissance Quarterly*, 41.1 (1988), 44–83 (pp. 57–58).

37. Stoughton, *The Christians Sacrifice*, sig. Z1^r.

38. For more on Frith's public performances, especially at the Fortune, see Raphael Seligmann, 'With a Sword by Her Side and a Lute in Her Lap: Moll Cutpurse at the Fortune', in Thomasin LaMay (ed.), *Musical Voices of Early Modern Women: Many-Headed Melodies* (London: Routledge, 2017), pp. 187–209 (the description of the St Paul's flashing episode is on p. 197). See also Paul Mulholland, 'The Date of *The Roaring Girl*', *The Review of English Studies*, 28.109 (1977), pp. 18–31.

39. Mulholland, 'The Date of *The Roaring Girl*', p. 31.

40. Thomas Middleton and Thomas Dekker, 'The Roaring Girl', in James Knowles (ed.), *The Roaring Girl and Other City Comedies* (Oxford: Oxford University Press, 2001), 2.127–132. For a full discussion of how we can look at Moll/Jack's trans possibility

across the whole play, see Marjorie Rubright, 'Transgender Capacity in Thomas Dekker and Thomas Middleton's *The Roaring Girl* (1611)', *Journal for Early Modern Cultural Studies*, 19.4 (2019), 45–74. The list here of ways Moll/Jack's gender is referred to is taken from Rubright's article, p. 46.

41. Dekker and Middleton, *The Roaring Girl*, 3.162, 3.165.

42. Ibid., 3.255, 5.67–107.

43. Ibid., 4.83.

44. Ibid., 4.79–87.

45. Jo Wheeler, 'Stench in Sixteenth-Century Venice', in *The City and the Senses: Urban Culture since 1500*, ed. by Alexander Cowan and Jill Steward (Aldershot: Ashgate, 2007), pp. 25–38; see also Filippo de Vivo, 'Walking in Sixteenth-Century Venice: Mobilizing the Early Modern City', *I Tatti Studies in the Italian Renaissance*, 19.1 (2016), 115–141; Alexander Cowan, 'Gossip and Street Culture in Early Modern Venice', in *Cultural History of Early Modern European Streets*, ed. by Riitta Laitinen and Thomas Cohen (Leiden: Brill, 2009), pp. 119–140.

46. Joanne M. Ferraro, 'Making a Living: The Sex Trade in Early Modern Venice', *The American Historical Review*, 123.1 (2018), 30–59 (pp. 40–41).

47. Lynne Lawner, *Lives of the Courtesans: Portraits of the Renaissance* (New York: Rizzoli, 1987), p. 14.

48. Santore, 'Julia Lombardo'.

49. Contemporaries wrote about this – see Margaret F. Rosenthal and Ann Rosalind Jones (eds.), *The Clothing of the Renaissance World: Europe, Asia, Africa, the Americas: Cesare Vecellio's Habiti Antichi et Moderni* (London: Thames & Hudson, 2008), p. 199.

50. For an example of these flap prints, see Pietro Bertelli, *Diversarum Nationum Habitus* (Padua: [Pietro Bertelli], 1594). For information about them, see Talvacchia, *Cultural History*, p. 17; Olwen Hufton, 'Istruzione, Lavoro e Povertà' ['Education, Work and Poverty'], in Sara F. Matthews-Grieco (ed.), *Monaca, Moglie, Serva, Cortigiana: Vita e Immagine della Donne tra Rinascimento e Controriforma* [*Nun, Wife, Servant, Courtesan: The Lives and Images of Women between the*

Renaissance and Counter-Reformation] (Florence: Morgana Edizioni, 2001), pp. 48-101 (p. 90). For more on Titian's painting, see Maureen McVeigh MacLure, 'The Allure of Artifice: Titian's Half -Lengths and the Courtesan as Masquerader', *Rutgers Art Review*, 32 (2017), 19–39.

51. Chambers and Pullan (eds.), *Venice: A Documentary History*, p. 123.

52. Margaret F. Rosenthal, *The Honest Courtesan: Veronica Franco, Citizen and Writer in Sixteenth-Century Venice* (University of Chicago Press, 2012), p. 65; see also Ferraro, 'Making a Living'.

53. See MacLure, 'The Allure of Artifice', p. 31.

54. Lawner, *Lives of the Courtesans*, p. 23.

55. Jill Liddington, *Female Fortune: Land, Gender and Authority: The Anne Lister Diaries and Other Writings, 1833–36* (London: River Orams Press, 1998), p. 100.

56. Helena Whitbread (ed.), *I Know My Own Heart: The Diaries of Anne Lister, 1791–1840* (New York: New York University Press, 1988), p. 145.

57. Helena Whitbread (ed.), *No Priest But Love: Excerpts from the Diaries of Anne Lister, 1824–1826* (Otley: Smith Settle, 1992), p. 127.

58. Whitbread, *No Priest but Love*, p. 152; Anna Clark, 'Anne Lister's Construction of Lesbian Identity', *Journal of the History of Sexuality*, 7.1 (1996), 23–50.

59. Clark, 'Anne Lister's Construction of Lesbian Identity', pp. 42–43.

60. Whitbread, *I Know My Own Heart*, p. 267; *No Priest but Love*, p. 85.

61. Clark, 'Anne Lister's Construction of Lesbian Identity', pp. 40–41.

62. On stone butches as 'untouchable', see Robin Maltz, 'Real Butch: The Performance/Performativity of Male Impersonation, Drag Kings, Passing as Male, and Stone Butch Realness', *Journal of Gender Studies*, 7.3 (1998), 273–286 (pp. 274–275).

Chapter 3

1. Paul Cohen-Portheim, *Time Stood Still: My Internment in England, 1914–1918* (London: Duckworth, 1931), pp. 84–85; Claire Corkill,

'Knockaloe First World War Internment Camp: A Virtual Museum and Archive' (unpublished doctoral thesis, University of York, 2013), pp. 64, 69.

2. Corkill, 'Knockaloe', p. 70.
3. Jennifer Kewley Draskau, 'Prisoners in Petticoats: Drag Performance and its Effects in Great War Internment Camps in the Isle of Man', *Proceedings of the Isle of Man Natural History and Antiquarian Society*, 12.2 (2009), 187–204 (pp. 187–188).
4. Corkill, 'Knockaloe', p. 53.
5. Ibid., pp. 53–54.
6. 'From the Archive, 13 May 1915: Anti-German Riots Spread', the *Guardian*, 13 May 2015, <https://www.theguardian.com/world/2015/may/13/anti-german-riots-lusitania-1915-first-world-war> [accessed 28 September 2021].
7. Corkill, 'Knockaloe', p. 57.
8. Ibid., pp. 12–13.
9. Ibid., pp. 63–64.
10. Ibid., pp. 39, 63.
11. Cohen-Portheim, *Time Stood Still*, pp. 43–44; Corkill, 'Knockaloe', pp. 69–71.
12. Corkill, 'Knockaloe', pp. 132–133.
13. Ibid., pp. 69–71, 135.
14. Cohen-Portheim, *Time Stood Still*, p. 85.
15. Iris Rachamimov, 'Camp Domesticity: Shifting Gender Boundaries in WWI Internment Camps', in Gilly Carr and Harold Mytum (eds.), *Cultural Heritage and Prisoners of War: Creativity Behind Barbed Wire* (New York: Routledge, 2012), pp. 291–305 (p. 292).
16. Iris Rachamimov, '"Er War für die Gefangenen, Was Er Darstellte": Geschlectertransgressionen in Kriegsgefangenenlagern des Ersten Weltkriegs' ['"He Was, for the Prisoners, What He Imitated": Gender transgression in Military Prison Camps of the First World War'], in Julia B. Köhne, Britte Lange and Anke Vetter (eds.), *Mein Kamerad – die Diva: Theater an der Front und in Gefangenenlagern des Ersten Weltkriegs* [*My Comrade, the Diva:*

Theatre at the Front and in Prison Camps of the First World War]
(München: Edition Text + Kritik, 2014), pp. 115–127 (p. 115).

17. Rachamimov, 'Er war für die Gefangenen', p. 115; Corkill, 'Knockaloe', p. 145.

18. Rachamimov, 'Er war für die Gefangenen', p. 115; Corkill, 'Knockaloe', pp. 69–71.

19. Corkill, 'Knockaloe', pp. 71, 144.

20. Draskau, 'Prisoners in Petticoats', pp. 190–191.

21. Panikos Panayi, '"Barbed Wire Disease" or a "Prison Camp Society": The Everyday Lives of German Internees on the Isle of Man, 1914–1919', in Panikos Panayi (ed.), *Germans as Minorities During the First World War: A Global Comparative Perspective* (Abingdon: Routledge, 2014), pp. 99–122 (pp. 118–119).

22. Panayi, 'Barbed Wire Disease', p. 119.

23. Corkill, 'Knockaloe', p. 155.

24. Draskau, 'Prisoners in Petticoats', p. 193.

25. Panayi, 'Barbed Wire Disease', p. 119.

26. Cohen-Portheim, *Time Stood Still*, p. 147. See also Iris Rachamimov, 'The Disruptive Comforts of Drag: (Trans)Gender Performances among Prisoners of War in Russia, 1914–1920', *The American Historical Review*, 111.2 (2006), 362–382 (pp. 377–378); Draskau, 'Prisoners in Petticoats', p. 198.

27. Anke Vetter, 'Einführung' ['Introduction'], in Köhne, Lange and Vetter (eds.), *Mein Kamerad – die Diva*, pp. 11–24 (p. 18).

28. Julia B. Köhne and Britte Lange, 'Mit Geschlechterrollen Spielen: Die Illusionsmaschine Damenimitation in Front- und Gefangenentheatern des Ersten Weltkriegs' ['Playing with Gender Roles: The Illusion Machine of Female Impersonation in Front and Prison Camp Theatre of the First World War'], in Köhne, Lange and Vetter (eds.), *Mein Kamerad – die Diva*, pp. 25–41 (p. 25); Rachamimov, 'Er war für die Gefangenen', p. 116.

29. Panayi, 'Barbed Wire Disease', p. 119; Clare Makepeace, *Captives of War: British Prisoners of War in Europe in the Second World War* (Cambridge: Cambridge University Press, 2017), p. 72.

30. Since the series aired, contestant Gigi Goode has come out as a trans woman; several other contestants, including Crystal Methyd, Dahlia Sin, Jackie Cox, Nicky Doll and Rock M. Sakura, are non -binary.

31. Detox . . ., *Twitter*, 23 January 2020, <https://twitter.com/ TheOnlyDetox/status/1220442901198536704> [accessed 28 September 2021]. See also Peter Piatowski, 'Where's the T? *RuPaul's Drag Race* and Transgender In/Exclusion', in Mike Perez, John C. Lamothe and Rachel Friedman (eds.), *Beyond Binaries: Trans Identities in Contemporary Culture* (Lanham: Lexington Books, 2021), pp. 69–81; Michelle Kim, 'Drag Race Alumni Criticize RuPaul's "Conscious Exclusion" of Trans Queens', *them.*, 24 January 2020, <https://www.them.us/story/ rupaul-drag-race-season-12-trans-queens-detox-carmen- carrera> [accessed 19 February 2021]; Hilary Weaver, 'Drag Race Winner Sasha Velour Is Not Done Addressing Those RuPaul Comments', *Vanity Fair*, 15 March 2018, <https://www. vanityfair.com/style/2018/03/drag-race-winner-sasha-velour- addresses-rupaul-comments-at-nightgowns-show> [accessed 3 September 2021].

32. Decca Aitkenhead, 'RuPaul: "Drag is a big f-you to male-domi- nated culture"', *Guardian*, 3 March 2018, <https://www.the guardian.com/tv-and-radio/2018/mar/03/rupaul-drag-race- big-f-you-to-male-dominated-culture> [accessed 3 September 2021].

33. Piatowski, 'Where's the T?', pp. 76–77.

34. Ibid., p. 70.

35. Ibid., pp. 70–71.

36. Zinnia Jones, 'The Worst Assimilation of All: How Modern-Day Drag Hurts Trans Women and Achieves Little or Nothing of Value', *The Orbit*, 26 April 2014, <https://the-orbit.net/zinnia- jones/2014/04/the-worst-assimilation-of-all-how-modern-day- drag-hurts-trans-women-and-achieves-little-or-nothing-of- value> [accessed 3 September 2021].

37. Jones, 'The Worst Assimilation'.

38. Andrea James, 'I F★cking Hate @RuPaul', *BoingBoing*, 4 April 2014, <https://boingboing.net/2014/04/04/rupaul.html> [accessed 10 September 2021]. Other trans people have agreed: see, for example, Baker A. Rogers, 'Drag As a Resource: Trans★ and Nonbinary Individuals in the Southeastern United States', *Gender & Society*, 32.6 (2018), 889–910 (p. 904); Samantha Riedel, 'A Brief History of How Drag Queens Turned Against the Trans Community', *them.*, 10 March 2018, <https://www.them.us/story/how-drag-queens-turned-against-the-trans-community> [accessed 3 September 2021].

39. James, 'I F★cking Hate @RuPaul'.

40. See also Piatowski, 'Where's the T?', pp. 72, 78.

41. Judith Butler, *Gender Trouble: Feminism and the Subversion of Identity*, 10th anniversary edn. (New York and London: Routledge, 1999); see also Laurence Senelick, *The Changing Room: Sex, Drag and Theatre* (London and New York: Routledge, 2000), p. 5.

42. Cohen-Portheim, *Time Stood Still*, p. 148.

43. Draskau, 'Prisoners in Petticoats', p. 198.

44. Ibid., p. 199.

45. Rachamimov, 'Disruptive Comforts', pp. 377–379; Draskau, 'Prisoners in Petticoats', p. 198; Senelick, *The Changing Room*, p. 336; Clare Makepeace, '"Pinky Smith Looks Gorgeous!" Female Impersonators and Male Bonding in Prisoner of War Camps for British Servicemen in Europe', in Linsey Robb and Juliette Pattinson (eds.), *Men, Masculinities and Male Culture in the Second World War* (Basingstoke: Palgrave Macmillan, 2017), 71–95 (p. 79).

46. Makepeace, 'Pinky Smith', pp. 75–76; Draskau, 'Prisoners in Petticoats', p. 200; Matthias Reiss, 'Liebe, Sexualität und Männlichkeit in der Lagergesellschaft: Das Beispiel der Deutschen Kriegsgefangenen in den Vereinigten Staaten im Zweiten Weltkrieg' ['Love, Sexuality and Masculinity in the Prison Camp Society: The Example of German Prisoners of War in the United States during the Second World War'], presented at *Ninth Symposium of the Working Group for Interdisciplinary Men's and Gender studies* (Stuttgart, Germany), 15 December 2013, <https://www.

fk12.tu-dortmund.de/cms/ISO/de/Lehr-und-Forschungsbereiche/soziologie_der_geschlechterverhaeltnisse/Medienpool/AIM_2013_Tagung/Reiss_Liebe_Sexualitaet_Maennlichkeit_in_der_Lagergesellschaft.pdf> [accessed 6 March 2018], p. 14.

47. Makepeace, 'Pinky Smith', pp. 79, 84–86.

48. Ibid., p. 79. For more details on people who played female roles onstage and lived as women offstage, in PoW camps and elsewhere, see Makepeace, 'Pinky Smith', pp. 75–76; Senelick, *The Changing Room*, pp. 334–339; Rachamimov, 'Disruptive Comforts', pp. 362–363, 377–378.

49. Senelick, *The Changing Room*, pp. 35–50, 115–142; Dominic Janes, 'The Varsity Drag: Gender, Sexuality and Cross-Dressing at the University of Cambridge, 1850–1950', *Journal of Social History*, forthcoming.

50. Senelick, *The Changing Room*, pp. 98–100.

51. Janes, 'Varsity Drag'.

52. Senelick, *The Changing Room*, pp. 176–179; see also CN Lester, *Trans Like Me: Conversations for All of Us* (London: Virago, 2017), pp. 152–154.

53. Simone Chess, 'Queer Residue: Boy Actors' Adult Careers in Early Modern England', *Journal for Early Modern Cultural Studies*, 19.4 (2019), 242–264.

54. Chess, 'Queer Residue', pp. 254–256.

55. Ibid., p. 258.

56. Senelick, *The Changing Room*, pp. 219–225; Jim Davis, '"Slap On! Slap Ever!": Victorian Pantomime, Gender Variance, and Cross-Dressing', *New Theatre Quarterly*, 30.3 (2014), 218–230 (p. 224); Chris O'Rourke, '"What a Pretty Man – or Girl!": Male Cross-Dressing Performances in Early British Cinema, 1898–1918', *Gender & History*, 32.1 (2020), 86–107 (p. 90).

57. O'Rourke, 'What a Pretty Man'.

58. Missouri Review, 'You Wouldn't Know Her From a Man: Male Impersonators of the Victorian Music Halls', *The Missouri Review*, 41.4 (2018), 83–93; Senelick, *The Changing Room*, pp. 311–312;

Robin Maltz, 'Real Butch: The Performance/Performativity of Male Impersonation, Drag Kings, Passing as Male, and Stone Butch Realness', *Journal of Gender Studies*, 7.3 (1998), 273–286.

59. Senelick, *The Changing Room*, pp. 240–248; Davis, 'Slap On', p. 220. In a wonderfully queer piece of history, Jack Sheppard – hero of the trans novel *Confessions of the Fox* – was one of these characters usually played by AFAB actors: in fact, he was 'the most popular transvestite criminal of the Victorian stage' (Senelick, *The Changing Room*, p. 245).

60. Senelick, *The Changing Room*, p. 222.

61. Leslie Feinberg, *Transgender Warriors: Making History from Joan of Arc to Dennis Rodman* (Boston: Beacon Press, 1996), p. 95; Senelick, *The Changing Room*, pp. 282, 288.

62. Simon Joyce, 'Two Women Walk into a Theatre Bathroom: The Fanny and Stella Trials as Trans Narrative', *Victorian Review*, 44.1 (2018), 83–98; Senelick, *The Changing Room*, pp. 279–281.

63. Senelick, *The Changing Room*, pp. 304–306.

64. Ibid., p. 306.

65. Ibid., pp. 243, 256–257.

66. Ibid., pp. 252, 355.

67. Draskau, 'Prisoners in Petticoats', p. 194; Alison Oram, 'Cross-Dressing and Transgender', in Harry Cocks and Matt Houlbrook (eds.), *Palgrave Advances in the Modern History of Sexuality* (Basingstoke: Palgrave Macmillan, 2006), pp. 256–285 (p. 260); Wolfgang Theis, 'Grusswort', in Köhne, Lange and Vetter (eds.), *Mein Kamerad – die Diva*, p. 9.

68. Oram, for example, refers to 'the theatrical convention of returning at the end of the act in "appropriate" clothes, thereby revealing the temporary nature of the subversion' ('Cross-Dressing', p. 260) – something explicitly missing from the way female presentation was typically handled in camps like Knockaloe. See also Senelick, *The Changing Room*, p. 282.

69. Draskau, 'Prisoners in Petticoats', p. 189.

70. Magnus Hirschfeld, *The Sexual History of the World War* (New York: Falstaff Press, 1937), pp. 253–254.

71. Christoph Jahr, '"Mr Goodhind, the Prima Donna of Ruhleben": Theater- und Geschlechterrollen im "Englanderlager Ruhleben" 1914–1918' ['"Mr Goodhind, the Prima Donna of Ruhleben": Theatre and Gender Roles in the "English Prison Camp Ruhleben" 1914–1918'], in Köhne, Lange and Vetter (eds.), *Mein Kamerad – Die Diva*, pp. 91–99 (p. 97).
72. Vetter, 'Einführung', p. 11; see also 19–20.
73. Draskau, 'Prisoners in Petticoats', p. 196.
74. Reiss, 'Liebe, Sexualität und Männlichkeit', p. 18. See also Makepeace, 'Pinky Smith', pp. 83–84.
75. Rachamimov, 'Er war für die Gefangenen', p. 124.
76. Cohen-Portheim, *Time Stood Still*, pp. 126–129.
77. Ibid., pp. 128–129; emphasis added.
78. Panayi, 'Barbed Wire Disease', p. 109.
79. Ibid., p. 110.
80. Makepeace, 'Pinky Smith', pp. 87–88.
81. Cohen-Portheim, *Time Stood Still*, p. 135.
82. Ibid., pp. 129–130.
83. Draskau, 'Prisoners in Petticoats', pp. 195–196; Reiss, 'Liebe, Sexualität und Männlichkeit', p. 17; Vetter, 'Einführung', p. 22; Köhne and Lange, 'Mit Geschlechterrollen Spielen', p. 36; Panayi, 'Barbed Wire Disease', p. 121. With some commitment to *avoiding* acknowledging the intersection of performance with trans history, Senelick argues that performers who underwent medical transition in the mid-twentieth century also did so 'in order to enhance stage illusion' (*The Changing Room*, pp. 359–362).
84. Makepeace, 'Pinky Smith', p. 73; Panayi, 'Barbed Wire Disease', p. 121; Rachamimov, 'Camp Domesticity'.
85. Draskau, 'Prisoners in Petticoats', p. 193.
86. Jason Crouthamel, '"Wir Brauchen Gauze Manner": Cross-Dressing, Kameradschaft und Homosexualität im Deutschen Heer wahrend des Ersten Weltkriegs' ['"We Need Complete Men": Cross-dressing, Comradeship and Homosexuality in the German Army during the First World War'], in Köhne, Lange and Vetter (eds.), *Mein Kamerad – die Diva*, pp. 65–75 (p. 65).

87. Draskau, 'Prisoners in Petticoats', p. 198.

88. I've written about this at more length – with more reference to historiographical theory, and with a consideration of its implications for curatorial practice – in my article 'Gender Nonconformity and Military Internment: Curating the Knockaloe Slides', *Critical Military Studies*, 6.3–4 (2020), 323–340.

89. Lisa Z. Sigel, '"Best Love": Female Impersonation in the Great War', *Sexualities*, 19.1–2 (2016), 98–118 (pp. 110–113).

90. Rachamimov, 'Disruptive Comforts', p. 382.

91. 'kinky, adj. and n.', *OED Online*, 3rd edn., 2020 <https://www.oed.com/view/Entry/103575 > [accessed 23 September 2021]; Sigel, 'Best Love', pp. 112–113.

92. Richard von Krafft-Ebing, *Psychopathia Sexualis*, trans. by Franklin S. Klaf (New York: Stein & Day, 1965), pp. 203–204.

93. Krafft-Ebing, *Psychopathia*, pp. 282–283.

94. Ibid., p. 221.

95. Senelick, *The Changing Room*, p. 282.

96. Roberta Cowell, *Roberta Cowell's Story, By Herself* (London: Heinemann, 1954), p. 33.

97. Hirschfeld, *Sexual History*, pp. 254–255; see also Jahr, 'Mr Goodhind', p. 93.

98. Ibid., pp. 150–151.

99. Sascha Förster and Peter W. Marx, '"Das Kampfbereich war der Schauplatz der Damendarsteller": Spannungsverhaltnisse des Kölner Kriegstheaterarchivs' ['"The Battlefield was the Stage of the Female Impersonators": Tensions in the Cologne War Theatre Archives'], in Köhne, Lange and Vetter (eds.), *Mein Kamerad – die Diva*, pp. 77–89 (p. 83).

100. Rachamimov, 'Er war für die Gefangenen', pp. 118–119.

101. Cohen-Portheim, *Time Stood Still*, p. 78.

102. Rachamimov, 'Er war für die Gefangenen', p. 117.

103. Ibid., pp. 117, 120; see also Jahr, 'Mr Goodhind', p. 92; Linsey Robb and Juliette Pattinson, 'Becoming Visible: Gendering the Study of Men at War', in Robb and Pattinson (eds.), *Men, Masculinities and Male Culture*, pp. 1–22 (p. 4).

104. Senelick, *The Changing Room*, p. 340.

105. Ibid., pp. 226–230, 366.

106. Piatowski, 'Where's the T?', p. 75; Betty Luther Hillman, '"The Most Profoundly Revolutionary Act a Homosexual Can Engage In": Drag and the Politics of Gender Presentation in the San Francisco Gay Liberation Movement, 1964–1972', *Journal of the History of Sexuality*, 20.1 (2011), 153–181.

107. See David Valentine, *Imagining Transgender: An Ethnography of a Category* (Durham, N.C.: Duke University Press, 2007). See also Hillman, 'The Most Profoundly Revolutionary Act', pp. 158–159, 163.

108. Hillman, 'The Most Profoundly Revolutionary Act'; Susan Stryker, 'Transgender History, Homonormativity, and Disciplinarity', *Radical History Review*, 100 (2008), 145–157 (pp. 151–152).

109. Senelick, *The Changing Room*, pp. 363–364.

110. Riedel, 'A Brief History'.

111. Jacob Tobia, *Sissy: A Coming-Of-Gender Story* (New York: G.P. Putnam's Sons, 2020), p. 195; Caroline Framke, 'How RuPaul's Comments on Trans Women Led to a Drag Race Revolt — and a Rare Apology', *Vox*, 7 March 2018, <https://www.vox.com/culture/2018/3/6/17085244/rupaul-trans-women-drag-queens-interview-controversy> [accessed 19 February 2021]; Tim Mulkerin, 'We Asked 3 Trans Drag Performers About the Present and Future of Drag. Here's What They Said', *Mic*, 9 February 2018, <https://www.mic.com/articles/187649/we-asked-3-trans-drag-performers-about-the-present-and-future-of-drag-heres-what-they-said#.wDSGKoHzz> [accessed 3 September 2021]; Rogers, 'Drag as a Resource'. Not everyone is able to feel comfortable enough in drag scenes to explore their gender identity, though – see Eve Shapiro, 'The Impact of Race on Gender Transformation in a Drag Troupe', in Sally Hines and Tam Sanger (eds.), *Transgender Identities: Towards a Social Analysis of Gender Diversity* (Abingdon and New York: Routledge, 2010), pp. 153–168 (pp. 165–166).

112. Rogers, 'Drag as a Resource'.

113. Senelick, *The Changing Room*, pp. 356–357; Heidi M. Levitt, Francisco I. Surace, Emily E. Wheeler, Erik Maki, Darcy Alcántara, Melanie Cadet, Steven Cullipher, Sheila Desai, Gabriel Garza Sada, John Hite, Elena Kosterina, Sarah Krill, Charles Lui, Emily Manove, Ryan J. Martin and Courtney Ngai, 'Drag Gender: Experiences of Gender for Gay and Queer Men who Perform Drag', *Sex Roles*, 78 (2018), 367–384 (pp. 377–378).

114. Senelick, *The Changing Room*, p. 362.

115. O'Rourke, 'What a Pretty Man', pp. 96–97; Janes, 'Varsity Drag', p. 6; Hillman, 'The Most Profoundly Revolutionary Act', pp. 172–173; Levitt et al., 'Drag Gender', p. 368; Elizabeth Schewe, 'Serious Play: Drag, Transgender, and the Relationship Between Performance and Identity in the Life Writing of RuPaul and Kate Bornstein', *Biography*, 32.4 (2009), 670–695 (p. 672); Senelick, *The Changing Room*, p. 230. Equally, though, the dismissal of drag-driven comedies like *Mrs Brown's Boys* by the British establishment can be classist too – see Luna Morgana, 'Mammy's Class War Part 1: Taste & Class', *GossipGrrrl*, 14 June 2021, <https://gossipgrrrl.substack.com/p/mammys-class-war-part-1> [accessed 28 September 2021]; Luna Morgana, 'Mammys Class War Part 2: The Working Classes are Revolting But We're Not the Most Bigoted', *GossipGrrrl*, 22 July 2021, <https://gossipgrrrl.substack.com/p/mammys-class-war-part-2> [accessed 28 September 2021].

116. Levitt et al., 'Drag Gender', pp. 373–374; Hillman, 'The Most Profoundly Revolutionary Act', pp. 153, 156–159, 163–165.

117. Riedel, 'A Brief History'.

118. O'Rourke, 'What a Pretty Man', p. 94; Peter Holland, 'The Play of Eros: Paradoxes of Gender in English Pantomime', *New Theatre Quarterly*, 13.51 (1997), 195–204 (p. 202); Children's Theatre Company, 'Not Your Punchline: The Need to Transform the Transphobic Panto Tradition', *OffBook*, 7 December 2020, <https://offbook.childrenstheatre.org/not-your-punchline-the-need-to-transform-the-transphobic-panto-tradition-6aa3f5efeb3a> [accessed 28 September 2021]; Rich Johnston, 'A Very British Flavour of Transphobia to Consider', *Bleeding Cool*, 27 June 2020,

<https://bleedingcool.com/pop-culture/very-british-transpho-bia> [accessed 28 September 2021].

119. Germaine Greer, *The Whole Woman* (London: Doubleday, 1999).

120. Sophie Labelle, cartoonist, *Twitter*, 16 May 2019, <https://twitter.com/assignedmale/status/1129052142910758913?lang=en> [accessed 28 September 2021].

121. See, for example, isshehungry, *Instagram*, <https://www.insta-gram.com/isshehungry> [accessed 28 September 2021]; Liana Satenstein, 'Salvia Is the New Age Instagram Drag Star With a Fantastical Take on Reality', *Vogue*, 27 February 2018, <https://www.vogue.com/vogueworld/article/salvjiia-personality-on-instagram-to-know> [accessed 28 September 2021]; justanneal-ien, *Instagram*, <https://www.instagram.com/justannealien> [accessed 28 September 2021].

122. Mulkerin, 'We Asked 3 Trans Drag Performers'.

123. Senelick, *The Changing Room*, p. 434.

124. Draskau, 'Prisoners in Petticoats', p. 199; Rachamimov, 'Er war für die Gefangenen', pp. 115–116.

125. Cohen-Portheim, *Time Stood Still*, p. 34; Corkill, 'Knockaloe', p. 72.

126. Ibid., p. 112.

127. Ibid., p. 133; see also Rachamimov, 'Er war für die Gefangenen', p. 125.

128. Draskau, 'Prisoners in Petticoats', p. 199.

129. Ibid., p. 196.

130. Cohen-Portheim, *Time Stood Still*, p. 132.

131. Laura Doan, *Disturbing Practices: History, Sexuality, and Women's Experience of Modern War* (Chicago: University of Chicago Press, 2013), p. 129. See also Rachamimov, 'Camp Domesticity', p. 291; Robb and Pattinson, 'Becoming Visible'; Karen Hagemann and Stefanie Schüler-Springorum, 'Preface', in Karen Hagemann and Stefanie Schüler-Springorum (eds.), *Home/Front: The Military, War, and Gender in Twentieth-Century Germany* (Oxford: Berg, 2002), pp. ix-xii.

Chapter 4

1. Gary P. Leupp, 'Capitalism and Homosexuality in Eighteenth-Century Japan', *Historical Reflections / Réflexions Historiques*, 33.1 (2007), 135–152 (p. 138).
2. For more on Edo's sex industry, see Yasuko Sato, 'Early Modern Prostitutes, Concubines, and Mistresses (Review)', *Journal of Women's History*, 28.2 (2016), 156–165.
3. Sato, 'Early Modern Prostitutes', p. 157; Rosina Buckland, *Shunga: Erotic Art in Japan* (London: British Museum, 2010), p. 15.
4. Buckland, *Shunga*, p. 15.
5. Sato, 'Early Modern Prostitutes', p. 157; Mark McLelland, 'Living More "Like Oneself"', *Journal of Bisexuality*, 3.3–4 (2003), 203–230 (p. 206).
6. Hubert C. Kennedy, 'The "Third Sex" Theory of Karl Heinrich Ulrichs', *Journal of Homosexuality*, 6.1/2 (1980/81), 103–111 (p. 105).
7. Kennedy, 'The "Third Sex" Theory', p. 104.
8. Richard von Krafft-Ebing, *Psychopathia Sexualis*, trans. by Charles Gilbert Chaddock (Philadelphia: F.A. Davis; London: F.J. Rebman, 1894), p. 280.
9. Joseph Gamble, 'Toward a Trans Philology', *Journal for Early Modern Cultural Studies*, 19.4 (2019), 26–44 (p. 32).
10. Havelock Ellis, *Studies in the Psychology of Sex, Vol. 1, Sexual Inversion* (London: The University Press, 1897), pp. 94–97.
11. Meg-John Barker and Jules Scheele, *Sexuality: A Graphic Guide* (London: Icon Books, 2021), p. 18.
12. Jules Gill-Peterson, *Histories of the Transgender Child* (Minneapolis: University of Minnesota Press, 2018), p. 115. For more on the treatment of intersex children, and the way they have been and continue to be forcibly assigned a binary gender, see Chapter 5.
13. Kennedy, 'The "Third Sex" Theory', pp. 105–106.
14. Krafft-Ebing, *Psychopathia*, pp. 279–280.
15. Kennedy, 'The "Third Sex" Theory', p. 105.

16. Krafft-Ebing, *Psychopathia*, pp. 197–216; see also Melanie A. Taylor, '"The Masculine Soul Heaving in the Female Bosom": Theories of Inversion and *The Well of Loneliness*', *Journal of Gender Studies*, 7.3 (1998), 287–296 (p. 289). Taylor points out that, while sexologists disagreed about the extent to which inversion manifested itself physically, the idea proved hard to shake off.

17. Ibid., pp. 222, 191.

18. Ibid., pp. 222–223, 197.

19. Ibid., pp. 223, 202–204.

20. Ibid., pp. 223, 216–220.

21. See Jay Prosser, 'Transsexuals and the Transsexologists: Inversion and the Emergence of Transsexual Subjectivity', in Lucy Bland and Laura Doan (eds.), *Sexology in Culture: Labelling Bodies and Desires* (Cambridge: Polity Press, 1998), pp. 116–131 (pp. 116–117); and see Gill-Peterson, *Histories of the Transgender Child*, pp. 15, 60, on how this fact necessarily complicates our research into trans history.

22. Ben Vincent, *Transgender Health: A Practitioner's Guide to Binary and Non-Binary Trans Patient Care* (London: Jessica Kingsley Publishers, 2018), p. 19.

23. Kennedy, 'The "Third Sex" Theory', p. 109; David Valentine, *Imagining Transgender: An Ethnography of a Category* (Durham, N.C.: Duke University Press, 2007), p. 42.

24. Jules Rylan, 'Non-Binary Lesbians Have Always Existed', *Medium*, 16 October 2020, <https://radiantbutch.medium.com/non-binary-lesbians-have-always-existed-7db6b9e7e646> [accessed 10 March 2021].

25. Chris Waters, 'Havelock Ellis, Sigmund Freud and the State: Discourses of Homosexual Identity in Interwar Britain', in Bland and Doan (eds.), *Sexology in Culture*, pp. 165–179. For a vivid and brilliant fictional depiction of how some people embraced inversion as an identity, see Juliet Jacques, 'A Wo/Man of No Importance', in *Variations* (London: Influx Press, 2021).

26. Magnus Hirschfeld, *Transvestites: The Erotic Drive to Cross Dress*, trans. by Michael A. Lombardi-Nash (Buffalo: Prometheus Books, 1991; first published 1910), p. 129.

27. Gill-Peterson, *Histories of the Transgender Child*, pp. 80–83, 142; Valentine, *Imagining Transgender*, pp. 57–58.

28. Prosser, 'Transsexuals and the Transsexologists', esp. p. 118.

29. Leah DeVun, 'Erecting Sex: Hermaphrodites and the Medieval Science of Surgery', *Osiris*, 30.1 (2015), 17–37 (p. 22); William Turner, *A Compleat History of the Most Remarkable Providences* (London: Printed for John Dunton, 1697), sig. 5B3ʳ; Nathaniel Wanley, *The Wonders of the Little World* (London: Printed for T. Basset, R. Cheswel, J. Wright, and T. Sawbridge, 1673), sig. H3ʳ.

30. Robert Mills, *Seeing Sodomy in the Middle Ages* (Chicago: University of Chicago Press, 2015), pp. 81–83, 95.

31. Rictor Norton, *Mother Clap's Molly House*, rev. edn. (Stroud: Chalford Press, 2006); Rictor Norton, 'The Raid on Mother Clap's Molly House, 1776', *Homosexuality in Eighteenth-Century England: A Sourcebook*, <http://rictornorton.co.uk/eighteen/mother.htm> [accessed 5 July 2021]; Rictor Norton, ed., 'The Mollies Club, 1709–10', *Homosexuality in Eighteenth-Century England: A Sourcebook*, 1 December 1999, updated 16 June 2008, <http://www.rictornorton.co.uk/eighteen/nedward.htm> [accessed 16 July 2021].

32. Giovanni Vitiello, 'The Dragon's Whim: Ming and Qing Homoerotic Tales from "The Cut Sleeve"', *T'oung Pao*, 78.4/5 (1992), 341–372 (pp. 360–361).

33. Jen Manion, *Female Husbands: A Trans History* (Cambridge: Cambridge University Press, 2021). For some particularly good examples of how sexuality intersected with the gender of 'female husbands', see pp. 9, 55, 227–228.

34. Hunt Janin, *The Pursuit of Learning in the Islamic World, 610–2003* (Jefferson: McFarland, 2005), p. 83.

35. Hadas Hirsch, 'Clothing and Colours in Early Islam: Adornment (Aesthetics), Symbolism and Differentiation', *Anthropology of the Middle East*, 15.1 (2020), 99–114 (p. 102).

36. Hirsch, 'Clothing and Colours', pp. 106–107.

37. Everett K. Rowson, 'The Effeminates of Early Medina', *Journal of the American Oriental Society*, 111.4 (1991), 671–693 (pp. 672–673).

38. Franklin Lewis, 'Sexual Occidentation: The Politics of Conversion, Christian-Love and Boy-Love in 'Attār', *Iranian Studies*, 42.5 (2009), 693–723; see also Jessica Hinchy, *Governing Gender and Sexuality in Colonial India: The Hijra, c.1850–1900* (Cambridge: Cambridge University Press, 2019), pp. 19–20.

39. Rowson, 'The Effeminates'.

40. Ibid., pp. 678, 681.

41. Ibid., p. 677.

42. Ibid., pp. 675–676, 680.

43. Ibid., pp. 691–692.

44. Ibid., p. 681.

45. Ibid., p. 693; Hinchy, *Governing Gender and Sexuality*, pp. 81–82.

46. Ibid., p. 685.

47. Afsaneh Najmabadi, *Women with Mustaches and Men Without Beards: Gender and Sexual Anxieties of Iranian Modernity* (Berkeley: University of California Press, 2005), p. 16.

48. E.g. Stephen O. Murray and Will Roscoe, 'Africa and African Homosexualities: An Introduction', in Stephen O. Murray and Will Roscoe (eds.), *Boy-Wives and Female-Husbands: Studies in African Homosexualities* (New York: Palgrave Macmillan, 1998) pp. 1–16; Elyse Semerdijan, ' "Because he is so Tender and Pretty": Sexual Deviance and Heresy in Eighteenth-Century Aleppo', *Journal for the Study of Race, Nation and Culture*, 18.2 (2012), 175–199 (p. 186).

49. Joshua S. Mostow, 'Wakashū as a Third Gender and Gender Ambiguity Through the Edo Period', in Joshua S. Mostow, Asato Ikeda and Ryoko Matsuba (eds.), *A Third Gender: Beautiful Youths in Japanese Edo-Period Prints and Paintings (1600–1868)* (Toronto: Royal Ontario Museum, 2016), pp. 49–70 (p. 38); Laurence Senelick, *The Changing Room: Sex, Drag and Theatre* (London and New York: Routledge, 2000), pp. 76–78.

50. Buckland, *Shunga*, p. 42; Gregory M. Pflugfelder, 'The Nation-State, the Age/Gender System, and the Reconstitution of Erotic Desire in Nineteenth-Century Japan', *The Journal of Asian Studies*, 71.4 (2012), 963–974 (pp. 966–967); Mori Rie, 'Nanshoku

Ōkagami ni Miru Dansei Fukushoku no Hyōgen: Wakashū no Furisode o Chūshin ni' ('The Expression of Male Clothes in *The Great Mirror of Male Love*: Focusing on the Wakashū Furisode'), *Bigaku*, 56.4 (2006), 41–54.

51. Asa Splinter, 'Japan's Pre-Modern Images of Intersexuality' (unpublished master's thesis, Universiteit Leiden, 2019–2020), pp. 22–23.

52. Pflugfelder, 'The Nation-State', p. 963.

53. Pflugfelder, 'The Nation-State', esp. p. 966; Joshua S. Mostow, 'The Gender of Wakashū and the Grammar of Desire', in Norman Bryson, Maribeth Graybill and Joshua S. Mostow (eds.), *Gender and Power in the Japanese Visual Field* (Honolulu: University of Hawaii Press, 2003), pp. 49–70 (p. 53).

54. Pflugfelder, 'The Nation-State', pp. 969–970.

55. Pflugfelder, 'The Nation-State', p. 968.

56. Leupp, 'Capitalism and Homosexuality', pp. 143–155; Senelick, *The Changing Room*, pp. 76–77.

57. Mostow, 'Gender of Wakashū', esp. pp. 50, 53–54.

58. Pflugfelder, 'The Nation-State', pp. 966–967; see Mostow, 'Gender of Wakashū', for analysis of an example of *shudō* literature.

59. Mostow, 'Gender of Wakashū', p. 49; Pflugfelder, 'The Nation-State', p. 967.

60. Mostow, 'Gender of Wakashū'; Ian Buruma, 'The "Indescribable Fragrance" of Youths', *New York Review of Books*, 11 May 2017, <https://www.nybooks.com/articles/2017/05/11/japanese-edo-indescribable-fragrance-youths> [accessed 16 July 2021].

61. Asato Ikeda, 'Curating "A Third Gender: Beautiful Youths in Japanese Prints"', *TSQ: Transgender Studies Quarterly* 5.4 (2018), 638–648 (p. 640); Pflugfelder, 'The Nation-State', p. 968.

62. Joshua S. Mostow, 'Utagawa *Shunga*, Kuki's "Chic" and the Construction of a National Erotics in Japan,' in *Performing "Nation": Gender Politics in Literature, Theater, and the Visual Arts of China and Japan, 1880–1940*, ed. by Doris Croissant, Catherine Vance Yeh and Joshua S. Mostow (Leiden and Boston: Brill, 2008),

pp. 383–424 (pp. 398–99, 403); Mostow, 'Wakashū as a Third Gender', p. 38; Senelick, pp. 77–78.

63. Paul Berry, 'Rethinking "Shunga": The Interpretation of Sexual Imagery of the Edo Period', *Archives of Asian Art* 54 (2004), 7–22 (p. 11).

64. Pflugfelder, 'The Nation-State', pp. 970–972.

65. Gregory M. Pflugfelder, *Cartographies of Desire: Male–Male Sexuality in Japanese Discourse, 1600–1950* (Berkeley and London: University of California Press, 1999), pp. 41–42, 268–269; Mostow, 'Gender of Wakashū', pp. 53–54, 68–69.

66. Leupp, 'Capitalism and Homosexuality', pp. 145–146.

67. Ibid., p. 147.

68. Ibid., p. 144.

69. Ikeda, 'Curating "A Third Gender"', p. 644.

70. Hayakawa Monta, 'Who Were the Audiences for Shunga?', *Japan Review*, 26 (2013), 17–36 (p. 23).

71. Anne Walthall, 'Masturbation and Discourse on Female Sexual Practices in Early Modern Japan', *Gender & History*, 21.1 (2009), 1–18 (p. 4).

72. Nicholas Bornoff, *Pink Samurai: The Pursuit and Politics of Sex in Japan* (London: Grafton, 1991), pp. 156–157. Clearly, the history of dildos is far from just a Japanese phenomenon: if you'd like to know more about their history in Europe, one fun place to start is Mills, *Seeing Sodomy*, pp. 83, 109–112.

73. Walthall, 'Masturbation', p. 5; Bornoff, *Pink Samurai*, p. 157.

74. Alfred Haft, 'Affirming the Life Erotic: Yoshida Hanbei's *Koshoku Kinmo Zui* (1686)', *Japan Review*, 26 (2013), 99–116 (p. 107); Walthall, 'Masturbation', p. 3. For an example of a sex toy catalogue, see British Museum, 'Keichū nyo'etsu warai-dōgu 閨中女悦笑道具 (Sex Toys for Women's Pleasure in the Bedroom) / Tō: harigata 冬: 張形 (Winter: Dildo)', museum number 2012,3051.4, <https://www.britishmuseum.org/research/collection_online/collection_object_details.aspx?objectId=3509620&partId=1&images=true> [accessed 16 July 2021].

75. British Museum, 'Fumi no kiyogaki 婦美の清書き (Neat Version

of a Love Letter (or Pure Drawings of Female Beauty))', museum number 1972,0724,0.3, image 3, <https://www.britishmuseum. org/research/collection_online/collection_object_details. aspx?objectId=779979&partId=1> [accessed 16 July 2021].

76. Allen Hockley, '*Shunga: Sex and Pleasure in Japanese Art*, edited by Timothy Clark et al., and *Shunga: Sex and Humor in Japanese Art and Literature*, edited by C. Andrew Gerstle and Timothy Clark, and *Shunga: Erotic Art in Japan*, by Rosina Buckland (review)', *Monumenta Nipponica*, 69.1 (2014), 132–136 (p. 135).

77. Berry, 'Rethinking "Shunga"', p. 9.

78. Allen Hockley, 'Review: Shunga: Function, Context, Methodology', *Monumenta Nipponica*, 55.2 (2000), 257–269 (p. 261); Hayakawa, 'Who Were the Audiences for Shunga?', pp. 18–19.

79. C. Andrew Gerstle and Timothy Clark, 'Introduction', *Japan Review*, 26 (2013), 3–14 (p. 3); Laura Moretti, 'The Distribution and Circulation of Erotic Prints and Books in the Edo Period', in Timothy Clark, C. Andrew Gerstle, Ishigami Aki and Akiko Yano (eds.), *Shunga: Sex and Pleasure in Japanese Art* (London: British Museum Press, 2013), pp. 300–317 (p. 300).

80. Gerstle and Clark, 'Introduction', p. 3; Ellis Tinios, 'Japanese Illustrated Erotic Books in the Context of Commercial Publishing, 1660–1868', *Japan Review*, 26 (2013), 83–96 (p. 85); Walthall, 'Masturbation', p. 1.

81. Walthall, 'Masturbation', pp. 3–5; Mostow, 'Gender of Wakashū', p. 69; see also Liang Shi, 'Mirror Rubbing: A Critical Genealogy of Pre-Modern Chinese Female Same-Sex Eroticism', *Journal of Homosexuality*, 60.5 (2013), 750–772 (p. 754), for a similar Chinese example.

82. Walthall, 'Masturbation', p. 4.

83. Shunga were produced by Japanese people, so this isn't the case here, but sometimes the depiction of concubines in closed compounds having sex with each other was also a racist, Orientalising fantasy: see Semerdijan, 'Because he is so Tender and Pretty', p. 182.

84. Fred G. Notehelfer (ed.), *Japan Through American Eyes: The Journal*

Of Francis Hall, 1859–1866 (Boulder: Westview Press, 2001), 26/11 /1859.

85. Walthall, 'Masturbation'.
86. Hayakawa, 'Who Were the Audiences for Shunga?', pp. 19–21.
87. Timothy Clark and C. Andrew Gerstle, 'What Was *Shunga*?', in Clark, Gerstle, Ishigami and Yano (eds.) *Shunga*, pp. 16–33 (p. 30).
88. Hayakawa, 'Who Were the Audiences for Shunga?', p. 19.
89. Victoria & Albert Museum Archive, Nominal File 'Bowles, R.R.', MA/1/B2095.
90. Walthall, 'Masturbation', pp. 5–7; Gary P. Leupp, 'The Floating World is Wide: Some Suggested Approaches to Researching Female Homosexuality in Tokugawa Japan', *Thamyris: Mythmaking from Past to Present*, 5 (1998), 1–40 (pp. 26–27).
91. Walthall, 'Masturbation', pp. 7–10.
92. Leupp, 'Capitalism and Homosexuality', p. 151.
93. James Welker, 'Toward a History of "Lesbian History" in Japan', *Culture, Theory and Critique*, 58.2 (2017), 147–165 (p. 154).
94. For two different perspectives on how people using dildos can disrupt gender, see Walthall, 'Masturbation', p. 5; Peter Lehman, 'The Prosthetic Penis and the Trans Penis: Changing Representations of and Cultural Discourses About the Penis', *Studies in Gender and Sexuality*, 21.4 (2020), 285–290 (pp. 287–288). For trans people's perspectives on how prosthetics can disrupt or affirm their experience of gender during sex, see Paul B. Preciado, *Testo Junkie: Sex, Drugs, and Biopolitics in the Pharmacopornographic Era*, trans. by Bruce Benderson (New York: Feminist Press, 2013), pp. 88, 328–329; Chris Straayer, 'Trans Men's Stealth Aesthetics: Navigating Penile Prosthetics and "Gender Fraud"', *Journal of Visual Culture*, 19.2 (2020), 255–271 (pp. 256–262); Tristan K. Martin and Deb Coolhart, '"Because Your Dysphoria Gets in the Way of You . . . It Affects Everything": The Mental, Physical, and Relational Aspects of Navigating Body Dysphoria and Sex for Trans Masculine People', *Sexual and Relationship Therapy* (2019), 1–18 (pp. 9–13).
95. Valentine, *Imagining Transgender*, pp. 51–52.

96. Ibid., pp. 4–5, 15–18, 61–62; Mills, *Seeing Sodomy*, pp. 88–89.
97. See, for example, Murray and Roscoe (eds.), *Boy-Wives and Female Husbands*, pp. 1–16, 19–21, 111–124; Semerdijan, 'Because he is so Tender and Pretty', p. 186; Stephen O. Murray, 'Gender-Mixing Roles, Gender-Crossing Roles, and the Sexuality of Transgendered Roles', *Reviews in Anthropology*, 31.4 (2002), 291–308 (pp. 302–303).
98. Valentine, *Imagining Transgender*; see also Shon Faye, *The Transgender Issue: An Argument for Justice* (London: Penguin Books, 2021), pp. 208–209.
99. Afsaneh Najmabadi, *Professing Selves: Transsexuality and Same-Sex Desire in Contemporary Iran* (Durham, N.C.: Duke University Press, 2013), p. 251.
100. Deborah P. Amory, 'Mashoga, Mabasha, and Magei: "Homosexuality" on the East African Coast', in Murray and Roscoe (eds.), *Boy-Wives and Female Husbands*, pp. 65–84.
101. Valentine, *Imagining Transgender*, pp. 42, 46.
102. Ibid., p. 46; Lillian Faderman, *Odd Girls and Twilight Lovers: A History of Lesbian Life in Twentieth-Century America* (New York: Columbia University Press, 1991), p. 180; Robin Maltz, 'Real Butch: The Performance/Performativity of Male Impersonation, Drag Kings, Passing as Male, and Stone Butch Realness', *Journal of Gender Studies*, 7.3 (1998), 273–286 (p. 277).
103. For more on this, see also Betty Luther Hillman, '"The Most Profoundly Revolutionary Act a Homosexual Can Engage In": Drag and the Politics of Gender Presentation in the San Francisco Gay Liberation Movement, 1964–1972', *Journal of the History of Sexuality*, 20.1 (2011), 153–181; Alison Oram, 'Cross-Dressing and Transgender', in Harry Cocks and Matt Houlbrook (eds.), *Palgrave Advances in the Modern History of Sexuality* (Basingstoke: Palgrave Macmillan, 2006), pp. 256–285 (pp. 272–273).
104. Some anti-trans campaigners try to undermine the genders of lesbian trans women by arguing that they've confused gender with sexuality: that they're not really trans, they're just aroused by the idea of themselves as women. For an explanation of why this argument and the theory that underlies it ('autogynephilia') is

inaccurate and unscientific, see Julia Serano, 'Autogynephilia: A Scientific Review, Feminist Analysis, and Alternative "Embodiment Fantasies" Model', *The Sociological Review Monographs*, 68.4 (2020), 763–778. For other examples of sexuality as one among many motivations for social or medical transition, see Najmabadi, *Professing Selves*, p. 285; Martin and Coolhart, 'Because Your Dysphoria Gets in the Way', p. 7.

105. For a good discussion of 'gender fraud' prosecutions and the assumptions behind them, see Straayer, 'Trans Men's Stealth Aesthetics'; CN Lester, *Trans Like Me: Conversations for All of Us* (London: Virago, 2017), pp. 130–132.

106. For a more detailed discussion of this, see Ynda Jas, 'Sexuality in a Non-Binary World: Redefining and Expanding the Linguistic Repertoire', *Journal of the International Network for Sexual Ethics and Politics*, 8 (2020), 71–92. See also Faye, *The Transgender Issue*, p. 211; Susan Stryker, 'Transgender History, Homonormativity, and Disciplinarity', *Radical History Review*, 100 (2008), 145–157 (pp. 145–147); Leslie Feinberg, *Transgender Warriors: Making History from Joan of Arc to Dennis Rodman* (Boston: Beacon Press, 1996), p. 92.

107. For more detail on this argument, and a historical perspective on why it's overly simplistic and erases the experience of trans people of colour, see Gill-Peterson, *Histories of the Transgender Child*, pp. 163–193.

108. Rylan, 'Non-Binary Lesbians'; Maltz, 'Real Butch', pp. 279–280.

109. See Maltz, 'Real Butch', pp. 277, 279–280.

110. Gill-Peterson, *Histories of the Transgender Child*, pp. 170, 175–176, 187–188, 191–192.

111. Rylan, 'Non-Binary Lesbians'; Faye, *The Transgender Issue*, p. 213; Amy Tooth Murphy, 'Butch on Butch: Historicising Butch Identity via Oral History', University of Plymouth, 10 March 2021. I'm really excited about Amy's newest project, a trans-inclusive oral history of butch identity: it promises to be an essential contribution to this discussion.

112. Gill-Peterson, *Histories of the Transgender Child*, p. 166.

113. Radclyffe Hall, *The Well of Loneliness* (London: Virago, 1987), p. 204; see also Taylor, 'The Masculine Soul', pp. 288–289.

Chapter 5

1. H.R. McIlwaine (ed.), *Minutes of the Council & General Court of Colonial Virginia, 1622–1632, 1670–1676, with Notes & Excerpts from Original Council & General Court Records, into 1683, Now Lost* (Richmond: The Colonial Press, Everett Waddey Co., 1924), pp. 194–195.

2. Kathryn Wichelns, 'From *The Scarlet Letter* to Stonewall: Reading the 1629 Thomas(ine) Hall Case, 1978–2009', *Early American Studies*, 12.3 (2014), 500–523 (p. 512). Wichelns's article is a great overview of the different ways in which Thomas(ine)'s case has been interpreted over the past few decades, and how the changing political and academic climate around queer identities has shaped those different interpretations.

3. Elizabeth Reis, 'Impossible Hermaphrodites: Intersex in America, 1620–1960', *The Journal of American History*, 92.2 (2005), 411–441 (p. 419).

4. The manuscript is *Virginia General Court, 1622–29, Cases, with Minutes*, ser. 8, vol. 15, Thomas Jefferson Papers, Library of Congress. You can see a scan at <https://www.loc.gov/resource/mtj8.064_0002_0573/?sp=496> [accessed 27 April 2021]: the Hall case is images 495–497. As Wichelns describes the damage: 'A small portion at the top right corner of the original parchment page, containing a few words . . . is missing'; 'it seems . . . likely that the section was lost because of normal wear; surrounding pages, and many others in the volume that contains these minutes, show similar damage' ('From *The Scarlet Letter* to Stonewall', pp. 506–507). On Thomas(ine)'s lack of access to (or expectation of) privacy, see Wichelns, 'From *The Scarlet Letter* to Stonewall', p. 505.

5. On the origin of the word 'intersex', see Iain Morland, 'Intersex',

TSQ: Transgender Studies Quarterly, 1.1–2 (2014), 111–115 (p. 111). On the conflict over the terminology of 'intersex' versus 'disorders of sex development', see Georgiann Davis, *Contesting Intersex: The Dubious Diagnosis* (New York: New York University Press, 2015), pp. 20–26, 44–46, 145–146.

6. Ben Vincent, *Transgender Health: A Practitioner's Guide to Binary and Non-Binary Trans Patient Care* (London: Jessica Kingsley Publishers, 2018), pp. 18–19; Melanie Blackless, Anthony Charuvastra, Amanda Derryck, Anne Fausto-Sterling, Karl Lauzanne and Ellen Leeb, 'How Sexually Dimorphic Are We? Review and Synthesis', *American Journal of Human Biology*, 12 (2000), 151–166.

7. Cristan Williams, 'The Ontological Woman: A History of Deauthentication, Dehumanization, and Violence', *The Sociological Review Monographs*, 68.4 (2020), 718–734 (p. 720); Claire Ainsworth, 'Sex Redefined', *Nature*, 518.7539 (2015), 288–291; Sally Hines, 'Sex Wars and (Trans)Gender Panics: Identity and Body Politics in Contemporary UK Feminism', *The Sociological Review Monographs*, 68.4 (2020), 699–717 (pp. 708–710).

8. *Gods Handy-Worke in Wonders Miraculously Shewen Upon Two Women, Lately Delivered of Two Monsters* (London: Printed [by George Purslowe] for I. W[right], 1615), sig. A3^v.

9. Ibid., sig. A4^r.

10. See Gabrielle M. W. Bychowski, Howard Chiang, Jack Halberstam, Jacob Lau, Kathleen P. Long, Marcia Ochoa, C. Riley Snorton, Leah DeVun and Zeb Tortorici, '"Trans*historicities": A Roundtable Discussion', *TSQ: Transgender Studies Quarterly*, 5.4 (2018), 658–685 (p. 671). For another example of this in an early modern text, see Robert Basset, *Curiosities: or The Cabinet of Nature* (London: Printed by N. and I. Okes, 1637), sig. C2^r.

11. Reis, 'Impossible Hermaphrodites', pp. 415–416; John Bulwer, *Anthropometamorphosis* (London: Printed by William Hunt, 1653), sigs. 3L2^v-3L3^v.

12. Bulwer, *Anthropometamorphosis*, sigs. 3L3^r-3L3^v.

13. Ibid., sigs. 3E4^r, 3L2^v; Nathaniel Wanley, *The Wonders of the Little*

World (London: Printed for T. Basset . . ., R. Cheswel . . ., J. Wright . . ., and T. Sawbridge . . ., 1673), sig. H2^v.

14. E.g. see Bulwer, *Anthropometamorphosis*, sigs. Z2^r-Z2^v; Leah DeVun, *The Shape of Sex: Nonbinary Gender from Genesis to the Renaissance* (New York: Columbia University Press, 2021).

15. Jenny C. Mann writes about the way the early modern medical discourse around intersex bodies encouraged this visual scrutiny, and how poetic discourse differed from this, in her article, 'How to Look at a Hermaphrodite in Early Modern England', *Studies in English Literature, 1500–1900*, 46.1 (2006), 67–91 (pp. 70–71).

16. See Davis, *Contesting Intersex*, p. 39, for more on how this issue united the early intersex rights movement.

17. Davis, *Contesting Intersex*, pp. 42, 45–46; see also pp. 3–4 for her personal testimony of the impact of this surgery and of the lies which intersex children are often told about their bodies.

18. Leah DeVun, 'Erecting Sex: Hermaphrodites and the Medieval Science of Surgery', *Osiris*, 30.1 (2015), 17–37 (p. 22); Lanfranco da Milano, 'Lanfranci Maioris', in *Cyrurgia Guidonis de Cauliaco: et Cyrurgia Bruni, Theodorici, Rogerij, Rolandij, Bertapalie, Lanfranci* (Venice, 1498), fol. 198^v; James Parsons, *A Mechanical and Critical Enquiry into the Nature of Hermaphrodites* (London: Printed for J. Walthoe, 1741), sigs. G7^v, B6^r; Onni Gust, 'Colonialism and the Idea of "Sex" in Eighteenth-Century Enlightenment Thought', University of York, 3 November 2020.

19. Davis, *Contesting Intersex*, pp. 7, 21, 70–83; Jules Gill-Peterson, *Histories of the Transgender Child* (Minneapolis: University of Minnesota Press, 2018), p. 118; Jemima Repo, 'The Biopolitical Birth of Gender: Social Control, Hermaphroditism, and the New Sexual Apparatus', *Alternatives: Global, Local, Political*, 38.3 (2013), 228–244 (p. 234); Veronica Sanz, 'No Way Out of the Binary: A Critical History of the Scientific Production of Sex', *Signs: Journal of Women in Culture and Society*, 43.1 (2017), 1–27 (p. 17).

20. Gill-Peterson, *Histories of the Transgender Child*.

21. Ibid., p. 16.

22. David Andrew Griffiths, 'Diagnosing Sex: Intersex Surgery and

'Sex Change' in Britain 1930–1955', *Sexualities*, 21.3 (2018), 476–495 (p. 481); Gill-Peterson, *Histories of the Transgender Child*, pp. 59, 63.

23. Roberta Cowell, *Roberta Cowell's Story, By Herself* (London: Heinemann, 1954), p. 31.

24. Ibid., pp. 36–37.

25. Ibid., p. 36.

26. Griffiths, 'Diagnosing Sex', p. 484. Zoe Playdon suggests that Cowell may also have started taking oestrogen before approaching a doctor – see *The Hidden Case of Ewan Forbes: The Transgender Trial that Threatened to Upend the British Establishment* (London: Bloomsbury, 2021), pp. 84–84. Playdon's book is a brilliant piece of investigative journalism as well as a great history of how trans rights and trans medical care developed in the UK in the 20th and 21st centuries; see e.g. pp. 94–95 for more information on how trans people in mid-twentieth-century Britain changed (or failed to change) their birth certificates.

27. Ibid., p. 51.

28. Ibid., p. 2.

29. Ibid., p. 5.

30. Ibid., p. 7.

31. Ibid., pp. 41–42.

32. Ibid., pp. 44–45.

33. Ibid., p. 52.

34. Ibid., p. 63.

35. Repo, 'The Biopolitical Birth of Gender', p. 232. See also Kadji Amin, 'Glands, Eugenics, and Rejuvenation in *Man into Woman*: A Biopolitical Genealogy of Transsexuality', *TSQ: Transgender Studies Quarterly*, 5.4 (2018), 589–605 (pp. 592–600), for an account of how these ideas are expressed in early-twentieth-century trans woman Lili Elbe's memoir *Man into Woman: An Authentic Record of a Change of Sex*.

36. Cowell, *Roberta Cowell's Story*, p. 42.

37. Ibid., p. 5.

38. Ibid., p. 43.

39. Ibid., p. 60.
40. Ibid., p. 43.
41. Ibid., p. 47; see also Playdon, *The Hidden Case of Ewan Forbes*, p. 45.
42. Ibid., p. 41.
43. Ibid., pp. 64–65.
44. Ibid., pp. 65, 44.
45. Ibid., p. 68.
46. Ibid., pp. 48, 51.
47. Ibid., pp. 67–70.
48. Ibid., p. 70.
49. Griffiths, 'Diagnosing Sex', p. 483.
50. Ibid., p. 484.
51. Ellis Martin and Zach Ozma (eds.), *We Both Laughed In Pleasure: The Selected Diaries of Lou Sullivan, 1961–1991* (New York: Nightboat Books, 2019), p. 338.
52. Gill-Peterson, *Histories of the Transgender Child*, pp. 16, 80.
53. Cowell, *Roberta Cowell's Story*, p. 64–65.
54. Playdon, *The Hidden Case of Ewan Forbes*, pp. 1–23.
55. Ibid., pp. 211–212
56. Ibid., pp. 150–151, 155, 173–175. Lesley-Anne Barnes Macfarlane, 'Gender Identity and Scottish Law: the Legal Response to Transsexuality', *Edinburgh Law Review*, 11.2 (2007), 162–186 (p. 170–171).
57. Macfarlane, 'Gender Identity and Scottish Law', pp. 169, 171.
58. Playdon, *The Hidden Case of Ewan Forbes*, p. 175.
59. See Playdon, *The Hidden Case of Ewan Forbes*, esp. pp. 52, 72, 130, 199.
60. Playdon, *The Hidden Case of Ewan Forbes*.
61. Ibid., pp. 225–227, 231, 277.
62. Ibid., p. 275.
63. Macfarlane, 'Gender Identity and Scottish Law', p. 169.
64. Jordy Rosenberg, *Confessions of the Fox* (London: Atlantic Books, 2018), pp. 148–150, nn. 7–8; p. 263, n. 2; p. 287, n. 2.
65. Ibid., p. 215, n. 5.
66. Ibid., p. 29, n. 4.

67. Ibid., p. 94, n. 1.
68. Eilish Fitzpatrick and Stella Maynard, 'Conversation with Jordy Rosenberg', *The Lifted Brow*, 11 November 2019, <https://www.theliftedbrow.com/liftedbrow/2019/11/11/a-conversation-with-jordy-rosenberg-by-eilish-fitzpatrick-and-stella-maynard> [accessed 18 February 2021].
69. Bogi Takács, '[NOVEL] CONFESSIONS OF THE FOX BY JORDY ROSENBERG', *Bogi Reads the World*, <http://www.bogireadstheworld.com/novel-confessions-of-the-fox-by-jordy-rosenberg> [accessed 26 April 2021]. I'm grateful to my friends and colleagues in The Book Club for flagging up this review to me.
70. Griffiths, 'Diagnosing Sex', p. 490.
71. For discussion of how we can interpret archaeological evidence in a way that validates the existence of trans and intersex people in the past, see Miller Power, 'Non-Binary and Intersex Visibility and Erasure in Roman Archaeology', *Theoretical Roman Archaeology Journal*, 3.1 (2020) pp. 1–19.
72. E.g. '1,000-Year-Old Remains in Finland May Be Non-Binary Iron Age Leader', the *Guardian*, 9 August 2021, <https://www.theguardian.com/world/2021/aug/09/1000-year-old-remains-in-finland-may-be-non-binary-viking-researchers-say> [accessed 5 October 2021].
73. DeVun, 'Erecting Sex', p. 32.
74. Mann, 'How to Look at a Hermaphrodite', p. 72.
75. Indira Falk Gesink, 'Intersex Bodies in Premodern Islamic Discourse: Complicating the Binary', *Journal of Middle East Women's Studies*, 14.2 (2018), 152–173 (pp. 155, 171).
76. Sanz, 'No Way Out of the Binary', pp. 5–6.
77. Richard von Krafft-Ebing, *Psychopathia Sexualis*, trans. by Franklin S. Klaf (New York: Stein & Day, 1965), p. 28. See also C. Riley Snorton, *Black On Both Sides: A Racial History of Trans Identity* (Minneapolis: University of Minnesota Press, 2017), pp. 17–53, 105; Snorton writes compellingly of how racism can 'un-gender' Black people and the consequences

this can have. See also Hines, 'Sex Wars and (Trans)Gender Panics', pp. 700–701.

78. Bulwer, *Anthropometamorphosis*, sig. 3E2ᵛ. Bulwer also lists numerous other racist ideas of bodily/sexual variation on sigs. 3E4ᵛ-3F4ᵛ. His claims about Florida are drawn from the narratives and images of French artist Jacques Le Moyne de Morgues – see *Narrative of Le Moyne, an Artist Who Accompanied the French Expedition to Florida under Laudonniere, 1564*, trans. by Frederick B. Perkins (Boston: James R. Osgood, 1875), pp. 7–8. Kames's quotation is from *Sketches of the History of Man*, 4 vols. (Dublin: Printed for James Williams, 1774–75), vol. 3, p. 90. For further context on these racist ideas, see also Martha Few, '"That Monster of Nature": Gender, Sexuality, and the Medicalization of a "Hermaphrodite" in Late Colonial Guatemala', *Ethnohistory*, 54.1 (2007), 159–176 (pp. 164, 170); Krystal Batelaan and Gamal Abdel-Shehid, 'On the Eurocentric Nature of Sex Testing: The Case of Caster Semenya', *Social Identities*, 27.2 (2020), 1–20 (p. 9).

79. Shon Faye, *The Transgender Issue: An Argument for Justice* (London: Penguin Books, 2021), p. 240.

80. GIRES, 'The Gender Recognition Act Discussion (July 2019)', *GIRES*, 22 July 2019, <https://www.gires.org.uk/the-gender-recognition-act-discussion-july-2019> [accessed 19 February 2021]. GIRES contrasts the UK's Gender Recognition Act with examples of good practice in other countries. Notably, they say Malta's procedure actually 'prohibits requests for medical information' – perhaps the only country to take seriously how invasive and unnecessary it is for officials to ask about the state of people's genitals.

81. Hines, 'Sex Wars and (Trans)Gender Panics', pp. 706, 710, 713.

82. Batelaan and Abdel-Shehid, 'On the Eurocentric Nature of Sex Testing', pp. 11, 5, 13; see also Shari L. Dworkin, Amanda Lock and Cheryl Cooky, '(In)justice in Sport: The Treatment of South African Track Star Caster Semenya', *Feminist Studies*, 39.1 (2013), 40–69.

83. Kevin Henderson, 'J.K. Rowling and the White Supremacist History of "Biological Sex"', *The Abusable Past*, 28 July 2020,

<https://www.radicalhistoryreview.org/abusablepast/j-k-rowl-ing-and-the-white-supremacist-history-of-biological-sex> [accessed 22 February 2021].

84. Ruth Pearce, Sonja Erikainen and Ben Vincent, 'TERF Wars: An Introduction', *The Sociological Review Monographs*, 68.4 (2020), 677–698 (pp. 680–681); Toby Beauchamp, *Going Stealth: Transgender Politics and U.S. Surveillance Practices* (Durham: Duke University Press, 2018), pp. 82–85, 98.

85. *Old Bailey Proceedings Online*, 9 September 1797, trial of Mary Tom House (t17670909–24), <http://www.oldbaileyonline.org> version 6.0, 17 April 2011 [accessed 7 October 2021].

86. *Old Bailey Proceedings Online*, September 1767 (s17670909–1), <http://www.oldbaileyonline.org>, version 8.0, 27 April 2021 [accessed 7 October 2021].

87. Sara Taylor, *The Lauras* (London: Heinemann, 2016), p. 203.

88. Taylor, *The Lauras*, pp. 153, 176.

89. Ibid., pp. 224–227.

90. Ibid., pp. 229–230.

91. Ibid., p. 237.

92. Ibid., p. 241.

Chapter 6

1. Claude E. Schaeffer, 'The Kutenai Female Berdache: Courier, Guide, Prophetess, and Warrior', *Ethnohistory*, 12.3 (1965), 193–236 (p. 194). Note that while Schaeffer's interview data is useful, the term 'berdache', long used in a pejorative manner, is now considered a slur by Two-Spirit people.

2. Schaeffer, 'The Kutenai Female Berdache', pp. 194–196.

3. Suzanne Crawford O'Brien, 'Gone to the Spirits: A Transgender Prophet on the Columbia Plateau', *Theology & Sexuality*, 21.2 (2015), 125–143 (p. 125).

4. Akwaeke Emezi, *Twitter*, 13 June 2021, <https://twitter.com/azemezi/status/1404113385915027457> [accessed 13 August 2021].

5. Emezi, *Twitter*, 13 June 2021.

6. See Akwaeke Emezi, *Dear Senthuran: A Black Spirit Memoir* (London: Faber & Faber, 2021), pp. 11–20, 154–156.

7. Akwaeke Emezi, *Twitter*, 10 August 2021, <https://twitter.com/azemezi/status/1425237644292857858> [accessed 27 August 2021].

8. Akwaeke Emezi and Saidiya Hartman, 'Spiritfirst: Akwaeke Emezi with Saidiya Hartman', *New York Public Library*, 8 June 2021, <https://www.nypl.org/events/programs/2021/06/08/spiritfirst -akwaeke-emezi-saidiya-hartman> [accessed 13 August 2021].

9. Emezi, *Dear Senthuran*, p. 16.

10. Emezi, *Twitter*, 10 August 2021.

11. Akwaeke Emezi, *Freshwater* (London: Faber & Faber, 2018), p. 5.

12. Emezi, *Freshwater*, p. 123.

13. Ibid., pp. 192–193.

14. Riki Anne Wilchins, *Read My Lips: Sexual Subversion and the End of Gender* (Ithaca: Firebrand, 1997), p. 30; see Evan B. Towle and Lynn M. Morgan, 'Romancing the Transgender Native: Rethinking the Use of the "Third Gender" Concept' in *The Transgender Studies Reader*, ed. by Susan Stryker and Stephen Whittle (New York: Routledge, 2006), pp. 666–684 (p. 669).

15. Towle and Morgan, 'Romancing the Transgender Native', p. 672 (though the whole article is very worth reading).

16. Joshua Whitehead, *Jonny Appleseed* (Vancouver: Arsenal Pulp Press, 2018), p. 221.

17. Michelle Cameron, 'Two-Spirited Aboriginal People: Continuing Cultural Appropriation by Non-Aboriginal Society', *Canadian Woman Studies*, 24.2 (2005), 123–127 (p. 123).

18. See Towle and Morgan, 'Romancing the Transgender Native', p. 670; see also Gregory D. Smithers, 'Cherokee "Two Spirits": Gender, Ritual, and Spirituality in the Native South', *Early American Studies: An Interdisciplinary Journal*, 12.3 (2014), 626–651 (p. 629); Sabine Lang, 'Native American Men-Women, Lesbians, Two-Spirits: Contemporary and Historical Perspectives', *Journal of Lesbian Studies*, 20.3–4 (2016), 299–323 (p. 301).

19. Kate Bornstein, *Gender Outlaw: On Men, Women, and the Rest of Us*, rev. edn. (New York: Vintage Books, 2016), p. 149.

20. Towle and Morgan, 'Romancing the Transgender Native', p. 672.

21. See Blake Gutt and Alicia Spencer-Hall (eds.), *Trans and Genderqueer Subjects in Medieval Hagiography* (Amsterdam: Amsterdam University Press, 2021); Siobhan M. Kelly, 'Multiplicity and Contradiction: A Literature Review of Trans* Studies in Religion', *Journal of Feminist Studies in Religion*, 34.1 (2018), 7–23 (pp. 12–13); Cheryl Myfanwy Morgan, 'Trans Lives in Rome', in Ardel Haefele-Thomas (ed.), *Introduction to Transgender Studies* (New York: Harrington Park Press, 2019), pp. 372–377.

22. Cameron, 'Two-Spirited Aboriginal People', p. 126; see also Towle and Morgan, 'Romancing the Transgender Native', p. 680.

23. Schaeffer, 'The Kutenai Female Berdache', p. 202; see also O.B. Sperlin, 'Two Kootenay Women Masquerading as Men? Or Were They One?', *The Washington Historical Quarterly*, 21.2 (1930), 120–130 (p. 120).

24. William E. Moreau (ed.), *The Writings of David Thompson, Volume 2: The Travels, 1848 Version, and Associated Texts* (Montreal: McGill-Queen's University Press, 2015), pp. 179, 237.

25. Moreau (ed.), *The Writings of David Thompson*, p. 237.

26. O'Brien, 'Gone to the Spirits', p. 126; Sperlin, 'Two Kootenay Women', pp. 120–121. For a list of all the white people who wrote contemporary accounts of Kaúxuma núpika, see Schaeffer, 'The Kutenai Female Berdache', p. 193.

27. O'Brien, 'Gone to the Spirits', pp. 135–136.

28. Moreau (ed.), *The Writings of David Thompson*, pp. 237–238.

29. Sperlin, 'Two Kootenay Women', p. 124.

30. O'Brien, 'Gone to the Spirits', pp. 125–128.

31. Ibid., p. 128.

32. Schaeffer, 'The Kutenai Female Berdache', p. 197.

33. Sperlin, 'Two Kootenay Women', pp. 120, 122.

34. Moreau (ed.), *The Writings of David Thompson*, p. 179; O'Brien, 'Gone to the Spirits', p. 135.

35. O'Brien, 'Gone to the Spirits', p. 138; Schaeffer, 'The Kutenai Female Berdache', pp. 198–201.

36. Claudia Jane Rogers, '"The People from Heaven"?: Reading Indigenous Responses to Europeans During Moments of Early Encounter in the Caribbean and Mesoamerica, 1492–c.1585' (unpublished doctoral thesis, University of Leeds, 2018).

37. O'Brien, 'Gone to the Spirits', pp. 138–139.

38. Ibid., pp. 129, 137.

39. Schaeffer, 'The Kutenai Female Berdache', p. 214; O'Brien, 'Gone to the Spirits', p. 138.

40. O'Brien, 'Gone to the Spirits', p. 128.

41. Ibid., pp. 131–133, 138.

42. Ibid., pp. 133–134.

43. Anita Hemmilä, 'Ancestors of Two-Spirits: Historical Depictions of Native North American Gender-Crossing Women through Critical Discourse Analysis', *Journal of Lesbian Studies*, 20.3–4 (2016), 408–426 (p. 410); Kai Pyle, 'Naming and Claiming: Recovering Ojibwe and Plains Cree Two-Spirit Language', *TSQ: Transgender Studies Quarterly*, 5.4 (2018), 574–588 (p. 577).

44. Qwo-Li Driskill, 'Stolen From Our Bodies: First Nations Two-Spirits/Queers and the Journey to a Sovereign Erotic', *Studies in American Indian Literatures*, 16.2 (2004), 50–64 (p. 52); see also Will Roscoe, *Changing Ones: Third and Fourth Genders in Native North America* (New York: St Martin's Press, 1998), p. III.

45. For criticisms of the term and the way it's used, see Lang, 'Native American Men-Women', p. 304; Mary Annette Pember, '"Two Spirit" Tradition Far From Ubiquitous Among Tribes', *Rewire News Group*, 13 October 2016, <https://rewirenewsgroup.com/article/2016/10/13/two-spirit-tradition-far-ubiquitous-among-tribes> [accessed 27 August 2021]; Carrie House, 'Blessed by the Holy People', *Journal of Lesbian Studies*, 20.3–4 (2016), 324–341 (p. 331); Robert Bittner, 'Hey, I Still Can't See Myself!: The Difficult Positioning of Two-Spirit Identities in YA Literature', *Bookbird*, 52.1 (2014), 11–22 (p. 15).

46. Pyle, 'Naming and Claiming', pp. 575–576.

47. Maia Sheppard and J.B. Mayo Jr., 'The Social Construction of Gender and Sexuality: Learning from Two Spirit Traditions', *The Social Studies*, 104.6 (2013), 259–270 (p. 262).

48. Roscoe, *Changing Ones*, pp. 6–9; Deborah A. Miranda, 'Extermination of the Joyas: Gendercide in Spanish California', *GLQ: A Journal of Lesbian and Gay Studies*, 16.1–2 (2010), 253–284 (pp. 265–266). For an example of an anti-trans perspective on this, see Carrie-Anne Brownian, 'Genderqueering the Dead', *4thWave-Now*, 12 January 2019, <https://4thwavenow.com/2019/01/12/genderqueering-the-dead> [accessed 23 February 2021]; for discussion of the ways in which European patriarchal ideology isn't applicable to Native American/First Nations cultures, see O'Brien, 'Gone to the Spirits', p. 129.

49. Roscoe, *Changing Ones*, pp. 182–183.

50. Lang, 'Native American Men-Women', pp. 310–311.

51. Journalists for Human Rights Indigenous Reporters Program, *Style Guide for Reporting on Indigenous People*, December 2017, <http://jhr.ca/wp-content/uploads/2017/12/JHR2017-Style-Book-Indigenous-People.pdf> [accessed 27 August 2021], p. 5.

52. House, 'Blessed by the Holy People', p. 329.

53. Roscoe, *Changing Ones*, p. 113; see also p. 198.

54. O'Brien, 'Gone to the Spirits', p. 138; Hemmilä, 'Ancestors of Two-Spirits', pp. 417–418; Roscoe, *Changing Ones*, p. 8; Thomas Loraine McKenney, *Sketches of a Tour to the Lakes: Of the Character and Customs of the Chippeway Indians and of Incidents Connected with the Treaty of Fond du Lac* (Baltimore: Fielding Lucas Jr., 1827), p. 315.

55. Roscoe, *Changing Ones*, p. 26.

56. Miranda, 'Extermination of the Joyas', pp. 266–267.

57. Lang, 'Native American Men-Women', pp. 306–307.

58. Roscoe, *Changing Ones*, p. 13. See also Laurence Senelick, *The Changing Room: Sex, Drag and Theatre* (London and New York: Routledge, 2000), pp. 15–34, on the intersections of gender, sexuality and spirituality in other cultural contexts.

59. Roscoe, *Changing Ones*, pp. 43–45.

60. For more on 'manifest destiny', see, for example, Albert Katz Weinberg, *Manifest Destiny: A Study of Nationalist Expansionism in American History* (New York: AMS Press, 1979).

61. Tisa Wenger, 'Indian Dances and the Politics of Religious Freedom, 1870–1930', *Journal of the American Academy of Religion*, 79.4 (2011), 850–878 (p. 855); Francis Paul Prucha, *Documents of United States Indian Policy*, 2nd edn. (Lincoln: University of Nebraska Press, 1990), p. 187.

62. Wenger, 'Indian Dances'.

63. Ibid., p. 856.

64. Ibid., pp. 850–851; Steve Talbot, 'Spiritual Genocide: The Denial of American Indian Religious Freedom, from Conquest to 1934', *Wicazo Sa Review*, 21.2 (2006), 7–39 (pp. 16, 18, 25).

65. Roscoe, *Changing Ones*, pp. 4, 26; Smithers, 'Cherokee "Two Spirits"', pp. 638–640 (see also p. 632); Miranda, 'Extermination of the Joyas', pp. 256–257 (see also p. 262).

66. Jonathan Burton, 'Western Encounters with Sex and Bodies in Non-European Cultures, 1500–1750', in Sarah Toulalan and Kate Fisher (eds.), *The Routledge History of Sex and the Body: 1500 to the Present* (London: Routledge, 2013), pp. 495–510 (pp. 499, 503).

67. Scott Lauria Morgensen, 'Theorising Gender, Sexuality and Settler Colonialism: An Introduction', *Settler Colonial Studies*, 2.2 (2012), 2–22; Leanne Betasamosake Simpson, *As We Have Always Done: Indigenous Freedom through Radical Resistance* (Minneapolis: University of Minnesota Press, 2017), p. 41.

68. Miranda, 'Extermination of the Joyas', pp. 257–258.

69. Ibid., pp. 264–265.

70. Ibid., pp. 263–264.

71. Roscoe, *Changing Ones*, pp. 34–35.

72. Miranda, 'Extermination of the Joyas', pp. 258–259.

73. John S. Milloy, *A National Crime: The Canadian Government and the Residential School System, 1879 to 1986* (Winnipeg: University of Manitoba Press, 1999), p. xv.

74. Morgensen, 'Theorising Gender, Sexuality and Settler Colonialism', pp. 11–12.

75. Craig Charbonneau Fontaine (ed.), *Speaking of Sagkeeng = Agadijindamin Sagkeeng* (Pine Falls, Manitoba: KaKineepahwitamawat Association, 2006), pp. 1–3.

76. Truth and Reconciliation Commission of Canada, *Canada's Residential Schools, The Legacy: The Final Report of the Truth and Reconciliation Commission of Canada*, 6 vols. (Montreal: Published for the Truth and Reconciliation Commission by McGill-Queen's University Press, 2015), <https://ehprnh2mwo3.exactdn.com/wp-content/uploads/2021/01/Volume_5_Legacy_English_Web.pdf> [accessed 27 2021], 5, 148.

77. Roscoe, *Changing Ones*, pp. 35–36.

78. Walter L. Williams, *The Spirit and the Flesh: Sexual Diversity in American Indian Culture* (Boston: Beacon Press, 1992), p. 180.

79. I'm grateful to my friend and former colleague Francesca Mussi, who has researched the Canadian TRC extensively, for bringing this to my attention.

80. Vinay Lal, 'Not This, Not That: The Hijras of India and the Cultural Politics of Sexuality', *Social Text*, 61 (1999), 119–140 (pp. 122–123).

81. For more information on gharanas, see Aniruddha Dutta, 'An Epistemology of Collusion: Hijras, Kothis and the Historical (Dis)continuity of Gender/Sexual Identities in Eastern India', *Gender & History*, 24.3 (2012), 825–849 (p. 830); Jessica Hinchy, *Governing Gender and Sexuality in Colonial India: The Hijra, c.1850–1900* (Cambridge: Cambridge University Press, 2019), pp. 155–156.

82. Chantal Zabus and Samir Kumar Das, 'Hijras, Sangomas, and Their Translects: Trans(lat)ing India and South Africa', *Interventions* (2020), 1–24 (p. 5).

83. Hinchy, *Governing Gender and Sexuality*, pp. 21, 146–147; Gayatri Reddy, *With Respect to Sex: Negotiating Hijra Identity in South India* (Chicago: University of Chicago Press, 2005), pp. 96–98, 109; Amen Jaffer, 'Spiritualising Marginality: Sufi Concepts and the

Politics of Identity in Pakistan', *Society and Culture in South Asia*, 3.2 (2017), 175–197 (pp. 190, 192–193). Overall, though some individual hijras might disagree, surgery is neither necessary nor sufficient for identification as a hijra – see Hinchy, *Governing Gender and Sexuality*, pp. 100–101; Roscoe, *Changing Ones*, p. 296.

84. Reddy, *With Respect to Sex*, pp. 89–09.

85. Ibid., pp. 97, 108–109.

86. Ibid., pp. 99–120.

87. Claire Pamment, 'Performing Piety in Pakistan's Transgender Rights Movement', *TSQ: Transgender Studies Quarterly*, 6.3 (2019), 297–314 (pp. 305–306).

88. Jaffer, 'Spiritualising Marginality', pp. 183–184; Pamment, 'Performing Piety', p. 304.

89. Pamment, 'Performing Piety', p. 304.

90. Reddy, *With Respect to Sex*, pp. 17–18, 39–40, 79, 84, 89; Jaffer, 'Spiritualising Marginality', pp. 182–183; Stephen O. Murray, 'Gender-Mixing Roles, Gender-Crossing Roles, and the Sexuality of Transgendered Roles', *Reviews in Anthropology*, 31.4 (2002), 291–308 (pp. 295–296).

91. Hinchy, *Governing Gender and Sexuality*, pp. 28–29, 40–41, 50.

92. Ibid., pp. 1–26 (this is the introduction, but the whole book is very much worth reading).

93. Ibid., p. 2; Aniruddha Dutta, 'Review: JESSICA HINCHY. *Governing Gender and Sexuality in Colonial India: The Hijra, c. 1850–1900*', *Journal of British Studies*, 59.4 (2020), 950–952 (p. 952); As historian and literary scholar Abdulhamit Arvas has pointed out, the integration of eunuchs into political systems simultaneously resulted in the unwilling castration of many, *and* provided an opportunity for voluntary medical transition for those who wanted it – see Abdulhamit Arvas, 'Early Modern Eunuchs and the Transing of Gender and Race', *Journal for Early Modern Cultural Studies*, 19.4 (2019), 116–136.

94. Hinchy, *Governing Gender and Sexuality*, pp. 11–12.

95. Ibid., p. 2.

96. Ibid., pp. 16–17.

97. Ibid., p. 216.

98. Ibid., p. 201.

99. Ibid., pp. 57–58.

100. Ibid., pp. 8–10, 44–45.

101. Ibid., pp. 19, 71–74

102. Arvas's consideration of consent with regard to eunuchs ('Early Modern Eunuchs') is a helpful, nuanced way into thinking about the issue of kidnap. See also Hinchy, *Governing Gender and Sexuality*, pp. 72–73, 103–104, 140, 157–162; Reddy, *With Respect to Sex*, pp. 78–79.

103. Hinchy, *Governing Gender and Sexuality*, pp. 74–75.

104. Ibid., pp. 19, 104

105. Whitehead, *Jonny Appleseed*, p. 221.

106. Miranda, 'Extermination of the Joyas', p. 259.

107. Lang, 'Native American Men-Women', p. 300; Cameron, 'Two-Spirited Aboriginal People', pp. 124–125; Pember, '"Two Spirit" Tradition'; Mark Rifkin, 'Queering Indigenous Pasts, or Temporalities of Tradition and Settlement', in *The Oxford Handbook of Indigenous American Literature*, ed. by James Cox and Daniel Heath Justice (Oxford: Oxford University Press, 2014), pp. 137–151 (p. 137); Sheppard and Mayo, 'Social Construction', p. 262; Driskill, 'Stolen From Our Bodies', pp. 52–54.

108. Willard Williams Hill, 'The Status of the Hermaphrodite and Transvestite in Navaho Culture', *American Anthropologist* 37.2 (1935), 273–279 (p. 7, p. 2 n. 3); Sheppard and Mayo, 'Social Construction', p. 270.

109. Cameron, 'Two-Spirited Aboriginal People', p. 124.

110. Hinchy, *Governing Gender and Sexuality*, pp. 80–92.

111. Ibid., pp. 264–267.

112. Dutta, 'Epistemology of Collusion', pp. 323, 331–334.

113. Ibid.

114. You can find other examples of this in Roscoe, *Changing Ones*, p. 204; Barbara Tedlock, *The Woman in the Shaman's Body: Reclaiming the Feminine in Religion and Medicine* (New York: Bantam Books, 2005), p. 250; Marjorie Mandelstam Balzer, 'Sacred Genders in Siberia: Shamans, Bear Festivals, and Androgyny', in Sabrina Petra

Ramet (ed.), *Gender Reversals and Gender Cultures: Anthropological and Historical Perspectives* (London: Routledge, 1996), pp. 164–182; Ifalade Ta'shia Asanti, 'Living with Dual Spirits: Spirituality, Sexuality and Healing in the African Diaspora', *Journal of Bisexuality*, 10.1–2 (2010), 22–30; Stephen O. Murray and Will Roscoe (eds.), *Boy-Wives and Female-Husbands: Studies in African Homosexualities* (New York: Palgrave Macmillan, 1998), pp. 19–40, 87–106, 137–144; Ifi Amadiume, *Male Daughters, Female Husbands: Gender and Sex in an African Society* (London: Zed Books, 2015), pp. 42–43.

115. Scott Larson, '"Indescribable Being": Theological Performances of Genderlessness in the Society of the Publick Universal Friend, 1776–1819', *Early American Studies*, 12.3 (2014), 576–600 (pp. 576–577).

116. Larson, 'Indescribable Being', p. 581.

117. Ibid., p. 585.

118. Ibid., p. 585.

119. Ibid., p. 578.

120. Ibid., pp. 599–600.

Epilogue

1. Shon Faye, *The Transgender Issue: An Argument for Justice* (London: Penguin Books, 2021), p. 174; emphasis added.

2. See, for example, Victoria Gagliardo-Silver, 'What I Mean When I Say I Want to Abolish the Police', *Independent*, 1 June 2020, <https://www.independent.co.uk/voices/acab-abolish-police-george-floyd-protests-cops-a9543386.html> [accessed 1 October 2021].

3. Alex, *Twitter*, 19 July 2021, <https://twitter.com/Axartsme/status/1417200818005098502> [accessed 1 October 2021]; [Star ver.Fall], *Twitter*, 21 February 2020, <https://twitter.com/StarSumiaki/status/1230997970339782656> [accessed 1 October 2021]; traaaaaaann nnnnnnnns, *Twitter*, 24 September 2020, <https://twitter.com/traabot

/status/1308947912026664960> [accessed 1 October 2021]. The same mockery is applied to historians' interpretation of evidence of same-sex relationships – see, for example, incorrect patrochilles quotes, *Twitter*, 21 October 2019, <https://twitter.com/wrongptrchlls/status/118637555 2548122624> [accessed 1 October 2021]; H U G I Y O, *Twitter*, 5 July 2020, <https://twitter.com/Hugoliine_/status/1279866585163988995> [accessed 1 October 2021].

4. Miller Power, 'Non-Binary and Intersex Visibility and Erasure in Roman Archaeology', *Theoretical Roman Archaeology Journal*, 3.1 (2020), 1–19 (pp. 12–13).

5. Christina Sharpe reflects on how this is also true of Black lives in her brilliant book *In the Wake: On Blackness and Being* (Durham, N.C.: Duke University Press, 2016), pp. 12–13.

6. See Margaret Middleton, 'Queer Possibility', *Journal of Museum Education*, 45.4 (2020), 426–436; Power, 'Non-Binary and Intersex Visibility'; Ben Taylor, 'Zines by Non-Binary Leeds', *West Yorkshire Queer Stories*, 14 July 2019, <https://wyqs.co.uk/stories/zines-by-non-binary-leeds> [accessed 30 September 2021].

7. Hil Malatino, *Trans Care* (Minneapolis: University of Minnesota Press, 2020), pp. 58–59; see also p. 7.

8. Jenn Shapland, *My Autobiography of Carson McCullers* (Portland: Tin House Books, 2020), pp. 161–162; Laura Doan, *Disturbing Practices: History, Sexuality, and Women's Experience of Modern War* (Chicago: University of Chicago Press, 2013), p. x.

9. Shapland, *My Autobiography*, p. 163.

10. Ibid, pp. 10, 23.

11. Rachel Cooke, '*My Autobiography of Carson McCullers* Review – Identity Parade', the *Observer*, 2 May 2021, <https://www.theguardian.com/books/2021/may/02/my-autobiography-of-carson-mccullers-review-identity-parade> [accessed 30 September 2021].

12. Leslie Feinberg, *Transgender Warriors: Making History from Joan of Arc to Dennis Rodman* (Boston: Beacon Press, 1996), pp. 81, xii-xiii; see also 36, 64, 75, 79–80.

13. CN Lester, *Trans Like Me: Conversations for All of Us* (London: Virago, 2017), pp. 146–147.

14. Malatino, *Trans Care*, p. 51.

15. Ellis Martin and Zach Ozma (eds.), *We Both Laughed In Pleasure: The Selected Diaries of Lou Sullivan, 1961–1991* (New York: Nightboat Books, 2019), p. 12; see also p. 13.

16. Shola von Reinhold, *LOTE* (London: Jacaranda Books Art Music, 2020).

17. Non-Binary Leeds, *Trancestors: A Non-Binary History Zine* (2019), <https://drive.google.com/drive/folders/1wiecteS1_mPn_cqYXkjaINTIE4be5ZYL> [accessed 30 September 2021], fol. 1ᵛ; see also 5ᵛ.

18. Malatino, *Trans Care*, p. 54; Non-Binary Leeds, *Trancestors*, fol. 2ᵛ.

19. Shapland writes movingly about the 'freedom' and 'abundance' that come from looking at the history of sexuality in the same way (*My Autobiography*, p. 233).

20. Faye, *The Transgender Issue*, p. xi; Feinberg, *Transgender Warriors*, p. 88. See also Feinberg, *Transgender Warriors*, pp. xi, 121; Lester, *Trans Like Me*. pp. 213–214.

21. Malatino, *Trans Care*, pp. 32–33.

22. Ursula K. Le Guin, 'Is Gender Necessary? Redux', in *Dancing at the Edge of the World: Thoughts on Words, Women, Places* (London: Gollancz, 1989), pp. 7–16.

23. Ursula K. Le Guin, *The Left Hand of Darkness* (London: Gollancz, 2018), pp. 248–249.

Index

Kit Heyam is a university lecturer, a queer history activist, and a trans awareness trainer who has worked with organizations across the United Kingdom. They live in Leeds, UK, with their partner Alex.